本书的出版得到了深圳大学语言与认知研究中心科研基金的全力资助（项目号：801），特此鸣谢。

SPATIAL LANGUAGE AND
EVENT SEMANTICS IN MANDARIN

汉语空间表达与事件语义学

邓湘君 著

中国社会科学出版社

图书在版编目（CIP）数据

汉语空间表达与事件语义学 / 邓湘君著 . —北京：中国社会科学出版社，2018.6
ISBN 978－7－5203－2668－1

Ⅰ.①汉… Ⅱ.①邓… Ⅲ.①汉语—语义学—研究 Ⅳ.①H13

中国版本图书馆 CIP 数据核字（2018）第 123558 号

出 版 人	赵剑英
责任编辑	刘　艳
责任校对	陈　晨
责任印制	戴　宽

出　　版	中国社会科学出版社
社　　址	北京鼓楼西大街甲 158 号
邮　　编	100720
网　　址	http://www.csspw.cn
发 行 部	010－84083685
门 市 部	010－84029450
经　　销	新华书店及其他书店
印　　刷	北京明恒达印务有限公司
装　　订	廊坊市广阳区广增装订厂
版　　次	2018 年 6 月第 1 版
印　　次	2018 年 6 月第 1 次印刷
开　　本	710×1000　1/16
印　　张	14.75
插　　页	2
字　　数	231 千字
定　　价	66.00 元

凡购买中国社会科学出版社图书，如有质量问题请与本社营销中心联系调换
电话：010－84083683
版权所有　侵权必究

Table of Contents

内容简介 ··· (Ⅳ)
Preface 序言 ··· (Ⅵ)
Acknowledgements ·· (Ⅸ)
Abbreviations ··· (Ⅺ)
Chapter 1   Space in Language ································ (1)
  1.1   Defining space ·· (2)
    1.1.1   Semantic primitives in motion events ············ (5)
    1.1.2   Syntactic realizations of semantic primitives ····· (7)
  1.2   Viewing space via event semantics: some
       preliminaries ·· (12)
    1.2.1   Argument structure of a verb ····················· (13)
    1.2.2   Event type and event structure ··················· (16)
  1.3   Objectives and organization of the book ··············· (21)
**Chapter 2   Ambiguities of Mandarin Spatial Modifiers: An
              Event-semantic Perspective** ······················ (24)
  2.1   Ambiguities in linguistic space ··························· (25)
  2.2   Explaining semantic ambiguity of spatial modifiers ··· (29)
    2.2.1   The principle of (sub)event modification ······· (29)
    2.2.2   The principle of aspect shift ······················· (44)
  2.3   Event semantics in framing Chinese motion events ··· (55)
  2.4   Remedies for ambiguity in linguistic space ············ (56)
  2.5   Summary ·· (59)

Chapter 3 Distribution of *zai* in Mandarin ......(61)

3.1 Verb classification based on event type ......(61)

3.2 Classification of spatial prepositions ......(69)

3.3 Spatial prepositional phrases headed by *zai* (*zai*-PPs) ......(74)

    3.3.1 Distribution of *zai*-PPs ......(75)

    3.3.2 An event-semantic account of the use of *zai*-PPs ......(77)

    3.3.3 Syntactic positions of *zai*-PPs ......(82)

    3.3.4 Cognitive constraints on the use of *zai*-PPs ......(92)

    3.3.5 Diachronic changes of *zai* ......(95)

3.4 Summary and discussion ......(101)

3.5 Acquisition of *zai* ......(105)

Chapter 4 Localizer Phrases, Locative Subjects, and Locative Object ......(117)

4.1 Syntax and semantics of localizers and localizer phrases ......(118)

4.2 Locative subjects ......(127)

    4.2.1 Information structure of locative subject sentences ......(128)

    4.2.2 Aspectual properties of locative subject sentences ......(131)

    4.2.3 One-argument locative subject sentences ......(145)

    4.2.4 Nature of locative subjects: subject or topic? ......(146)

4.3 Syntax and semantics of locative objects ......(158)

4.4 Summary ......(162)

4.5 Acquisition of the localizer phrase and the locative subject construction ......(163)

Chapter 5 Linguistic Space, Perception, and Cognition ......(167)

5.1 Frames of reference, reference strategies and Figure-Ground asymmetry ......(168)

5.2 Effects of cognitive development on language development ......(176)

5.2.1 Frames of reference and reference strategies used
by children .... (176)

5.2.2 Acquisition sequence of localizers .... (183)

5.2.3 Early awareness to Figure-Ground asymmetry .... (193)

5.2.4 Summary .... (193)

Chapter 6 Beyond the Domain of Spatial Language .... (195)

6.1 The application of event semantics to the study of
spatial encoding in Mandarin .... (195)

6.2 A better understanding of linguistic space from the
perspective of perception and cognition .... (198)

6.3 Other contributions .... (199)

References .... (202)

内容简介

人们如何解读含有空间短语的句子，又如何表达空间概念？本书以汉语普通话为例考察事件类型和事件结构对空间表达的影响。全书共分六章。第一章介绍空间表达的句法语义基础，以及事件语义学的一些基本概念，包括论元结构和事件结构。第二章通过中英文对比探讨空间短语作为事件修饰语的歧义现象。第三、四章分别讨论汉语普通话表达空间关系最重要的几种句式：含有"在"引领的空间介词短语的句子、处所主语句和处所宾语句。作者将 Davidson（1967）和 Parsons（1990）等学者建构的事件语义学应用到这些句式的考察中，发现事件语义原则可以统一地描写或解释"在"引领的空间介词短语和处所主语句的句法语义特征。第五章介绍了空间参照系统或参照策略的选择、目的物-参照物非对称性两个现象，并以此来讨论空间语言、知觉及一般认知系统之间的关系。第六章讨论了用事件语义学来分析汉语空间表达主要句式的优势所在，以及这种分析给我们带来的新的认识。

本研究中讨论的事件语义学语义原则包括：动词的事件类型转换（Smith 1997；Rothstein 2004），以及空间介词短语是事件修饰语（Parsons 1990）。这些普遍的语义原则使我们能够解释和描述汉语普通话中"在"引领的空间介词短语的分布和解读，它们是由与"在"连用的动词的事件结构决定的（Fong 1997；Liu 2009）。当"在"短语出现在放置类动词（一种完成体动词）前时，它们可能会有歧义，因为它们可以修饰两个子事件中的任何一个。当"在"短语出现在姿态类动词后时，它们表达一个静态位置或是一个动作的结果位置，因为动词经历了从状态体（它的预设事件类型）到成就体（它的衍生事件类型）的事件类型转换。在普通话口语中，只有事件结构中含有动态或结果状态的动词可以后接"在"短语。能进入双论元处所主语句的动词的事件结构中也必须含有动态或结果状态。除了可以被事件语义学解释的一系列语法现象外，汉语普通话空间表达还有一些独特性和复杂性：参照物的轴向信息在普通话中是由方位词表达的，方位词的词类是名词还是后置词仍在讨论之中；方位词短语的构成规则很复杂，根据方位词所带的名词短语的性质不同有不同的变体。

总而言之，汉语空间表达是一个复杂的系统，既有规律性，又有不规则性。在事件语义学的理论框架下，本书以跨语言的视角来研究汉语普通话中空间表达方式的句法语义问题，对比考察了英语、德语、Chichewa语和上海话等语言或方言中的对应词汇、句法表达。我们的理论框架以及研究方法使我们能从复杂的语料中整理出一条清晰的思路，对汉语普通话中一些基于普遍语义原则的语言现象以及一些独特性有了全新的更为深入的认识。此外，本书将语言学理论和儿童语言习得联系起来，介绍了儿童空间语言习得的相关研究。我们相信本书对理论研究者、儿童语言研究者、汉语学习者、语文教师及对外汉语教师都有益处，能够帮助他们加深对汉语空间语言和事件语义学的了解。

Preface 序言

叶彩燕（Virginia Yip）

邓湘君是我在香港中文大学语言学及现代语言系指导的专攻儿童语言习得的博士生。本书是在她 2014 年完成的博士论文《Space, Events and Language Acquisition in Mandarin》的基础上修改加工而成的。她的博士论文从语言学中事件语义学的理论角度出发，通过语料库及几种不同的实验手段，研究了 2 至 6 岁汉语普通话儿童对空间表达，尤其是方位词、"在"字句、处所主语句的习得。由于本书旨在介绍 Davidson（1967）、Parsons（1990）等学者创立的事件语义学，以及事件语义学如何解释汉语空间表达中的相关现象，目标群体为语言学理论研究者、语言学或对外汉语教学研究生、汉语教学工作者、汉语学习者，她选取了自己的博士论文中的相关章节进行了修订。目前，此书包含了事件语义学的介绍，对国内外关于空间表达的经典理论和最新动态的综述，以及对相关儿童习得文献的回顾和总结。

本书的新颖之处在于用汉语普通话语料来验证并充实了一些事件语义学原则，如动词的事件类型转换、空间介词短语为事件修饰语等。动词是句子的核心，影响句子的解读，包括句子中空间修饰语的解读。本书运用事件语义学的核心原理，将动词按事件类型分为状态体（State）、活动体（Activity）、成就体（Achievement）、完成体（Accomplishment）。这样的动词分类，使我们看到动词与空间修饰语互动的本质以及同一个动词在不同类型间的转换。动词的事件类型转换、空间介词短语为事件修饰语这两个语义原则非常有力地解释了汉语"在"字句的一些歧义现象。

此外，本书还用汉语语料验证了一些前人提出来的语言共性，如目的物-参照物非对称性。本书的意义在于通过对空间概念在语言中的编码进行对比研究，使读者更深入了解到汉语普通话的语言独特性以及各语言、方言潜藏在表层差异下的语言共性。我觉得这是一本可读性很强的理论探讨书籍，因此将它推荐给读者。

Deng Xiangjun received her PhD degree from the Department of Linguistics and Modern Languages at the Chinese University of Hong Kong under my supervision. This book is adapted from her 2014 dissertation "Space, Events and Language Acquisition in Mandarin". Under the framework of the linguistic theory of event semantics, her dissertation investigates Mandarin-speaking 2- to 6-year-olds' acquisition of spatial expressions, including localizers, sentences with *zai* '(be) at', and locative subject sentences, through a corpus study and a number of experiments. To produce this book, she selected and revised relevant chapters from her dissertation with a view to introducing event semantics based on Davidson (1967) and Parsons (1990) and its application to the linguistic encoding of space in Mandarin Chinese. The target readers are researchers in theoretical linguistics, postgraduate students with an interest in linguistics or teaching Chinese as a second language as well as teachers of Chinese and students of Chinese. The book includes an introduction to event semantics, a review of classic theories and cutting-edge research on spatial language at home and abroad, and a review of the literature on children's acquisition of spatial language.

The originality of this book lies in confirming and enriching principles in the theory of event semantics, such as aspect shift of the verb, and spatial modifiers as event modifiers, based on data from Mandarin Chinese. A verb is the core of a clause, determining the interpretation of the whole sentence, including its spatial modifiers. The most basic theoretical tenet of event semantics is its classification of verbs into State, Activity,

Achievement and Accomplishment on the basis of the verb's event type and event structure. Applying this classification to Mandarin verbs allows us to see the nature of the interaction between the verb and the spatial modifier and the shift of verbs between different event types, as this book shows. The two principles of aspect shift and spatial modifier as event modifier provide a powerful explanation of the ambiguities of Mandarin sentences with *zai* ' at '.

In addition, this book uses Mandarin data to support some proposed language universals, for instance, the Figure-Ground asymmetry. The significance of this book consists in the detailed comparison of the linguistic encoding of spatial concepts in different languages, and the revelation of the specificity of Mandarin Chinese as well as the commonalities underneath the superficial variation between Mandarin and other languages or dialects. I hope readers will find this book of great theoretical interest and be engaged by its rich and fascinating analyses. I highly recommend it.

Virginia Yip

Co-Director, University of Cambridge-Chinese University of

Hong Kong (CUHK) Joint Laboratory for Bilingualism

Director, Childhood Bilingualism Research Centre, CUHK

Professor, Department of Linguistics and Modern Languages, CUHK

Acknowledgements

This book has grown out of my PhD dissertation done at the Chinese University of Hong Kong. I would like to take this opportunity to thank the professors, colleagues and friends there, especially my supervisor Virginia Yip, for their inspiration and support. My thesis committee members Boping Yuan, Thomas Lee and Candice Cheung, as well as Stephen Matthews and Audrey Li generously shared their insights with me. My heart-felt gratitude also goes to the following colleagues and friends: Ziyin Mai, Jiahui Yang, Haoze Li, Donald White, Aijun Huang, Zhuang Wu, Natsumi Shibata, Hinny Wong, Haoyan Ge, Jing Yang, Jess Law, Yu'an Yang and Li Yang.

I am also indebted to my colleagues at Shenzhen University, Yinglin Ji, the director of the Research Centre for Language and Cognition, Xiaobei Zheng, and other collegues at the School of Foreign Languages, for helping me in various ways in the publication of this book. The financial support from Shenzhen University Social Sciences Foundation (project code: 801) is acknowledged.

Part of the contents in this book has been published in the form of journal articles. An abridged version of Chapters 2 to 4 serves as the theoretical background in the article "The linguistic encoding of space in child Mandarin: A corpus-based study" published in *Linguistics* vol. 53 (5), 1079 – 1112 (Copyright 2015 by De Gruyter, Berlin, Germany). An adapted edition of Chapter 5 appeared in *Journal of Chinese Linguistics*, as the introduction and literature review in "Cognition and perception in the linguistic encoding of space in child Mandarin" vol. 44(2), 287 – 325 (Copyright 2016 by *Journal of Chinese linguistics*). I am very grateful to the editors and publishers for permission to reprint.

Lastly, I owe profound gratitude to my beloved family members. I thank Keqing, Tongtong, Xianchuan and Yuxin for their sacrifice and support. This book is dedicated to the memory of my late mother Jinggui for her endless love.

Abbreviations

BA	marker of the *ba* construction
BEI	marker of the passive construction in Mandarin
CL	classifier
CP	complementizer phrase
DE	modification marker, genitive marker, or nominalizer *de*
DP	determiner phrase
DUR	durative aspect suffix *-zhe*
EXP	experiential aspect suffix *-guo*
GEN	genitive marker
L	localizer
LE	sentence-final particle *le* signaling inchoativity or current relevance
LP	localizer phrase
N	noun
NP	noun phrase
P	preposition
Perf	perfective aspect marker *-le*
PLU	plural marker *-men*
PP	preposition phrase
Q	question particle
RE	reference entity
RVC	resultative verb compound

sfp	sentence-final particle
TOP	topic marker *a*, *ma*, *ne* and so on
TP	tense phrase
V	verb
VP	verb phrase

The following symbols are used in the transcription:

*	Unacceptable sentence
?	Marginally acceptable sentence
#	Sentence with semantic anomaly

Chapter 1　　Space in Language

As an enduring object of intellectual inquiry, 'language and space' arouses extensive interest in the cognitive sciences, including linguistics, psychology, philosophy, and brain sciences (Levinson 1996a). Although the notion of space has not stirred the intellect of linguists to the degree that time and aspect have, there are still hundreds of monographs, and journal papers dedicated to this topic (Kracht 2002). Space, time, and aspect all fall under the broader linguistic study of I-semantics, which is concerned with intrinsic human knowledge of the relation between language and concepts. According to Jackendoff (1996a), I-semantics is preoccupied by the research of spatial expressions, because the field is rich, and judgments of truth and ambiguity for sentences with spatial relationships are perceptually verifiable and highly structured. Recently, the field has also attracted generative syntacticians, who endeavor to reveal the universal underlying structure for spatial expressions across languages (Cinque 2010).

The specific focus of this book is to connect space with verbal aspect, namely to take an aspectual, or event-semantic perspective to understand spatial expressions in Mandarin Chinese.① It also aims to be an interdisciplinary psycholinguistic study addressing the broader issue of the

---

① In this book, Mandarin is used interchangeably with *Putonghua*, the official spoken language of mainland China. In its normal, broad use, 'Mandarin' refers to a group of related varieties or dialects spoken across most of northern and southwestern China based on which *Putonghua* was developed. We use 'Mandarin' in a more restricted way.

relationship between language, perception and cognition in the field of space, and exploring the possibility to link linguistic theory and child language development. In this study, the syntax and semantics of Mandarin spatial phrases (SPs), including spatial prepositional phrases (PPs), verb phrases (VPs), and localizer phrases (LPs), functioning as spatial adjuncts, predicates, and locative subjects or objects, will be examined. The Mandarin data will be compared with various languages, especially English and other varieties of Chinese. The comparison will shed light on the specific properties of Mandarin spatial language as well as the properties shared by other languages. Through the investigation of various aspects of this linguistic-space system, the present study will contribute to the understanding of how space and events are represented in human mind in general, and in Chinese speakers in specific.

1.1 Defining space

Space is a semantic domain covering location and motion. Location refers to the position of an entity in relation to other entities, whereas motion denotes a moving object passing through many locations in space successively. All animals have the ability to perceive the location of food, and undergo motion to get it. While some animals can communicate the location of food in an elementary way, human beings are unique in their ability to use spatial language to locate an object. Spatial language provides a window through which the interaction of human perception, spatial cognition, and language faculty can be surveyed and understood.[1] The

---

[1] In this study, language is defined as a computational system interfaced with other organism-internal systems with a phonological system and a semantic system (Hauser, Chomsky, and Fitch 2002). In perception, 'the sense organs transduce physical energy from the outside world, which is encoded and delivered to the brain via sensory neurons for interpretation by the perceptual system' (Styles 2005, 7). Cognition is the collection of mental processes and activities, including perceiving, remembering, thinking, understanding, and so on (Ashcraft 2006, 11).

primacy of spatial organization for human cognition is well noted: it is the common ground for the essential faculties of vision, touch and action; it has evolved long before language; and spatial metaphors are extended to nonspatial domains (Miller and Johnson-Laird 1976, 375; Lakoff and Johnson 1980, chs. 4 and 9; Jackendoff 1983, 210).

The present study distinguishes three senses of space: absolute space, P(erceptual)-space, and L(inguistic)-space (see H. Clark 1973; Miller and Johnson-Laird 1976). In perceiving the location of an entity, a coordinate system must be established in which the point of origin coincides with the viewer, or a reference entity. The position of the located entity can be calculated by measuring its distance from the axes of the coordinate system. Absolute space enables a speaker to label locations by their coordinate values precisely. In Marr's (1982) discussion about vision, at the level of the 3D(imensional) model representation, viewers construct an object-centered representation out of the parts they perceive from a certain perspective.[1] Marr's 3D model representation is a perspective-free system, which is the closest copy to absolute space in our mind. P-space, on the other hand, is not perspective-free: an individual's physical and biological environment places a priori constraints on how the location of objects is perceived and described. The linguistic system of spatial language interfaces with, but does not duplicate, non-linguistic cognitive systems. L-space also has coordinates but normally only involves spatial relations between several entities that are perceptually relatable (Miller and Johnson-Laird 1976, 380). In contrast to absolute space and P-space, L-space does not attempt to specify an object's exact location: the relative indeterminacy of locative expressions is demonstrated by the use of *at* in *the*

---

[1] Marr (1982) made distinctions between representational stages for deriving shape information from images. The primal sketch makes explicit information about the 2D image. A 2½-D sketch conveys the shape information in a viewer-centered coordinate frame while the 3-D model representation describes it in an object-centered coordinate frame.

man at the desk, *the man at the office* and *the man at the university* (ibid., 387). In these expressions, the exact position of the man is not specified in relation to the reference entity.

In L-space, human beings have the major means listed in (1) to locate a referent or describe its movement. The conceptual core of space originates with our own body. By using space deixis, we refer to a place close to us as *here* and a distal place as *there*. The body is the first reference entity that humans learn to use; later this egocentric space is supplemented with decentered spatial systems (Miller and Johnson-Laird 1976, 394). In (1a), topological relationships including proximity ('nearby'), separation, order ('before'), surrounding ('in', 'between') and continuity are widely used to locate an entity in space (Piaget and Inhelder 1948). In using named locations, or proper names such as *Beijing*, the speaker can pick out a unique referent merely by mentioning its name. Besides these methods, one may also use the coordinate system of the reference entity to locate an object, which is called the object-centered frame of reference. If a speaker uses ego to project the coordinate system, he adopts the viewer-centered frame of reference. When cardinal directions in the environment such as north and east are used, the environment-centered perspective is adopted.

(1) a. No coordinate systems employed

    deixis

    topological relations

    named locations

  b. Coordinate systems or frames of reference employed

    object-centered or intrinsic

    viewer-centered or relative

    environment-centered or absolute

(adapted from Levinson 1996b)

Our mental representation of space interfaces with conceptual structure, which is characterized as an algebraic representation of the world as we conceptualize it (Jackendoff 1996b). Even though conceptual structure is universal, languages can differ in their overall semantic organizations: they may diverge in what elements of conceptual structure they require the speaker to express in syntax; they can have different strategies in bundling up conceptual elements into lexical items (e.g. Talmy 1985; Bowerman 1996). The following two sections will introduce some universal semantic primitives as well as language variations in encoding these primitives cross-linguistically.

1.1.1 Semantic primitives in motion events

The universality of semantics is open to dispute in the study of space. Some argue that grammars and lexicons of all languages are broadly similar, and linguistic categories and structures are straightforward mappings from preexisting concepts (Li and Gleitman 2002). A similar view is that L(inguistic)-space is universal because it is conditioned by P(erceptual)-space, a human universal (H. Clark 1973). Conversely, a number of researchers argue that few, if any, lexical concepts occur universally (Levinson 2003). Levinson (1996a, 1996b, 2003) and Levinson and Wilkins (2006) observed that languages make different uses of frames of reference.

To account for the similarities and differences across languages, the present study will invoke the independent level 'semantics' intervening between syntax and concept. While conceptual structure might be universal, semantic structure varies cross-linguistically, depending on what conceptual distinctions are grammaticized (Talmy 1985; Choi and Bowerman 1991). In mapping concepts onto language, people may make the same semantic distinctions, which the present study will refer to as the semantic universals. Nevertheless, in packaging the universal semantic primitives into lexical items or functional categories and mapping them to certain syntactic positions, languages may differ.

Candidates for the semantic primitives include, for instance, Figure, Ground, Motion, and Path as proposed by Talmy (1975, 1985, 2000) in analyzing motion events in various languages. Definitions of these concepts are given in (2).

 (2) Figure: the moving or located object

   Ground: a reference frame, or a reference object with respect to which the Figure moves

   Motion: the moving or located state that the Figure is in with respect to the Ground

   Path: the course followed by the Figure with respect to the Ground

Talmy's definition of motion covers both moving and located states. Semanticists and syntacticians make a fundamental distinction between the two (Nam 2000; Kracht 2002; Cinque 2010; den Dikken 2010). In a motion event, we are concerned about the Path of an entity, but in a located state, the Place or Location of an entity is relevant.[①] A location can be viewed as a point in a path since a moving object passes through many locations successively. Thus, the sequence of locations forms a path. The origin and terminus of a path are distinct from other points in this path: the origin is called Source and the terminus Goal, which are lexicalized, for instance in English, as *from* and *to*, respectively.

[①] Besides the distinction between static location vs. motion as shown by the contrast between (ia) and (ib), there is a further distinction within motion events, the translocational motion vs. the non-translocational one as exemplified by (ic) and (ib), respectively (Yinglin Ji, personal communication).

 (i) a. John is on the playground.   [location]
   b. John is jumping up and down on the playground. [motion: non-translocational]
   c. John is jumping across the playground.   [motion: translocational]

1.1.2 Syntactic realizations of semantic primitives

In this section, we will introduce the syntactic realizations of the semantic primitives mentioned above in Mandarin, in comparison with English.

It is generally agreed that objects are represented by basic units that have an axial structure: the generating axis around which the cone or surface is elaborated, plus up to two orthogonal orienting axes (reviewed in Landau and Jackendoff 1993). For instance, the three axes of a three-dimensional telephone determine that it has a top and a bottom, a front and a back, and two sides. A large number of prepositions in English, such as *on top of*, *under*, *in front of*, and *beside*, make reference to an object's axial structure. They are called Axial Part, or AxPart expressions (Cinque 2010; Svenonious 2010). The Mandarin counterparts of English AxPart words are localizers (Ls), including a closed set of monosyllabic Ls, such as *qian* 'front' and *li* 'inside', and disyllabic ones formed by adding one of the suffixes, *-bian* 'side', *-mian* 'face', and *-tou* 'end' to monosyllabic Ls (e. g., Chao 1968; Zhu 1982). The suffixes *-bian*, *-mian* and *-tou* have lost both their tones and concrete semantic content when occurring as the second component of disyllabic Ls (Huang, Li and Li 2009). The suffix *-fang* 'position' is comparatively formal and less used. Table 1-1 summarizes the frequently used Ls. A tick in the cell indicates that the combination of the monosyllabic L and the suffix is possible. A horizontal line means that the combination does not exist in Mandarin. There are some peripheral cases such as *fujin* 'vicinity', *zhouwei* 'surrounding', *zhongjian* 'middle', *liang-pang* 'side' (N. Liu 1994), which could also be viewed as localizers.

Table 1–1   Localizers in Mandarin

Localizer	Meaning	边-bian (er) 'side'	面-mian (er) 'face'	头-tou (er) 'end'	方-fang 'position'
上 shang	'top'	✓	✓	✓	✓
下 xia	'bottom'	✓	✓	✓	✓
前 qian	'front'	✓	✓	✓	✓
后 hou	'back'	✓	✓	✓	✓
里 li	'inside'	✓	✓	✓	—
外 wai	'outside'	✓	✓	✓	—
左 zuo	'left'	✓	✓	—	✓
右 you	'right'	✓	✓	—	✓
东 dong	'east'	✓	✓	—	✓
南 nan	'south'	✓	✓	—	✓
西 xi	'west'	✓	✓	—	✓
北 bei	'north'	✓	✓	—	✓
旁 pang	'side'	✓	—	—	—
中 zhong	'middle'	—	—	—	—

In perceiving and describing an object's location, three elements must be considered: the object to be located (Figure), the reference entity (Ground), and the relationship between the two. We use the term 'reference entity (RE)' rather than Ground hereafter because the latter is associated with the concept of 'background', which may contain irrelevant entities other than the reference entity.① In English, the Figure and RE are encoded by noun phrases, while their relationship is encoded by around 80 prepositions (Ps) (Landau and Jackendoff 1993). There are three basic spatial relations expressed by spatial prepositional phrases (PPs): static locations as in 'the baby is (sitting) on the bed', motion within general

---

① The Figure and reference entity are also called theme and relatum in the discussion of reference frames (see P. Li 1988).

locations as in 'the baby is running (around) in the kitchen' and changes of location as in 'the baby ran into the kitchen' (Hickmann 1995). Close examination reveals that the last spatial relation involves change of location, or Path, while the first two do not—the spatial PPs just specify the general location of the state or activity. The distinction between Location and Path is a basic split in our conceptual structure and semantic structure. As represented in (3), the notion Path projects into a Path head which is higher than Place, the node for static Location (Svenonius 2010).① In English, cooccurrence of Path and Place elements such as *from* and *at* is forbidden as shown in example (3). The same is true for Mandarin Path and Place elements such as *cong* 'from' and *zai* 'at', as exemplified in (4).

(3) [$_{PathP}$ from [$_{PlaceP}$ (*at) behind the table]]

(4) 从/到(*在)桌子后边

    cong/dao (*zai) zhuozi hou-bian

    from/to (*at) desk back-side

    'from/to behind the table'

The distinction between Path and Location are encoded by grammatical Case in some languages. For example, Finnish differentiates between directional Cases (Illative, Elative, Allative and Ablative) and non-directional ones (Adessive and Inessive) (Fong 1997). In German, the Dative Case is used for general location, and the Accusative Case for change of location (Hickmann 1995; Bierwisch 1996). Mandarin, on the other hand, uses word order to encode such a distinction: preverbal spatial

---

    ① Path is morphosyntactically outside Place because there are languages where the directional preposition is hierarchically higher than the stative preposition as exemplified in the Romanian sentence (i) (Cinque 2010; Svenonious 2010).

  (i) Ion vine de la magazin.

    Ion is coming from at store

    'Ion is coming from at store.' (Romanian [Zegrean 2007, cited in Cinque 2010])

PPs headed by the locational preposition *zai* 'at' (simplified as *zai*-PPs hereafter) express Location, while postverbal *zai*-PPs convey Goal as exemplified in (5) (see Wang 1957, 1980; Zhu 1978).① In (5a), horseback is the general location of the action of jumping, and in (5b), horseback is the end point of the action of jumping.

(5) a. 他在马背上跳。

　　　Ta　zai　mabei　　shang　tiao.②　　(Location-V)

　　　he　at　horseback　top　　jump

　　　'He was jumping on the horse's back.'

　b. 他跳在马背上。

　　　Ta　tiao　zai　mabei　　shang.　　(V-Goal)

　　　he　jump　at　horseback　top

　　　'He jumped to the horseback.'

Thus far, we have discussed three types of spatial phrases (SPs) - Path, Place and AxPart phrases. As Path and Place elements do not co-occur in an English or Mandarin phrase, they can be argued to occupy

---

①　Apart from grammatical means, Mandarin also has lexical means to encode Path: it can be encoded by directional complements in a directional resultative verb compound, such as *chu* 'exit' in *fei-chu* 'fly-exit'; it can also be encoded by directional verbs or prepositions such as the Goal-denoting *dao* 'reach, to'.

　The *zai*-PP is very special in Mandarin Chinese, being the only type of spatial PP that demonstrates such a meaning contrast in preverbal vs. postverbal positions. Preverbal and postverbal phrases headed by *dao* 'reach, to' also demonstrate meaning contrast as in (i), but both readings express Goal, one being projected Goal, and the other reached Goal (Tai 1975).

(i) a. Ni　dao　zhe-bian　xie.
　　　you　come　this-side　write
　　　'You come here and write.'

　b. Ni　xie　dao　zhe-bian.
　　　you　write　to　this-side
　　　'you write up to here.'

②　Without context, this type of Chinese sentence can be translated into English in either present or past tense. Mandarin third-person singular pronoun *ta* has three forms: 他 (male), 她 (female), and 它 (animal or inanimate object). For the reason of simplicity, we gloss *ta* as 'he' in this book.

the same node in a syntactic tree. A PathP/PlaceP in the two languages can be simply viewed as having two layers—SP_H and SP_L as shown in (6) (N. Zhang 2002). The S_H encodes locative relation, while the S_L hosts Axial Part information. The word order for English SPs can be directly derived from the hierarchical structure. For instance, in (7a) S_H and S_L are realized by the preposition *in* and the noun *front*, respectively. In (7b), both S_H and S_L are realized by prepositions. Sometimes, Path/Place and AxPart are lexicalized into one preposition as shown by *in* in (7c). On the other hand, the word order for Chinese SPs, as in (8), is derived by movement or by setting the head parameter for the SP_L as head-final (N. Zhang 2002; Huang 2009; Huang, Li and Li 2009). The Mandarin counterpart of (7) in (8) shows that in Mandarin, SP_H can be realized by a VP or PP headed by *zai* '(be) at', and SP_L by a localizer phrase (LP). The morpheme *zai* '(be) at' could be a verb as in (9a) or a preposition as in (9b). Here we treat *zai* '(be) at' which is not the main verb of a stand-alone sentence as a preposition. The morpheme *zai* 在 can also be a progressive aspect marker, which falls outside of our discussion of spatial phrases. The categorial status of the locational *zai* is debatable, which will be further discussed in section 3.2.

(6) SP_H
       /   \
     S_H SP_L
           /   \
         S_L DP[①]   (based on N. Zhang 2002, 47)

(7) a. [$_{PP}$ in [$_{NP}$ front of the table]]
    b. [$_{PP}$ from [$_{PP}$ behind the table]]
    c. [$_{PP}$ in the box]

[①] This book does not make a distinction between NP and DP (the phrase which is headed by a determiner, such as *a*, *the* and *this*, and takes an NP as its complement). Both are used to refer to nominal phrases.

(8) a. [$_{VP/PP}$ zai [$_{LP}$ zhuozi   qian-mian]]
          at   table   front-face
     b. [$_{PP}$ cong [$_{LP}$ zhuozi   hou-mian]]
          from   table   behind-face
     c. [$_{VP/PP}$ zai [$_{LP}$ hezi   li-mian]]
          at   box   inside-face

(9) a. 他在地下。
       Ta   zai   di   xia.
       he   be at ground   bottom
       'He was on the ground.'

    b. 他在地下玩。
       Ta   zai   di   xia   wanr.
       he   at   ground   bottom   play
       'He was playing on the ground.'

By comparing English and Mandarin, we find that S_H and S_L may be instantiated by different syntactic categories across or within languages. Cross-linguistically, S_H is a preposition in English, but can be either a verb or preposition in Mandarin. Within English, S_L is realized by preposition or noun, whereas in Mandarin, S_L is exclusively realized by L.

So far, we have shown that space is encoded in Mandarin by localizers, prepositions, verbs and the phrases that they project into. We will examine them in detail in Chapters 2 to 4.

1.2   Viewing space via event semantics: some preliminaries

An event happens in space, and space is one of the elements that define events. This study attempts to understand space through the perspective of event semantics. In this section, the reader will be familiarized with basic notions in event semantics. We will first introduce arguments in the argument structure of an event-denoting verb, and then go on to discuss different eventualities that verbs encode and the internal structures of these eventualities.

1.2.1 Argument structure of a verb

An important observation in the generative literature is that the nominal phrases associated with a verb in a sentence realize fixed roles out of a limited pool of thematic roles, or theta-roles, including Agent, Experiencer, Theme, Goal, Source, and Location. In this study, Theme is defined as the event participant that undergoes motion, be it physical motion or nonconcrete types of motion (Gruber 1965, 48; Jackendoff 1972, 29 - 30).[①] Agent has a will or volition toward the action expressed by the sentence (Jackendoff 1972, 32). In (10a) and (10b), *the rock* is obviously the Theme as it is the entity that is conceived as moving. In (10b), *John* is the Agent, whereas in (10c) *John* is both the Agent and the Theme as he has volition toward the movement on the one hand, and undergoes movement on the other hand. Now let's turn to Location, Goal, and Source, theta-roles that are closely related to the present discussion of space. Location goes with locative verbs such as *stand*, whereas Source and Goal go with verbs of motion such as *move* and *roll*.

(10) a. The rock moved away.

　　　b. John rolled the rock from the dump to the house.

　　　c. John moved away.　　　(based on Jackendoff 1972, 29)

For the sake of simplicity, all spatial arguments will be referred to as Location hereafter, unless further distinction between static Location, Source, and Goal is required. When Location is obligatorily required by a verb, such as the English verb *put* as in (11a), it is considered an

---

[①]　There is a lack of agreement among linguists as to the definition of a few theta-roles. Our definition of Theme here is broader than some in the literature. For instance, in (10c), *John* is not considered as Theme by some researchers.

argument of the verb. When it can be omitted as shown by *from the dump to the house* in (10b), it is an adjunct, also called adverbial or modifier. Therefore, Location in English has a chameleon character as either a core or peripheral element in event representation, depending on the co-occurring verb. Different from English *put*, the Mandarin verb *fang* 'put' can go without a Location argument as in (11b). There seems to be a spectrum with adjuncts on one end and arguments on the other, and Mandarin Location is closer to the adjunct end than English Location.

(11) a. John put a book *(on the desk).

b. 张三放了一本书（在桌上）。

Zhangsan fang-le yi-ben shu (zai zhuo shang).
Zhangsan put-Perf one-CL book at desk top
'Zhangsan put a book (on the desk).'

The nominal phrases associated with a verb are said to receive theta-roles and serve as the arguments of the verb. Argument structure is the relationship between a verb's arguments and the verb in syntax. Linguists are very interested in the linking problem—how are the theta-roles mapped onto different syntactic positions. The Uniformity of Theta Assignment Hypothesis (UTAH) states that identical thematic relationships between items are represented by identical structural relations between these items at the D(eep)-structure level (Baker 1988, 46). As a corollary to this hypothesis, theta-roles are projected based on a thematic hierarchy: the higher its position in the semantic hierarchy, the higher its projection in syntax, and vice versa. The universal thematic hierarchy assumed in Jackendoff (1972, 43) and Grimshaw (1990, 8) is shown in (12), in which Location is higher than the most embedded Theme.

(12) (Agent (Experiencer (Goal/Source/Location (Theme))))

However, the hierarchical relationship between Theme and Location is controversial: in contrast to the view that Location is higher than Theme as in (12), Bresnan and Kanerva (1992) and Lin (2001, 23) argued for the reverse ordering. There is cross-linguistic evidence from Chishona and Kichaga showing that Theme ranks higher than Location (Bresnan and Kanerva 1992). It was observed by Jackendoff (1972, 43) that the passive *by*-phrase must be higher than the derived subject on the thematic Hierarchy. There are Chishona examples like (13) in which the *by*-phrase contains a Theme, and the derived subject is the Location. Therefore, Theme should be higher than Location. Data from Chishona and similar examples from Kichaga lead Bresnan and Kanerva (1992) to contend that Theme is higher than Location. ① In addition to thematic hierarchy, other linguistic factors, for instance, the aspectual hierarchy that ranks Cause higher than other arguments in a sentence, also influence the argument structure (Grimshaw 1990). ②

(13) Mu-tsime m-a-w-ir-w-a　　　　　ne-mbudzi.
　　　18-well　18 SU-PRF-fall-AP-PAS-FV　by-9 goat
　　　'The well has been fallen into by a goat.'

---

① The difference between English and Chishona with regard to the passivization of < Theme Location > verbs is attributed to the Intrinsic Classification parameter on passivization (Bresnan and Kanerva 1992).

② Some psych verbs like *frighten* seem to allow the least prominent Theme to be realized as the most prominent subject as in (i), which was explained by the aspectual hierarchy in (ii) that ranks Cause argument (*thunder* in this case) higher than other arguments in a sentence (Grimshaw 1990, 24).

(i) Thunder frightens them.
(ii) (Cause　(other (…)))
　　　subject　object

Event structure breaks down events into subparts. An Accomplishment, for instance, is comprised of two aspectual subparts—the causing activity and a resulting state. A cause is part of the first sub-event, so it is aspectually more prominent than arguments that participate in the second sub-event. When the thematic hierarchy and the aspectual hierarchy are in conflict, the former gives way to the latter. In (i), the thematically least prominent Theme is also the Cause as shown by its paraphrase in (iii). As the most prominent Cause, it is realized in the most prominent syntactic position—the subject position.

(iii) Thunder caused them to experience fear.

1.2.2 Event type and event structure

Each verb has associated with it an event structure, which determines the aspectual properties of the verb and the entire clause (Grimshaw 1990; Pustejovsky 1991, 1995, inter alia). One important goal of this study is to show that the event structure of a verb and its event type influences the way in which spatial phrases are interpreted. Aspect has two components—lexical aspect and grammatical aspect (Smith 1991, 1997). The lexical aspect of some lexical categories constrains the perspective that a speaker adopts to present a situation and contributes significantly to the aspectual interpretation of a sentence. The most heatedly discussed lexical aspect is verb aspect, also called aktionsart, situation aspect or verb phrase aspect in the literature.[①]

Four major types of aktionsarten or event types, including State, Activity, Achievement and Accomplishment, have been identified (Vendler 1957; Dowty 1979; Parsons 1990; Smith 1997; Rothstein 2004).[②] In the literature, Activity is also called Process, while Achievement and Accomplishment are also termed Event or Transition. Smith (1997, 20) proposed that three underlying features [+/− dynamic], [+/− durative] and [+/− telic] interact to determine the four lexical aspectual classes. Rothstein (2004, 12) reduced the features to two: [+/− event of change] and [+/− extended minimal events]. Employing Occam's razor, the present study adopts the simpler system. The interaction of the two features yields four event types as shown in Table 1 − 2. Events with the feature [+ event of change], corresponding to Smith's (1997) [+ telic], have a set terminal point as determined by the inherent properties of

---

[①] Verb aspect is also called verb phrase aspect, because the arguments of the verb, including the subject, also play a role (Smith 1997, 2).

[②] Smith (1997) and Rothstein (2004) also discussed a fifth event type, Semelfactive, which is irrelevant to the present discussion.

the events. Accomplishment and Achievement are telic. For instance, the event of drawing a circle has an inherent culmination, namely, the point when the circle is drawn. State and Activities are atelic, as they can go on indefinitely if there is no interference from an external force. An accomplishment is an extended event of change over an interval. It lasts long enough to allow the event to reach its completion incrementally. On the other hand, an Achievement such as *recognize* is nearly instantaneous and not extendable. It is a minimal event of change that consists of two instants: one instant when ϕ holds and the other when the negation of ϕ holds. The shortest possible state can hold at an instant and thus is not extended, whereas the shortest possible activity must hold at an interval. Take the shortest activity that counts as walking as an example. It consists of lifting one foot, moving it in the air and putting it down on the ground. Obviously, the whole process is an extended one. The classification of verbs into the four event types reflects 'basic cognitive distinctions that appear generally in language' (Smith 1990). Mandarin verbs can also be classified according to these four event types (Smith 1990, 1997). There are finer distinctions in dealing with eventualities. The division of states into dynamic and static is also relevant to the present discussion. According to Bach (1986), posture verbs like *sit*, *stand*, and *lie* are dynamic states whereas *love*, *know*, and *hungry* are static ones.

Table 1 – 2　Classification of event types based on Rothstein (2004, 194)

Event types	[+/– Extended minimal events]	[+/– Event of change]	Examples
States	–	–	*love, know*
Activities	+	–	*run, push a cart*
Achievements	–	+	*reach, recognize*
Accomplishments	+	+	*run a mile, draw a circle*

In the framework of Pustejovsky (1991, 1995) and Grimshaw (1990), event structure is a distinct lexical representation that exists alongside subcategorization and argument structure. The event structure comprises the primitive event types—State, Process and Transition, the rules of event composition, and the mapping rules of lexical structure. The event type of state stands for a single event, process stands for a sequence of events, and transition is an event evaluated relative to its opposition as shown in (14). Transition subsumes Achievement and Accomplishment, both of which share the same primitive event types, Process and State. However, their representations differ in that for Accomplishment, the activity leading to a state change is more prominent than the state change, whilst for the Achievement, the culmination part is more prominent than the development. The more prominent subpart in an event is the head of the event as marked by the asterisk in (15).

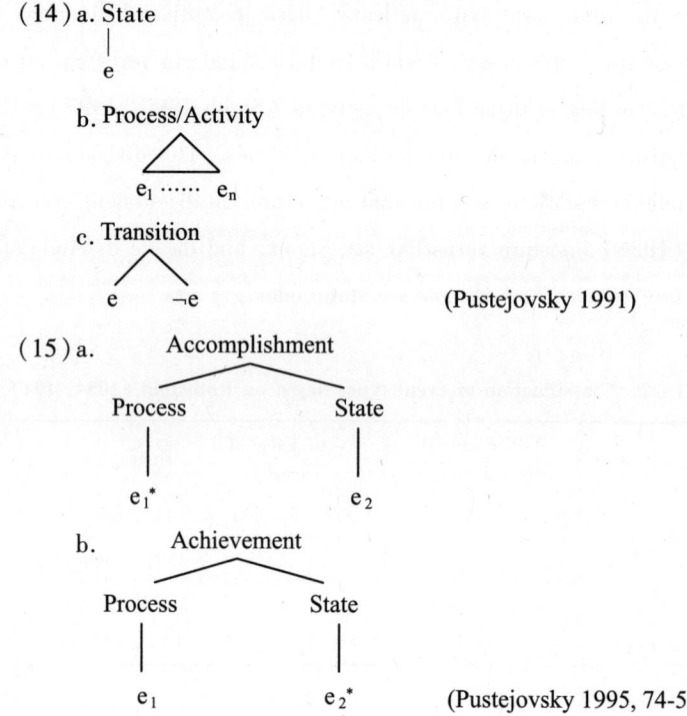

One of the motivations for positing a head in an event structure is to explain the situation where an adverbial modifies the head of an event rather than the entire event (Pustejovsky 1995, 74 – 5). In (16a), the durative adverbial modifies the result state of the achievement verb *die*, as it is not the process of dying that lasts for two days, but the state of being dead that lasts for two days. Therefore, the result state is the more prominent part, namely, the head of Achievement. In (16b), the manner adverbial *quietly* modifies the activity of drawing, which brought the picture into existence. It indicates that the process is the head of Accomplishment. Some Accomplishments, however, have both subevents as heads in the event structure (Nam 2000). For instance, the Accomplishment *drive the remote-controlled car behind the house* is doubly headed, as the adverbial *for an hour* can either modify the activity subpart or the result state subpart as shown by the two interpretations in (17). ①

(16) a. My terminal died for two days.

    b. Mary quietly drew a picture.　　(Pustejovsky 1995, 74 – 5)

(17) He drove the remote-controlled car behind the house for an hour.

    i. He drove for an hour.

    ii. The remote-controlled car was behind the house for an hour.

The event types of Process/Activity, Accomplishment and Achievement correspond to three syntactic configurations as in (18) (see Rappaport 1999; Lin 2001, 55 – 6). Following Larson's (1988) *v*P-shell analysis, a causative verb has two layers of VP structures, which correspond to the two subevents of Accomplishment. As shown in (18b), the upper component *v* encodes the causing activity while the lower VP

---

① Nam's (2000) original example under the two interpretations in (i) was judged as marginal by some native speakers. The example in (17) was from Donald White.

  (i) John loaded the hay on the truck all day long.

    a. John spent the whole day loading the hay on the truck.

    b. The hay was on the truck all day long.

encodes the result. The result can be a final state represented by an adjective phrase (AP) or a result location realized by a spatial PP. The V/v positions in the V-DP, v-VP and V-AP/PP sequences host semantic primitives DO, CAUSE and BECOME, respectively. The syntactic template of the Achievement is seen as the second subpart of that of the Accomplishment.

(18) a. Process/Activity

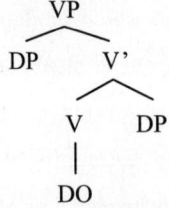

b. Accomplishment

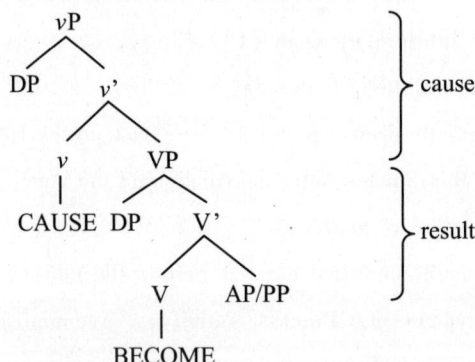

c. Achievement

(Rappaport 1999)

The second component of aspect is grammatical aspect or viewpoint aspect. A situation is always presented by speakers from a particular perspective or viewpoint. Perfective aspect focuses on a situation in its entirety, while imperfective aspect focuses on an interval, and neutral viewpoints include the initial point and at least one stage of a situation (Smith 1997, 62). ① Grammatical aspect is encoded by a limited number of morphemes, such as English *-ing*, in the verb-inflectional system of a language. Mandarin Chinese has two perfective aspect markers, *-le* and *-guo*, two imperfective aspect markers *zai* and *-zhe*, and a neutral viewpoint (see Li and Thompson 1981; Smith 1997). Grammatical aspect interacts closely with event types. What information a viewpoint presents is limited by the event structure of the verb, while viewpoint aspect can also induce change of the event type of the verb. For example, as we will show in section 2.1.3, the progressive aspect, one of the imperfective aspects, triggers the operation of aspectual shift from Achievement to Accomplishment.

1.3 Objectives and organization of the book

This study aims to provide a unified account of the linguistic encoding of space in Mandarin from a cross-linguistic perspective. To understand L (inguistic)-space in Mandarin, its semantics and syntax must be examined vis-à-vis other languages. We will investigate the ways in which Mandarin is aligned with universal patterns in encoding semantic primitives such as Location, and Path/Direction, and the ways in which it demonstrates its own unique characteristics. Specifically, the book focuses on three important issues:

---

① Sentences that lack viewpoint morphemes have a neutral viewpoint. For instance, sentence (i) does not have aspect markers and time adverbials, but it presents a situation that may be ongoing, terminated or completed (Smith 1997, 277).
  (i) Zhangsan xiuli yi-tai diannao.
    Zhangsan repair one-CL computer
    'Zhangsan repaired / is repairing a computer.'

a) How can we account for the placement and interpretation of spatial phrases headed by *zai* '(be) at' from the perspective of event semantics?

b) How are localizer phrases formed? Which syntactic positions do they fit in? Can the properties of the locative subject construction be captured by event semantics?

c) What is the relationship between language, perception and general cognition, three important cognitive systems in the discussion of space?

In the following chapters, a systematic description of L-space in Mandarin will be provided first, and then explanations will be proposed for some underlying patterns. The representation of L-space by Mandarin-speaking children will also be touched upon. The present chapter has introduced the basic syntactic and semantic structures of the spatial phrases in natural languages, including Mandarin. The rest of the book is structured as follows. Chapter 2 discusses the ambiguities of some spatial modifiers from the perspective of event semantics. Event structure and Davidsonian event argument are employed to explain the mechanisms of aspect shift and (sub)event modification. The ambiguities do not affect communication in a noticeable way, as there are syntactic means, contextual cues and real world knowledge to solve the ambiguity.

In Chapter 3 and Chapter 4, an aspectual hypothesis is proposed to account for the distribution and interpretation of the PPs headed by *zai* 'at', and the locative subject construction in Mandarin. We will show that the event type of the verb is pivotal in understanding the two structures. They are governed by universal principles of event semantics. However, the two structures also demonstrate some language-specific properties.

Chapter 5 examines the interaction between language, perception and cognition. Besides theoretical analyses, this book also features review and discussion of acquisition studies. In the last sections of Chapter 3 to Chapter 5, relevant empirical data, especially child language data, including children's use of *zai*, their choice of reference frames or strategies, and their acquisition of spatial terms are discussed. With the theoretical background, Mandarin-speaking children's acquisition of spatial terms and constructions is viewed from a linguistic perspective. By comparing patterns found in first language acquisition of Mandarin with those reported for adult learners of Mandarin, and children speaking other languages, especially English, this book aims to shed light on language universals and specificities, as well as the development of non-linguistic spatial cognition and general cognition in early childhood.

Chapter 6 discusses the contributions that this study makes to linguistic theory. There are some concluding remarks about the significance of this study in the current understanding of the linguistic encoding of space.

In summary, this book discusses the ambiguity of L-space, distribution of *zai*, and locative subject sentences in adult and child Mandarin under the framework of event semantics. Going beyond the domain of spatial language, it also investigates the interaction between language, perception and cognition.

Chapter 2 Ambiguities of Mandarin Spatial Modifiers: An Event-semantic Perspective

Natural language is rife with vagueness and ambiguities.[①] Even though it is possible for spatial language to communicate the positions of entities precisely, it is seldom the case. One prominent characteristic of spatial reference is its vagueness: a point in space is rarely specified precisely by a speaker as shown by the phrase *the man at the desk/office/ university*, in which the man's location is not specific in relation to the reference entity. It is not only indeterminate, but also ridden with ambiguity. In section 2.1, we will have an introduction of the ambiguities in L-space. Even though Mandarin does not display the English type of syntactic ambiguity discussed in section 2.1, both languages have the semantic ambiguity given by the event semantics of the verb which the spatial expression modifies. In section 2.2, we will elaborate on two types of semantic ambiguity from a cross-linguistic perspective. In Mandarin, spatial modifiers with placement verbs and those with posture verbs are potentially ambiguous between a directional reading and a locational reading. This section is devoted to explain the ambiguities under the

---

[①] An abridged version of this chapter and Chapter 3 and Section 4.1 appeared as the first three sections (pp. 1080 – 1094) of the following article: Deng, Xiangjun and Virginia Yip. 2015. The linguistic encoding of space in child Mandarin: A corpus-based study. *Linguistics* 53(5): 1079 – 1112.

framework of event semantics developed by Davidson (1967) and Parsons (1990). In section 2.3, we explain why the framework of event semantics is adopted for this study.

Even though L-space is relatively indeterminate and ambiguous, we do not often suffer from breakdown in communication, as our construal of a sentence is constrained in specific ways by our grammar and semantic principles on the one hand, and contextual cues, either linguistic or extra-linguistic, as well as our encyclopedic knowledge on the other. In section 2.4, we reflect on factors that give rise to ambiguous utterances and discuss how such utterances are disambiguated.

2.1 Ambiguities in linguistic space

In comparison with other languages, word order disharmony in Chinese gives rise to many structural ambiguities that are typical in Chinese but are not commonly found in other languages (D. Liu 1999). For instance, Chinese has object noun phrases (NPs) following verbs (V), relative clauses (Rel) preceding NPs, and genitive phrases (GP) before NPs. The cooccurrence of the three word orders is not found in 30 languages sampled in Greenberg (1966, cited from D. Liu 1999). For example, the vast majority of the languages in the world do not have the type of structural ambiguity in (19a) with two possible underlying structures shown in (19b) and (19c).

(19) a. 关心自己的孩子

    guanxin   ziji   de   haizi
    care   self   DE   child

    i. care about one's own child

    ii. the child who cares about himself   (D. Liu 1999)

b. [$_{VP}$ guanxin [$_{DP}$[$_{GP}$ ziji] de [$_{NP}$ haizi]]]

c. [$_{DP}$[$_{Rel}$ guanxin ziji] de [$_{NP}$ haizi]]

By comparing Mandarin and English, we found another typological difference in the availability of structural ambiguity. Both languages have the V-DP-PP word order. The structure is potentially ambiguous in English, but not in Mandarin. In English, a spatial PP can modify an NP or a VP. For instance, in (20), the PP *in the garage* can be adjoined to the N' in an X-bar tree, thereby modifying the NP projected by *car* as in (21a), and the corresponding meaning is in (20i). If the PP is adjoined to the V' modifying the VP *kept the car* as in (21b), then the sentence gets the meaning in (20ii). This type of syntactic ambiguity is also found in German (see Kratzer 1995). Cross-linguistically, the possible attachment sites of PPs in a sequence containing V, DP and PP give rise to ambiguity (see Schütze 1995).

(20) John kept the car [$_{PP}$ in the garage].

    i. The car that John kept was the one in the garage.

    ii. The garage was where John kept the car. (Guasti 2002, 6 - 7)

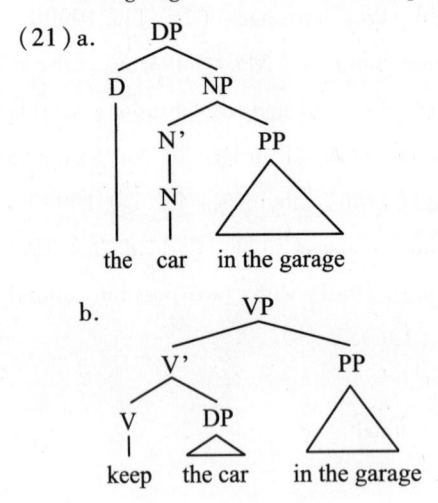

(21) a.
```
            DP
           /  \
          D    NP
              /  \
             N'   PP
             |   /  \
             N  
             |
        the car   in the garage
```

b.
```
              VP
            /    \
           V'     PP
          /  \   /  \
         V   DP
         |   /\
        keep the car  in the garage
```

In Mandarin, the V-DP-PP word order is rare, as Mandarin adjuncts normally precede V (Tai 1973; Huang 1982). As an exception, placement verbs like *fang* 'put' allow the V-DP-PP word order as in (22). Nevertheless, the spatial PP in this construction does not modify the

NP because spatial PPs never modify NPs in Mandarin as shown by (23). Unlike English, PPs in Mandarin Chinese can only adjoin to V in the V-DP-PP sequence: restricted adjunction determines that Mandarin does not have the type of structural ambiguity in English. The most literal Mandarin translation of (20) under the NP-modifying reading is (24), in which *zai cheku* 'be at garage' is in the relative clause modifying the NP.① As we will discuss in section 3.2, *zai* '(be) at', when used without a verb in a stand-alone sentence, is itself a verb.

(22) 他放了一本书在桌上。

    Ta fang-le [$_{DP}$ yi-ben shu] [$_{PP}$ zai zhuo shang].
    he put-Perf one-CL book at desk top
    'He put one book on the desk.'

(23) *从中国（的）学生

    *[$_{PP}$ cong Zhongguo] (de) xuesheng②
    from China (DE) student
    Intended meaning: 'the student from China'

(24) 张三留着在车库的车。

    Zhangsan liu-zhe [$_{VP}$ zai cheku] de che.
    Zhangsan keep-DUR be at garage DE car
    'Zhangsan kept the car which was in the garage.'

It is also important to recognize that not all the ambiguities in English are caused by the multiple adjunction sites of the locative PP. There are cases where the locative PP cannot possibly modify the DP in a V-DP-PP sequence, just as the case in Mandarin, and yet ambiguity still arises. In (25), the PP *in the tree* could not possibly modify the indefinite DP *a*

---

① The Mandarin counterpart for (20) under the (ii) reading is as follows.
(i) Zhangsan ba che liu-zai-le cheku.
    Zhangsan BA car keep-at-Perf garage
    'Zhangsan kept the car in the garage.'
② In Chinese, NP modifiers always precede the NP.

character. What he wrote was not 'a character on the tree', since before the writing, a character did not exist, let alone existed on the tree. An indefinite DP in the V-DP-PP structure disallows spatial modification. For instance, changing *the* into *a* in (20) renders the ambiguous sentence unambiguous. Even though the spatial PP in (25) has only one adjunction site, the sentence is still ambiguous: either he or the character was located in the tree. The indefinite Themes of verbs of creation, such as *write*, *draw*, and *build*, cannot be modified by spatial PPs in V-DP-PP sequences, but ambiguity does arise, so the ambiguity cannot be attributed to structural reasons.

(25) He wrote a character in the tree.

　　i. He wrote a character while he was in the tree.

　　ii. He wrote a character onto the tree.

The Mandarin counterpart of (25) in (26) demonstrates the same type of ambiguity. In section 1.1.2, we have pointed out that Mandarin has the two word orders PP-V and V-PP, PP being the prepositional phrase headed by *zai* 'at', to encode the spatial concepts Location and Goal. The real picture is far more complex. Many PP-V sentences are found to be ambiguous, expressing locational or directional meanings as shown in (26). It is hard to find one structural reason to account for this type of ambiguity. Meanwhile, some V-PP sentences are also ambiguous between a locational reading and a directional reading as exemplified in (27). As other V-PP sentences do not demonstrate this type of ambiguity, word order cannot explain the ambiguity in (27). The two types of ambiguity are well documented in the literature, but there is no satisfactory explanation for them.

(26) 他在树上写了一个字。

　　　　Ta　　zai　　shu shang　　xie-le　　　yi-ge　　　zi.

　　　　he　　at　　tree top　　write-Perf　　one-CL　　character

　　　i. 'He wrote a character while he was in the tree.' (location)

ii. 'He wrote a character onto the tree.' (direction)

(27) 阿姨坐在椅子上。

Ayi zuo zai yizi   shang.
auntie sit at chair top

i. 'Auntie sat on the chair.' (location)
ii. 'Auntie sat down on the chair.' (direction)

In this section, we have reviewed some types of ambiguity in L-space by comparing Mandarin with English and other languages. The ambiguity in (25), (26), and (27) cannot be explained by structural reasons, but are caused by some universal semantic principles to be discussed in the next section.

2.2 Explaining semantic ambiguity of spatial modifiers

So far, we have shown that the cause of the ambiguity of spatial modifiers in Mandarin Chinese and English is not always structural, due to syntactic or semantic restrictions. The main thrust of the present chapter will focus on two types of semantic ambiguity, arising from (sub)event modification and aspect shift respectively.

2.2.1 The principle of (sub)event modification

This principle of (sub)event modification presupposes the notion of event. We will first address why the Davidsonian approach posits 'event' in semantics, discuss its influence on the interpretation of spatial modifiers, and then identify the type of ambiguity given by event or subevent modification.

2.2.1.1 Davidsonian approach

It is informative to consider why multiple modifiers are possible in a single sentence as in (28). The intuition is that these modifiers all modify the same event: Jones buttering the toast. Davidson (1967) argued that each event-denoting verb has an event argument about which an indefinite number of things can be said. For instance, the logical form of (29a), shown in (29b), indicates that the verb *fly* contains an extra event argument *e*, which recurs in the two conjuncts representing the predicate and the spatial PP in the original sentence, and, therefore, links them. Using the terminology of predicate logic, the spatial modifiers are called predicates of the event.

(28) Jones buttered the toast slowly, deliberately, in the bathroom, with a knife, at midnight.

(29) a. I flew my spaceship to the Morning Star.

b. ($\exists$ e) (Flew (I, my spaceship, e) & To (the Morning Star, e))

'There is an evente such that e is a flying of my spaceship by me and e is to the Morning Star.'

(adapted from Davidson 1967)

In Parson's (1990) analysis, Agent and Theme, previously incorporated into the verb as in (30b), appear as separate conjuncts in the logical form as shown in (30c). Agent and Theme should not be automatically built into the meaning of a verb, because they are optional in cases like 'Brutus stabbed, but he missed' and 'I was stabbed in a dream, but not by anybody' (Parsons 1990, 96 – 99).

(30) a. I flew my spaceship.

b. ($\exists$ e) (Flew (I, my spaceship, e)) (adapted from Davidson 1967)

c. ($\exists$ e) [Flying (e) & Agent (e, I) & Theme (e, my spaceship)] (based on Parsons 1990)

Why can the event e in (29b) and that in (30c) be existentially quantified as indicated by the existential quantifier symbol '$\exists$'? This symbol is normally used to represent quantified NPs such as *an apple* or *someone*. In order to quantify entities, they must first be individualized, and much controversy has arisen over how events are individuated. Davidson (1980, 179, cited in Quine 1985) proposed that two events are identical if and only if they cause and are caused by all and the same events. This view was challenged by Quine (1985) who pointed out the circularity in the argumentation: two events are individuated by quantifying over other events as indicated by the universal quantifier *all*, but how can other events be individuated? Quine reified events as physical objects or as constructs upon physical objects. As physical objects are identical if and only if spatiotemporally coextensive, events that take the same place-time are identical. Quine's argumentation is not without problems. Suppose a ball is simultaneously rotating and heating up. In this case, is the event of ball's rotating identical to the event of its heating up? More seriously, if it is rotating rapidly and heating slowly, can we say that the event is both rapid and slow? To solve this problem, Quine retreated to conclude that an event is the pair of a physical object and a distinctive set of some sort. A third view, proposed by Kim (cited in Parsons 1990, 154), argues that the event of one's singing is distinct from the event of one's singing loudly. This fine-grained definition of event gives rise to a proliferation of events. There are many different possible descriptions of the same event. Should the entities corresponding to all the descriptions be considered different events? None of the accounts satisfactorily answer what counts as an event. Despite imperfect theories of event individuation at this stage, there are some intuitive arguments for events being countable individuals (Parsons 1990, 145 – 146). First, they are located in space and time: there may be generic stabbing, but there is a clear distinction between stabbing in the marketplace and stabbing at home, and the distinction between stabbing in the morning and that in the evening. Second, they can be perceived: in *Mary saw Brutus stab Caesar*, Mary's perception of the event is clearly denoted by the sentence *she saw the stabbing* in which the stabbing is the event that was perceived.

Numbers, functions and other classes are not visible entities, but they are considered categories in our mind, as they play an indispensable role in natural science (Quine 1985). The same line of reasoning justifies the ontological categorization of events. When events are treated as ontological categories (e.g. spatiotemporal regions or physical objects), it helps to explain a number of facts about language. The decisive evidence for the theory of underlying events comes from its power to capture the logic of modifiers in natural language. Firstly, it explains the entailment relationship between (29a) and (30a) (Davidson 1967). If the former is true, the latter is necessarily true. Thus, the former entails the latter. As the logical form of (30a) in (30b) is one conjunct of the logical form of (29a), it follows that (29a) entails (30a) based on predicate logic.

Second, the entailment relationship in (31) can be accounted for with the underlying event argument (Parsons1990, 14). Even though (31a) entails (31b) and (31c), (31b) and (31c) do not entail (31a). That is to say even though Brutus stabbed Caesar in the back and he stabbed Caesar with a knife, he did not necessarily stabbed Caesar in the back with a knife. Perhaps he stabbed Caesar in the back with an icepick, and in the thigh with a knife. The logical form in (32) reveals why the entailment does not hold. The stabbing event e in (32b) may be different from that in (32c). So the conjunction of (32b) and (32c) does not entail (32a). The underlying event analysis enables us to explain logical relations between sentences with modifiers.

(31) a. Brutus stabbed Caesar in the back with a knife.

b. Brutus stabbed Caesar in the back.

c. Brutus stabbed Caesar with a knife.

(32) a. ($\exists e$) [Stabbing(e) & Agent(e, Brutus) & Theme(e, Caesar) & In(e, back) & With(e, knife)]

'For some event e, e is a stabbing, and the agent of e is

Brutus, and the Theme of e is Caesar, and e is in the back, and e is with knife. '

b. (∃e) [Stabbing (e) & Agent (e, Brutus) & Theme (e, Caesar) & In(e, back)]

c. (∃e) [Stabbing (e) & Agent (e, Brutus) & Theme (e, Caesar) & With(e, knife)]

(Parsons 1990,13 – 14)

Spatial modifiers provide a third piece of evidence for a Davidsonian position. Kratzer (1995) pointed out the contrast between the two German sentences in (33) and (34). The spatial PP *in dieser Stadt* 'in this city' in (33) either modifies the NP *Flüchtlinge* 'refugees', leading to the (ⅰ) reading, or the verb *umgekommen* 'perished', yielding the (ⅱ) reading. (33) is ambiguous whereas (34) is not. The contrast can be explained by the distinction between stage-level predicates and individual-level predicates. According to Carlson (1977), an individual can be a kind or an object. Examples for individual-level predicates include *black*, *know French*, and *be named 'Hans'*. A stage is spatiotemporal part of an individual. Stage-level predicates include *perish*, *bite*, *sit*, and so on. Kratzer (1995) argued that not all kinds of predicates have an event argument. Individual-level predicates are not confined to time, so they do not contain an underlying event variable in their logic forms. Spatial expressions cannot modify individual-level predicates, because they do not have an event variable in its logical form. In (34), the individual-level predicate 'be black' does not have an event variable, so the spatial PP cannot modify the predicate, but can only modify the NP *swans*, while in (33), the stage-level predicate 'perish' has an event variable which allows spatial modification. This example in (33) clearly demonstrates ambiguity given by event modification. Similar cases can be found in English. In (35), the individual-level predicate *be a dancer* does not have an event variable, resisting modification by spatial PPs, in contrast to the stage-level predicate *dance* in (36).

(33) ···weil fast alle Flüchtlinge in dieser Stadt umgekommen sind.

since almost all refugees in this city perished are

i. ' ···since almost all of the refugees in this city perished. '

ii. ' ···since almost all the refugees perished in this city. '

(34) ···weil fast alle Schwäne in Australien schwarz sind.

since almost all swans in Australia black are

' ···since almost all swans in Australia are black. '

(35) a. Manon is a dancer (* on the lawn).

b. dancer (Manon)

(36) a. Manon is dancing on the lawn.

b. [dancing (Manon, l) & on-the-lawn (l)]

' Manon is dancing at l, and the spatial extension of l consists of the surface of the lawn. ' ①

(Kratzer 1995)

To summarize, the logic of modifiers validates the existence of an underlying event argument. The theory of event semantics is very powerful in explaining the semantics of modifiers, including spatial modifiers (Davidson 1967; Parsons 1990; Kratzer 1995). In what follows, we will use this theory to account for the logic of spatial modifiers headed by *zai* ' at ' in Mandarin.

2.2.1.2 Event modification

The semantic orientation of spatial modifiers has generated much

---

① In this logical form, ' l ' is a variable ranging over spatiotemporal locations. Different from the Davidsonian view that the verb introduces an event variable, Kratzer (1995) does not commit herself to the precise nature of the Davidsonian argument. It may simply be an argument for spatiotemporal location. In the logical form, the unbound ' l ' may become bound by quantifiers when the sentence appears as part of a more complex sentence, or gets its value from the context.

discussion in the literature. In this vein, one line of research posits that the spatial phrase orient towards an argument (Teng 1975; Kracht 2002). The question then becomes which argument it orients towards. In Mandarin, for example, Teng (1975) pointed out that with transitive verbs, preverbal locative PPs are ambiguous between being subject-oriented and object-oriented as shown in (26), while postverbal ones are unambiguously oriented towards the argument in the object position. Following the Davidsonian approach, we argue that all Mandarin spatial PPs are event modifiers. Argument orientation is only a surface reflection of the deep-level modification.

Firstly, spatial PPs are independent of arguments, modifying events rather than arguments. In (37a), both the Agent 'he' and the Theme 'the character' could not be on the keyboard. Instead, the character is on the computer screen. In other words, the spatial modifier *zai jianpan shang* 'on the keyboard' modifies the writing event rather than the Agent and the Theme. In (37b), under the scenario where he lay on the bed and turned on the light on the ceiling by pressing a button on the headboard, both 'he' and 'the lamp' are not on the headboard. In the extreme case of (37c), all the three arguments Agent 'he', Goal 'Lisi' and Theme 'one thing' are not on the phone. Now it should be clear that spatial PPs are independent of arguments present in a sentence. It is still necessary, however, to demonstrate that spatial PPs do indeed modify the event. The location of an event is the union of all the places occupied by the participants during that event (Kracht 2002). All three sentences in (37) have spatial PPs that signify the location of the event's Instrument: the keyboard, the power switch and the telephone, respectively. In this sense, these spatial modifiers modify events, encoding the locations of the events.

(37) a. 他在键盘上打字。

Ta   zai   jianpan   shang   da   zi.
he   at   keyboard   top   type   character

'He is typing on the keyboard. '

b. 他在床头开了屋里的灯。

   Ta   zai   chuang-tou   kai-le   wu   li   de   deng.
   he   at   bed-head   open-Perf   room inside DE   lamp

   'He turned on the room's lamp on the headboard. '

c. 他在电话里告诉了李四一件事。

   Ta   zai   dianhua   li   gaosu-le   Lisi   yi-jian   shi.
   he   at   telephone inside   tell-Perf   Lisi   one-CL   thing

   'He told Lisi something on the phone. '

Spatial modifiers are not alone in this regard, as manner modifiers also predicate on events rather than on arguments. In (38), the VP modifiers *shishi-de* 'wetly' and *cuicui-de* 'crisply' seem to be semantically oriented towards the Themes as shown by the English glosses. The present study argues, however, that the manner adverbials still modify the event, rather than the arguments. In (39) and (40), the (b) sentences do not have the same meaning as the (a) sentences.① The unacceptability of (39b) and (40b) is due to the semantic incompatibility of the modifier and the predicate. A blow-drying event cannot be wet and a buying event cannot be crisp, even though the hair can be wet, and the peanut can be crisp. In a word, manner adverbials do not modify one argument of the event, but the event *per se*.

(38) a. 头发湿湿地贴在脸上。

   Toufa   shishi-de   tie   zai   lian   shang.
   hair   wet-DE   stick   at   face   top

   'Wet hair stuck on the face. '

b. 他脆脆地炸了一盘花生米。

   Ta   cuicui-de   zha-le   yi-pan   huashengmi.
   he   crisp-DE   deep-fry-Perf   one-dish   peanut

---

① Jess Law, personal communication.

'He deep fried a dish of crisp peanuts.'

(39) a. 湿湿的头发吹干了。
   Shishi-de toufa chui-gan le.
   wet-DE hair blow-dry LE
   'The wet hair was blown dry.'

 b. *头发湿湿地吹干了。
   *Toufa shishi-de chui-gan le.
   hair wet-DE blow-dry LE

(40) a. 他买了一盘脆脆的花生米。
   Ta mai-le yi-pan cuicui de huashengmi.
   he buy-Perf one-dish crisp DE peanut
   'He bought a dish of crisp peanuts.'

 b. *他脆脆地买了一盘花生米。
   *Ta cuicui de mai-le yi-pan huashengmi.
   he crisp DE buy-Perf one-dish peanut

A piece of indirect evidence comes from English perceptual idioms in which a perceptual verb is followed by a tenseless clause as in (41). Parsons (1990, 15 – 17) argued that it is the event that is perceived rather than the event participants. One might feel Mary shuffling her feet without feeling Mary. Suppose John were blind and sitting in a canoe with Mary. He would be able to feel the percussion of the canoe and infer that Mary was shuffling her feet without actually seeing or feeling Mary. The predication of spatial PPs on events in Mandarin, and the logic of perceptual idioms in English lend further support to the underlying event theory. As events can be perceived alongside event participants, we can verbally locate events in space.

(41) John felt Mary shuffle her feet.   (Parsons 1990, 16)

Equipped with the evidence presented above, the modification relationship between an event and the spatial PPs can now be formalized. Following Parsons (1990), the logical form for sentences with transitive verbs and preverbal spatial modifiers such as (42), is provided below in (43). The logical form shows that the spatial modifier is predicated on the event only. It has no direct association with event participants. The event participants might happen to be present at the location as exemplified in readings i, ii, and iii for (42), but they do not have to be as exemplified in reading iv. To conclude, spatial modifiers are event predicates, and are not directly associated with arguments present in a sentence.

(42)张三在桌上写信。

    Zhangsan zai zhuo shang xie xin.

    Zhangsan at desk top write letter

    i. 'Zhangsan wrote letters on the desk but he was not on the desk.'

    ii. 'Zhangsan sat on the desk and wrote letters at another place.'

    iii. 'Zhangsan sat on the desk and wrote letters on the desk.'

    iv. 'Zhangsan wrote letters on a computer at the desk (neither Zhangsan nor the letters were on the desk).'

(43) ($\exists$e)[Agent(e, Zhangsan) & Theme (e, letters) & on (e, desk)]

Among a wide range of Chinese ambiguous structures discussed in G. Huang (1985), the ambiguity of PPs, both spatial and non-spatial ones, in the structure of PP-V, can be explained in the same way, demonstrating the explanatory power of the event-modification account. For example, in (44a), the manner PP *anzhao butong zhuangye* 'according to different majors' can be semantically oriented towards the subject, or the object of the preposition *he* 'with'. Since the manner PP, as an event modifier, predicates on the event of talking rather than on a particular argument, it can be freely associated with the two arguments of the event-denoting verb *jiaotan* 'talk'—*wo-men* 'we' and *ta-men* 'they'. Event modification also explains the ambiguity of spatial PPs in the topic position. In (44b), the spatial PP *zai dianyingyuan li* 'in the cinema' is the topic, as it precedes the subject *wo* 'I', occupying the Specifier position of the Complementizer Phrase (CP, namely the sentence) (see Radford 2004, ch. 9). This topic PP is structurally higher than, and has scope over the predicate *quan* 'persuade' in the main clause and the predicate *xiyan* 'smoke' in the subordinate clause.① Therefore, it may modify either of the two events, giving rise to the two readings: either the event of persuading or the event of smoking happened in the cinema.

(44) a. 我们按照不同专业和他们交谈。

      Wo-men anzhao   butong   zhuangye he   ta-men jiaotan.
      we   according to different majors   with they   talk

      i. 'We talked with them according to our majors.'

      ii. 'We talked with them according to their majors.'

b. 在电影院里,我劝他不要吸烟。

      Zai dianyingyuan li,   wo quan   ta   bu   yao   xiyan.
      at   cinema   inside I   persuade he   not   want   smoke

      i. 'In the cinema, I persuaded him not to smoke.'

      ii. 'I persuaded him not to smoke in the cinema.'

(G. Huang 1985)

2.2.1.3 Subevent modification

Another type of ambiguity associated with spatial modification involves external and internal readings, as observed by Dowty (1979, 261) in time adverbials. In order to explain the ambiguity in (45a), Dowty proposed meaning postulates in (45b) and (45c). In the meaning postulates, CAUSE is a kind of two-place sentential connective that relates an activity and a result state. The operator BECOME takes an embedded clause which depicts the result state. In the first reading, *again* is within the scope of

---

① Topic PPs occupy the specifier position of CP, and thus c-command TP, the main clause. The structural relationship determines that semantically, the topic PP has scope over the main clause and the embedded clause. For a tree representation of spatial PPs as topics, please refer to section 3.3.3.

BECOME, while in the second reading, it has scope over the entire event, including both CAUSE and BECOME. The decomposing of a causing event such as closing a door into CAUSE and BECOME in the meaning postulates successfully explains the ambiguity of *again*. The ambiguity of time adverbials provides a strong argument for decomposing an Accomplishment into an activity and a result state.

(45) a. John closed a door again.

    i. John closed the door at least once before.

                                        (external reading)

    ii. John caused the door to be closed again, but he did not close the door in an earlier occasion. (internal reading)

b. again' ($\wedge$[$\vee$ x[door'(x) $\wedge$ $\vee$ P[P{j} CAUSE BECOME close'(x)]]])   (external reading)

c. $\vee$ x[door'(x) $\wedge$ $\vee$ P[P{j} CAUSE BECOME again' ($\wedge$[close'(x)])]]   (internal reading)

                                                    (Dowty 1979, 261)

Pustejovsky (1995, 74) showed that adverbials can indeed modify individual subevents. It is generally assumed that only Activity and State can be modified by durative adverbials. Nevertheless, the Achievement *die* in (46) is also compatible with the durative adverbial *for two days*. The modification is fine, because in the event structure of *die*, there is a result state for the durative adverbial to modify (for the event structure of Achievement, see (15b) in Chapter 1). The modification yields the meaning that it has been two days since his death.

(46) He died for two days.   (Pustejovsky 1995, 74)

To explain the ambiguity of spatial PPs in sentences like (47a), Parsons (1990) also decomposed Accomplishments into two subevents. He argued that if there is only one event, it is hard to see how (47a) can have two distinct interpretations. The only solution is to admit that there are two underlying events in a causative sentence. The modifier may go with either of the two. The ambiguity is captured by the logical form in (47b). The verb *fly* introduces an event which can be decomposed into two subevents e and e' with the former causing the latter. The modifier of the verb modifies either e or e', giving rise to ambiguity.

(47) a. Mary flew her kite behind the museum.
      i. Mary did something behind the museum.
      ii. The kite flew behind the museum.
   b. $(\exists e)$[Agent(e, Mary) & $(\exists e')$[Flying(e') & Theme(e', kite) & Behind(_, museum) & CAUSE(e, e')] (the blank may be filled by either e or e') (Parsons 1990, 118)

Summarizing Dowty (1979), Parsons (1990) and Pustejovsky (1995), we found that even though these researchers resorted to different techniques in representing and explaining the ambiguity of temporal or spatial modifiers, there was a shared intuition that a modifier may modify either subevent in an event with complex event structure, giving rise to ambiguity. Following this line of reasoning, it is tempting to hypothesize that the ambiguity of the spatial PP in a Mandarin sentence such as (48) is also caused by subevent modification. In (48), *chuang shang* 'in the bed' could be either the general location of the event of pasting photos, or the end location of the photos as a result of the pasting. The two readings are called the locational reading, and the directional or Goal reading, respectively. Abstracting from tense and aspect, we provide the logical forms for the two readings in (49). The accomplishment verb *tie* 'stick' has a complex event structure which can be decomposed into a causing event e, and a caused event e' which leads to a result state s. [①] The spatial

---

[①] There is controversy as to whether Activities and States can be counted or not. Löbner (1989), for instance, argued that States and Activities cannot be individualized or counted, whereas Ahievements and Accomplishments, events in his terminology, are abstract individuals allowing classification and counting. Following Parsons (1990), we treat Activities as a type of event and States as countable. The existentially quantified Activity and State in the logical forms can be conceived as a chunk of activity and a chunk of state measured out by a time interval.

modifier, in boldface, can modify either the causing event *e* or the result state *s*.

(48) 他在床上贴了两张照片。

      Ta   zai   chuang   shang   tie-le   liang-zhang   zhaopian.
      he   at   bed   top   stick-Perf two-CL   photo

    i. 'He was in the bed and pasted two photos on another place.'

(location)

    ii. 'He pasted two photos onto his bed.'   (direction)

(49) a. (∃e) [Agent (e, he) & At (e, bed) & (∃e') [Theme (e', two photos) & CAUSE (e, e') & (∃s) [Being-stuck (s) & Theme (s, two photos) & BECOME (e', s)]]]

(location)

   b. (∃e) [Agent (e, he) & (∃e') [Theme (e', two photos) & CAUSE (e, e') & (∃s) [Being-stuck (s) & Theme (s, two photos) & At (s, bed) & BECOME (e', s)]]]

(direction)

Besides spatial PPs modifying events with complex event structure, it turns out that those modifying simple events also lead to ambiguity. In (50), the predicate *xi pingguo* 'wash apple' is Activity. Yet the preverbal *zai*-PP is still ambiguous. Sentences with simple event structures have two readings, just like sentences with complex event structures. Despite this, the two readings for (50) do not include a directional reading. *Pen li* 'inside of the basin', be it associated with the Agent or the Theme, is not understood as the result location of the action of washing apples.

(50) 他在盆里洗苹果。

        Ta   zai   pen   li   xi   pingguo.
        he   at   basin inside wash apple

    i. 'He washed apples and the apples were in the basin.'

    ii. 'He was in the basin and washed apples.'

Given cases such as (50), the present study proposes that all the preverbal *zai*-PPs with transitive verbs in Mandarin are potentially ambiguous. Being modifiers of the event rather than a particular argument, they could be associated with either Agent or Theme of the verb. The *zai*-PP with accomplishment verbs is a special case. These verbs have an internal event structure that contains a causing activity and a result state. It is logical to contend that the spatial PP associated with the Agent, which takes part in the causing activity, will have the locational reading while the spatial PP associated with the Theme, which is involved in the result state, will have the directional reading. The question is whether the ambiguity of the spatial PP between the locational reading and the directional reading is caused by subevent modification suggested by Dowty (1979) and Parsons (1990) or free association with Agent or Theme in event modification as discussed in section 2.2.1.2. It is hard to tease apart the two by looking into spatial PPs as they could modify both Argument DPs and verbs as shown by English and German data that we discussed in section 2.1. Even though Mandarin *zai*-PPs do not modify DPs, they still could hold a predication relationship with Arguments since *zai* '(be) at' could also be a verb. A better case to tease apart the two analyses is the sentence such as (45) discussed in Dowty (1979). The adverb *again* could not possibly modify the arguments *John* and *door*. The ambiguity of *again* is solely caused by subevent modification in the event structure of the verb *close*. Spatial PPs, being another type of adverbials, should behave the same as other event modifiers such as *again*.

The ambiguity of *zai*-PPs is no longer perplexing if viewed from the perspective of event semantics. In all the Mandarin examples in this section, spatial PPs modify the event, as encoded by the verb, rather than the event participant(s). All the preverbal *zai*-PPs with transitive verbs in Mandarin are potentially ambiguous, as being modifiers of the event, they could be associated with either Agent or Theme. However, the directional reading of spatial PPs is given by the complex event structure of the verb and subevent modification.

2.2.2 The principle of aspect shift

As a starting point, consider the ambiguity in (51). Many previous studies have claimed that English prepositions (e.g. *over*, *under*, *on*, *in*, *above*, *below*, *in front of*, *in back of*, *behind*, *before*, *ahead* and *between*) can have both a locational and a directional reading (Gruber 1965, 85; Jackendoff 1983; Svenonius 2010). Jackendoff (1983) asserted that these prepositions are locational, but can have a directional reading as they contain an unpronounced silent *to* in their conceptual structures. Conceptual structure is a level of mental representation at which linguistic, sensory, and motor information are compatible. It is at the interface between language and other cognitive systems. The conceptual structure for the prepositional phrase *under the table* is shown in (51). For the conceptual structure of *under*, it could either be the locational UNDER or UNDER plus the directional TO, hence the ambiguity.

(51) The cat ran under the table.
  i. [$_{Place}$ UNDER ([$_{Thing}$ TABLE])]
  ii. [$_{Path}$ TO ([$_{Place}$ UNDER ([$_{Thing}$ TABLE])])]

(Jackendoff 1983)

The lexical ambiguity account was later challenged by Fong (1997). If a locational preposition such as *under* is ambiguous between a locational and directional reading, then this ambiguity should be evident elsewhere. Fong claimed, however, that this prediction is not borne out as in (52): the only reading for (52) is that the road is wholly beneath and covered by the bridge. The road cannot pass under the bridge in an orthogonal manner. In other words, *under* in a noun phrase such as *a road under the bridge* has no directional reading, according to Fong (1997). However, some English native speakers do feel that (52) has the directional reading 'a road which leads under the bridge' (Stephen Matthews, personal communication), which calls Fong's analysis into question. We find that there are more convincing examples indicating that prepositions *per se* are not ambiguous. In (53), even though the (a) sentence is ambiguous, the phrase in (b) is not. Critically, the road in (53b) cannot pass through the trees. Therefore, *behind*, as shown by (53b), is not ambiguous. The ambiguity in (51) and (53a) is not caused by prepositions, but by other elements in these sentences.

(52) a road under the bridge

(53) a. The road extends behind the trees.

　　b. a road behind the trees

It is the aspect shift of the verb that explains this type of ambiguity (Fong 1997, 80). The directional reading of (51) is caused by the verb *run* shifting from Activity into Accomplishment. In the event structure of an Accomplishment, there is a result state which, when modified by a spatial modifier, gives rise to a change-of-state/directional reading. Examples of verbal aspect shift are abundant in language. Posture verbs can show State-Achievement alternation in combination with non-directional PPs as in (54), and internally caused change-of-state verbs also show such pattern as in (55) (Fong 1997, 72 – 74).

(54) He crouched behind the bush.　　　(State/Achievement)

(55) a. The tree blossomed for ten days.　(State)

　　b. The tree blossomed in a day.　　(Achievement)

(Fong 1997, 80)

Why is the aspect shift from Activity to Accomplishment and from State to Achievement possible? Some argue that a bounded PP induces the shift. Besides verbs, prepositions are also argued to have 'aspect' in a wider sense of the term involving the linguistic presentation of meanings as 'bounded' or 'unbounded' (Zwarts 2005).① The PPs headed by bounded prepositions, such as *to* and *from*, are bounded, whereas those headed by unbounded prepositions, such as *along* and *towards*, are unbounded. It has long been observed that an activity verb becomes an Accomplishment when followed by some bounded PPs as shown in (56a) (e. g. Dowty 1979, 60). Verkuyl and Zwarts (1992) show the compositional steps in deriving the sentence in (56a). The DP *the store* bears the [+ bounded] feature, which can be represented by finite cardinality and nonemptiveness of a set. The directional preposition *to* is also bounded. It turns the reference place into a bounded region. The predicate *walk* first applies to the spatial Path to yield a spatial-temporal Path, and then combines with the Theme of *walk* to form the event. The final event is bounded due to the boundedness of the spatial PP. In (56b), however, the spatial PP *along the river* is unbounded. Thus the event formed with the same verb *walk* and the unbounded PP is unbounded.

(56) a. John walked to the store.

b. John walked along the river.

(Verkuyl and Zwarts 1992)

Smith (1997, 53) provided a similar account: the feature value of an external form (adverbial, progressive aspect) overrides the value of the verb constellation, and gives rise to aspect shift. The aspectual coercion

---

① There are three types of prepositional aspect, exemplified in (i) (Verkuyl and Zwarts 1992; Nam 2000; Zwarts 2005).

(i) Bounded: to, into, from, away from, past, via

Unbounded: along, towards

(Un)bounded: around, across, down, over, through, up

The last type could be either bounded or unbounded. For instance, 'run around' can go with either 'for an hour' or 'in an hour' as shown in (ii), suggesting that it can be Activity or Accomplishment. In the former case, 'around' is unbounded, and in the latter, it is bounded.

(ii) a. He ran around the lake for an hour.

b. He ran around the lake in an hour.

account proposed by Pustejovsky (1995) and Jackendoff (1997, 51 – 53) is essentially in the same spirit.① Apart from the aspect shifts discussed above, Smith (1997, 52 – 53) proposed that time adverbials trigger Accomplishment to shift into Activity as in (57).② The sentences in (58) present State as Activity because the progressive viewpoint ascribes dynamism to the situation. A nominal variant of the dynamic verb with the copular verb as in (59) renders Activity into State.

(57) Accomplishment to Activity

John walked to school for ten minutes.

(58) State to Activity

a. I'm hating zoology class.

b. The river is smelling particularly bad these days.

(59) Activity to State

The ship was in motion.

(Smith 1997, 52 – 53)

Rothstein (2004, ch. 2) discussed two more types of aspect shift. The progressive aspect triggers the achievement verbs *die* and *reach* to shift into Accomplishment in (60), and triggers the achievement verbs *spot* and *notice* to switch into Activity in (61). As observed by Dowty (1979, 133), Accomplishment but not Activity induces the imperfective paradox in

---

① Coercion is defined as 'a semantic operation that converts an argument to the type which is expected by a function, where it would otherwise result in a type error' (Pustejovsky 1995, 111). This concept encompasses aspectual coercion as well as other kinds of type shifting. For instance, in *he began a book*, the governing verb *begin* requires an event-denoting complement, so it coerces the physical object-denoting NP *a book* into an event denotation to avoid a type error.

② In Jackendoff (1997, 51 – 53) and Pustejovsky (1995, 14 – 15), the type shift from Accomplishment to Activity is also discussed. For instance, in sentence (ia), the verb *keep* which requires its argument to be an ongoing process coerces the Accomplishment *cross the street* into a compatible event type Activity. In (ib), the accomplishment verb *build* becomes Activity when followed by a bare plural object.

(i) Accomplishment to Activity

a. Bill kept crossing the street.

b. Brown and Root Inc. builds runways in Southwest Asia.

the progressive as shown in (62). The progressive Achievements in (61) are different from those in (60), because the former do not induce the imperfective paradox, in contrast to the latter, as shown in (63).

(60) Achievement to Accomplishment
 a. The old man is dying.
 b. Jane is reaching the summit.

(61) Achievement to Activity
 a. Mary is spotting her enemy at the party at the moment.
 b. The critic is noticing the new picture.
(Rothstein 2004, 56)

(62) a. Jane is/was running ENTAILS Jane ran. (Activity)
 b. Jane is/was building a house DOES NOT ENTAIL Jane built a house. (Accomplishment)

(63) a. The old man is/was dying DOES NOT ENTAIL he died.
(Achievement → Accomplishment)
 b. The critic is/was noticing the new picture ENTAILS s/he noticed it. (Achievement → Activity)

In Mandarin, we identified three more event-type shifts. Individual-level predicates differ from stage-level predicates in not falling into any of the four event types (Kratzer 1995). Yet with the help of the sentence-final particle *le* signaling inchoativity (Chao 1968/2004, 800), change of state (Soh 2009) or currently relevant state (Li and Thompson 1981, 240), individual-level predicates can shift into inchoative achievement predicates, which, as a subtype of Achievement, encode the beginning of a state, as exemplified in (64). Another interesting type shift is shown in (65) where agentless placement verbs, originally Accomplishments, shift into state verbs without any external trigger.① Some manner-of-motion verbs such as *pao* 'run' and *zou* 'walk' are normally conceived of as Activities

---

① We will provide diagnostics for the shift between the two event types in section 3.3.2.

as shown by (66i), but they can be turned into Achievement as in (66ii). In this sentence, *pao* 'run' under the 'escape' reading is Achievement as it can go with the punctually locating expression 'at x time' as shown in (67). This property is the hallmark of Achievement and State to be introduced in Section 3.1.

(64) Individual-level predicate to inchoative Achievement

    a. 他聪明了。

        Ta   congming   le.

        he   intelligent   LE

        'He became intelligent.'

    b. 他白了。

        Ta   bai   le.

        he   white   LE

        'He became white.'

(65) Accomplishment to State

    相片贴在床上。

    Xiangpian   tie   zai   chuang   shang.

    photo   stick   at   bed   top

    'Photos are stuck on the bed.'

(66) Activity to Achievement

    他跑了。

    Ta   pao   le.

    he   run   LE

    i. 'He has run.'

    ii. 'He escaped.'

(67) 他九点半跑了。

    Ta   jiu   dian   ban   pao   le.

    He   nine   o'clock   half   escape   LE

    'He escaped at half past nine.'

There are two logical possibilities to account for why aspect shift arises. The first is a compositional view — an adverbial or an aspect marker coerces the aspect shift at the sentential level, which has already been introduced above. The second is a non-compositional one: aspect shift is solely given by the inherent feature of the verb (see Fong 1997, 81). The present study rejects the compositional analysis for adverbials. In sentences (51) and (54), the aspect shift (from State/Activity to Achievement/Accomplishment) occurs when the PPs are not bounded. Mandarin provides converging evidence. As observed by Fong (1997, 91), Mandarin posture verbs, just like English posture verbs, can shift between State and Achievement. In (68a), for instance, when the posture verb *zuo* 'sit' is used as State, the sentence gets the locational reading, and when it is used as Achievement, the directional reading arises. The locational morpheme *zai* '(be) at' does not have the change-of-location meaning when used alone or used with a State such as *heng* 'lie', as shown in (68b) and (68c) respectively. The change-of-location meaning in (68a) is non-compositional: it comes solely from the verb, rather than the combination of the verb and the adverbial. If the meaning of the whole does not equal the combined meanings of the parts, then the entire structure is not compositional. Therefore, aspect shift in (68a) is non-compositional. The adverbials do not override the aspectual value of the verb constellation, but instead trigger the aspect shift when the verb has the potential to undergo the shift. Nevertheless, in the case of the progressive aspect, it works on the aspectual value of the verb phrase, and changes the interpretation of the verb phrase at the sentential level as shown in (58), (60), and (61). This type of aspect shift is compositional: the perspective that a speaker chooses to present a situation coerces the aspect shift.

(68) a. 阿姨坐在椅子上。

  Ayi zuo zai yizi shang.

  auntie sit at chair top

i. 'Auntie sat on the chair.'　　　　　(State →location)

ii. 'Auntie sat down on the chair.'　(Achievement → direction)

b. 阿姨在椅子上。

Ayi　　zai　　yizi　　shang.

auntie　be at　chair　top

'Auntie is/was on the chair.'

c. 大桥横在江上。

Da　qiao　heng　zai　jiang　shang.

big　bridge　lie　at　river　top

'The big bridge lies above the river.'

Thus far, the present study has demonstrated that a verb can switch between Achievement and State as shown in (54), between State and Activity in (58) and (59), between Accomplishment and Activity as in (56a) and (57), as well as between Achievement and Activity in (61) and (66). Achievement can also shift into Accomplishment as shown in (60). Accomplishment may shift into State as in (65). Each of the four event types has an aspect-shift relationship with the other three event types.① However, some of the aspect shifts occur less naturally than others. For instance, the Achievement-to-Activity shift in (61) is less natural, or more coerced, than the shift from Achievement to Accomplishment in (60) (Rothstein 2004, 58). Within the alternation pairs, one event type is considered a more prototypical use of the verb than the other. The former is called basic-level and the latter the derived-level (Smith 1997, 18). In (60a), for example, the verb *die* is normally considered as Achievement and its use as Accomplishment is considered derived.

---

① The mechanism is universal but there may be crosslinguistic differences in the availability of some types of aspect shift.

Why is aspect shift between event types possible? There are three possible explanations. First, the porousness of event-type boundaries may be ascribed to commonalities in feature values. Among the four event types, there may be a shared feature value in every possible pairing combination. It is widely assumed that if different lexical categories share a syntactic feature value, they may behave the same in some respects. For instance, the feature [+/− N(oun)] determines whether a lexical category can assign Case or not (Stowell 1981, 21 − 23). Prepositions (with the feature cluster [− N] & [− V(erb)]) and verbs ([− N] & [+ V]) both have the [− N] feature, so they can be Case-assigner, while adjectives ([+ N] & [+ V]) and nouns ([+ N] & [− V]) have the [+ N] feature and thus both cannot take an object without the help of a Case-assigner. The same line of reasoning may be used in explaining aspect shift. For instance, the feature value [− extended minimal event] is shared by State and Achievement as shown in Table 1 − 2 in section 1.2.2. This may be the reason that a verb can switch between the two event types. However, there are obvious counterexamples: e. g. Accomplishment ([+ event of change] & [+ extended minimal events]) does not share a feature value with State ([− event of change] & [− extended minimal events]), but it can shift into State. One way out is to argue that the number of features in Rothstein's (2004) two-feature system is not enough to capture the overlap between four event types. However, Smith's (1997) three-feature system also cannot cover all the possible shifts. This system can explain the aspect shift from Accomplishment to State as the two share the feature value [+ durative], but this time it fails to explain the shift between State (with the feature cluster [+ static], [+ durative] and [− telic]) and Achievement (with the opposite feature values for all the three features). In a word, feature sharing is not a necessary condition for aspect shift.

The second possible explanation is that aspect shift is a by-product of the more general semantic class shift. Levin and Rappaport Hovav (1996) discussed semantic class shift from verbs of sound to verbs of directed motion. Verbs of sound such as *yell* and *creak* are unergative as they do not have underlying objects, so a fake object such as *oneself* must be inserted for a resultative phrase to predicate on as in (69). [①] Verbs of directed motion, however, are unaccusative verbs that have underlying objects. Verbs of sound show unaccusative behavior when they shift into verbs of directed motion as in (70). They do have an underlying object in this sense, so the resultative phrase can predicate on the trace of the object (represented as *t* which is assigned the same index i as the subject to indicate movement and coreference), which has moved to the subject position. (69) and (70) demonstrate that verbs of sound can undergo meaning shift, and occur in the resultative patterns associated with both unergative and unaccusative verbs. Besides verbs of sound, manner-of-motion verbs (e.g. *run*, *shuffle*, *walk*) and verbs of exerting force (e.g. *push*, *pull*) can become verbs of directed motion in the presence of a directional phrase as exemplified by (71).

(69) yell oneself hoarse

(70) The curtains$_i$ creak t_i open.

(71) Kim pushed the stroller into the store.

(based on Levin and Rappaport Hovav 1996)

We hold the third view that aspect shift is possible because there is overlap in event structure between some event types. In particular, an eventuality of Transition overlaps with the subevent that serves as its head (see (15) in section 1.2.2), and aspect shift between the two is natural. Accomplishment and its aspectual head Activity can serve as an example. Aspect shift occurs naturally between the two, as observed by Bach (1986) who drew attention to the parallels between the mass-count distinction in the nominal system, and the distinction between event and process

---

[①] Unergative and unaccusatives verbs will be introduced in section 3.1.

(Transition and Activity in our terms) in the aspectual classification of verbs. He provided a series of evidence to demonstrate the parallels. English allows switching back and forth between count and mass, event and process without change in the form. Practically any count noun can be used as a mass one, e. g. *dog* in *there was dog splattered all over the road*. Conversely, a mass noun can also be used as a count noun. For instance, the mass term *mud* can be pluralized to refer to kinds of mud. Similarly, practically any process verb can denote a bounded event if the context is right. *Look for* is a process verb as it cannot follow *finish*. For instance, *I finished looking for a unicorn* is anomalous. However, in the context of a library, the sentence *I finished looking for a book* is perfectly acceptable. The count-mass shift and the event-process shift are possible because all things or events can be decomposed into small granules of material or process. The boundary of events and processes are 'more an artifact of our language or conceptualizations of the world than something about the world itself' (Bach 1986, 15). The head of Achievement is State. Aspect shift between the two is also very natural as shown by the posture verbs *crouch* in (54). State could also be the head of Accomplishment in English under special circumstances as shown by (17) in section 1.2.2, so aspect shift between the two is also possible. Such shift is also productive in Mandarin as shown by the case in (65). Even though the activity subevent of an Achievement is negligible, Achievement shares the same event structure with Accomplishment as shown by (15) in section 1.2.1. Thus we see cases like (60) where Achievement shifts into Accomplishment. Activity is one subevent in the event structure of Achievement, so shift between the two is also possible; but as Activity is not the head of Achievement, the shift is not that natural as shown in (61). Activity and State do not overlap in event structure. So shift between the two must be coerced: external forms such as the progressive aspect exemplified in (58), or change of form as in (59) are called for.

Our account is compatible with the second explanation based on Levin and Rappaport Hovav (1996). In aspect shift or semantic-class shift, verb semantics, including the aspectual features of the verb, undergoes change. The capacity to shift between different event types is determined by the verb *per se*, but the actual shift may be induced by the context.

2.3 Event semantics in framing Chinese motion events

Event semantics of an event-denoting verb, including its event type and event structure, is key to understanding a wide spectrum of phenomena in language. In particular, the theory of event semantics has proven to be useful in explaining the logic of modifiers, including spatial modifiers (Davidson 1967; Parsons 1990; Kratzer 1995). In this study, we extend this theory to spatial modifiers headed by *zai* 'at' in Mandarin, and find that it is capable of accounting for their interpretation. This is the motivation for adopting event semantics as the framework for the present study, and extending it to cover more data in Mandarin in the following two chapters. In Chapters 3 and 4, we will show that this approach is more powerful than previous approaches in accommodating Mandarin data.

The event-semantic theory helps us to explain the ambiguity of spatial PPs in English and Mandarin. The multiple readings of preverbal *zai*-PPs with transitive verbs, and the directional reading of *zai*-PPs preceding placement verbs are well captured by this theory. Spatial PPs modify the event rather than the event participant. As being modifiers of the event, they could be associated with either Agent or Theme. This explains why all preverbal *zai*-PPs with transitive verbs in Mandarin are potentially ambiguous. The directional reading of a spatial PP is given by the complex event structure of the verb and subevent modification. When the result state subevent in the verb is modified by a spatial PP, a directional meaning arises. The event-semantic theory also helps us explain the ambiguity of the postverbal zai-PPs with posture verbs. Verbs can undergo aspect shift. The types of shift that have been identified in English and Mandarin include Activity-Accomplishment alternation, State-Achievement alternation, State-Activity alternation, the shift from Achievement to Accomplishment, the shift from Accomplishment to State, and the shift from individual-level predicate to inchoative Achievement. Posture verbs in Mandarin, just like those in English, can shift between Achievement and State (Fong 1997). Therefore, the corresponding directional reading and locational reading are potentially possible for zai-PPs following posture verbs. Positing the mechanism of aspect shift enables us to explain why a verb can occur in different syntactic structures, such as the verb *tie* 'stick' in (48) and (65), and why the same structure may have multiple readings as in the case of the posture V-*zai* structure.

2.4 Remedies for ambiguity in linguistic space

Even though ambiguity in L-space is pervasive, human beings have no difficulty in resolving ambiguity in communication. The number of possible interpretations for any given sentence is limited by syntactic, semantic, and cognitive constraints. A sentence can only be interpreted in certain structured ways. For instance, as discussed in section 2.1, the string V-DP-PP can only have two possible structural representations as exemplified in (21), each corresponding to one of the two readings of the sequence. Spatial adverbials are used to modify the event so they predicate on events rather than arguments as shown by the logical form in (43) for a Mandarin sentence in (42) in section 2.2.1.2. There are only four possibilities that match with the logical form in (43) truth-conditionally: (a) neither Agent nor Theme are on the desk, (b) Agent is on the desk, (c) Theme is on the desk and (d) both of them are on the desk. The logical possibilities of association between the spatial modifier and the two arguments present in the sentence give rise to the four readings. Spatial modifiers may be associated with event participants not present in the sentence as shown in section 2.2.1.2, but this type of association is restricted to Instrument. In short, the ambiguity of L-space is not whimsical, but is constrained in specific ways.

Many sentences discussed so far are ambiguous only when presented without context. Most ambiguities of L-space can be resolved in extralinguistic context. What concerns us here is the linguistic means to resolve ambiguity. Different word orders, for instance, can be employed to disambiguate spatial expressions. In Mandarin, a spatial PP headed by *zai* 'at' can either precede a placement verb such as *fang* 'put' or follow it. When preceding the verb, it is ambiguous. Postverbally, however, the ambiguity disappears (Teng 1975). In other words, one can choose to put the *zai*-PP in postverbal position to avoid ambiguity. The syntactic means will be discussed in section 3.3.3, after we have laid out the particularities of *zai*.

Co-occurring phrases within the same sentence also helps to disambiguate a sentence. Some manner adverbials which are frequently used with events, such as *xunsu-de* 'quickly', *manman-de* 'slowly' and *xiaoxin-de* 'carefully', bring out the directional reading for the posture V-*zai* structure while discouraging the locational reading. In (72a), for instance, the use of the adverbial *yi-pigu* 'one-buttock = quickly' forces the otherwise ambiguous sentence to have the directional reading only. One may argue that the directional reading comes from the adverbial. But when this adverbial is attached to a corresponding stative sentence as in (72b), no directional meaning arises. So the directional meaning in (72a) does not come from the adverbial *yi-pigu* 'one-buttock = quickly' but from the predicate. Similarly, manner adverbials which are frequently used with States, such as *anjing de* 'quietly', and *yidongbudong de* 'motionless' bring out the locational reading while discouraging the directional one. In contrast to (72a), the only reading for (73) is a locational one.

(72) a. 阿姨一屁股坐在地上。

    Ayi   yi-pigu   zuo zai di   shang.

    auntie one-buttock sit   at   ground top

    'Auntie sat down on the ground quickly.'

b. #阿姨一屁股在地上坐。

    #Ayi   yi-pigu   zai di   shang   zuo.

    auntie one-buttock at   ground top   sit

    Intended meaning: 'Auntie sat down on the ground quickly.'

(73) 阿姨一动不动地坐在地上。

    Ayi   yidongbudong-de   zuo zai di   shang.

    auntie motionless-DE   sit   at   ground top

    'Auntie sat on the ground motionlessly.'

Real world knowledge, which is stored in our long-term memory, also plays a significant role in resolving ambiguity (Schütze 1995). Spatial modifiers can be disambiguated by our encyclopedic knowledge. For instance, the English sentence (74a) is ambiguous whereas (74b) is not, because actress is normally conceived as being on the stage. There are similar cases in Mandarin. The two sentences in (75) have the same syntactic structure, but (75b) is unambiguous, in contrast to (75a). The availability of ambiguity is determined by the localizer phrases that follow the spatial Ps. The place denoted by the localizer phrase *qiang shang* 'on the wall' could only be the Goal according to our world knowledge, as a man could not possibly stay on the wall to write under normal conditions, whereas *chuang shang* 'on the bed' could be either the Location or Goal of writing. There is another example. In Mandarin, the posture V-*zai* structure is potentially ambiguous between a locational reading and a directional reading, but rarely so in real world communication. For instance, the directional reading is not possible for the localizer phrase *fangjian li* 'inside the room' in (76), as in the real world, one could not sit down in one room and end up in another. Therefore, (76) is unambiguous.

(74) a. John saw the actress on the train.

b. John saw the actress on the stage.

(75) a. 张三在床上写了一个字。

Zhangsan zai chuang shang xie-le yi-ge zi.
Zhangsan at bed top write-Perf one-CL character
i. Zhangsan wrote a character while he was in bed.
ii. Zhangsan wrote a character on the bed.

b. 张三在墙上写了一个字。

Zhangsan zai qiang shang xie-le yi-ge zi.
Zhangsan at wall top write-Perf one-CL character
'Zhangsan wrote a character on the wall.'

(76) 阿姨坐在房间里。

Ayi zuo zai fangjian li.
auntie sit at room inside
'Auntie sat in the room.'

To sum up, this section has demonstrated that the ambiguity of L-space is not whimsical, but constrained by syntactic, semantic, and cognitive constraints. Linguistic context and real world knowledge help to resolve ambiguity in L-space.

2.5 Summary

L-space has plentiful ambiguities that may cause misunderstanding in communication. One type of ambiguity is given by aspect shift. Verbs can undergo aspect shift, and the types of shift that have been identified in English and Mandarin include the State-Achievement alternation of the posture verb, and so on. Another type of ambiguity arises from (sub)event modification. Spatial PPs modify the event, as embodied by the verb, rather than the event participant. All preverbal *zai*-PPs with transitive verbs in Mandarin are potentially ambiguous: as being modifiers of the event, they could be associated with either event participant—Agent or Theme.

The current study argues for the psychological reality of the category of 'event', alongside 'entity'. It could be a particular type of entity that figures in the denotations of verbs (Löbner 1989; Kracht 2002). Semanticists like Davidson (1967), Parsons (1990) and Kratzer (1995) have provided much evidence to demonstrate its existence. The interpretation of spatial PPs offers another window through which its psychological reality can be seen. Spatial PPs do not modify any particular participant in an event, but the event *per se*. That is why they can be potentially associated with any of the participants, and the event participants present in a sentence could, but do not have to, be located at the place specified by the spatial PP. Moreover, the directional reading of spatial-PPs is given by the complex event structure of the verb and subevent modification. The spatial modifier can modify either of the two subevents, leading to ambiguity. Without the category of event and its internal structure, the rampant ambiguities of spatial PPs cannot be explained.

In this chapter, we have also shown that languages differ in the linguistic encoding of space. For instance, Mandarin does not have the English type of ambiguity in the adjunction site of prepositional phrases (PPs) in V-DP-PP sequences.

Chapter 3　Distribution of *zai* in Mandarin

The first two chapters have discussed the general encoding of space in natural language, and the ambiguities of Mandarin spatial modifiers under the framework of event semantics. Chapter 3 will continue to examine the syntax and semantics of spatial modifiers formed by the prepositional phrases headed by *zai* '(be) at' (abbreviated as *zai*-PPs hereafter) in Mandarin Chinese from the perspective of event semantics. Following Davidson (1967) and Parsons (1990), adverbials are treated as modifiers of events. *Zai*-PPs, being one type of adverbials, are also event modifiers. Section 3.1 introduces the classification of Mandarin verbs based on their event types, which will be used to describe and explain the syntax and semantics of *zai*-PPs that co-occur with the verbs. Section 3.2 introduces various Mandarin spatial prepositions. Section 3.3 provides an event-semantic account of the syntax and semantics of *zai*-PPs, and elaborate on the influences of syntactic positions, cognition, and language change on the use of *zai*-PPs. Section 3.4 summarizes the theoretical analyses in previous sections, and the last section delves into child language acquisition of *zai* and *zai*-PPs.

3.1　Verb classification based on event type

Similar to other languages, Mandarin verbs can be categorized, according to their syntactic properties, as unaccusative, unergative, transitive, causative and ditransitive verbs (Huang 2007, inter alia). Unaccusative verbs, such as *lai* 'come' and *si* 'die', do not have an external argument. Unergative verbs, such as *xiao* 'laugh' and *chao* 'quarrel', have a single, external argument. Transitive verbs are exemplified by *chi* 'eat' and *da* 'hit' which take two arguments Agent and Theme in a clause. Causative verbs include verbs such as *chen* 'sink' and *kai* 'open'. In an event encoded by a causative verb such as *kai* 'open' in *Zhangsan kai men* 'Zhangsan opened the door', the Cause *Zhangsan* precipitates a change of state in the Theme *the door*. Ditransitive verbs, e.g., *gei* 'give' and *qiang* 'rob', have three arguments Agent, Theme and Recipient in their argument structures.

While such syntactic classification has many applications, it does not adequately account for the distribution and interpretation of spatial modifiers, as our discussion on the PP-V and V-PP constructions and the locative subject construction below will show. Therefore, we go for semantic classification. Many aspects of a verb's behavior are determined by membership in a certain semantically coherent class (Levin and Rappaport Hovav 1996). Verbs fall into numerous narrow classes with similar meanings and distributions (Pinker 1989, ch. 4). For instance, Fong (1997, 13 – 16) distinguished four major types of Finnish verbs—verbs of motion, 'abstract motion' verbs, stative verbs and verbs with posterior/anterior entailments. Verbs of motion were further divided into verbs of plain motion, verbs of inherently directed motion, verbs of manner of motion, verbs of 'putting' and so on. The classification helps to explain the distributional properties of Finnish Directional Locative Cases.

Verbs or verb phrases differ in the kinds of eventuality that they denote. The aspectual property of a verb is an important part of verb semantics. One of the semantic classifications for verbs is based on event type or Aktionsart introduced in Chapter 1. Liu (2009), for instance, classifies Mandarin verbs that can take postverbal *zai*-PPs into telic, atelic dynamic, and stative verbs. Telic verbs include directional verbs (e. g. , *dao* 'fall' and *diu* 'throw'), (dis)appearance verbs (*chuxian* 'appear'), placement verbs (*fang* 'put'), combining verbs (*he* 'combine'), change of state verbs (*lan* 'rot'), and other accomplishments such as *da* (*yi xia*) 'hit (one hit)'.① Atelic dynamic verbs have two subclasses—motional process verbs such as *zou* 'walk', and non-motional process verbs such as *wan* 'play'. Stative verbs include posture verbs such as *kao* 'lean on', and verbs of existence such as *zhu* 'live'. The present study will basically follow Fong's (1997) and Liu's (2009) classifications, as verb semantics, especially the event type or Aktionsart of verbs, has been proven powerful in explaining the interpretation of various spatial phrases. The syntactic behavior of verbs is fundamentally shaped by their lexical semantics. Unaccusative verbs, for instance, are usually Achievements, and unergative verbs are Processes/Activities (see Levin and Rappaport Hovav 1996; Rappaport 1999).

The current study will look closely at seven types of verbs. We used two diagnostics to determine the event types of these verbs. As introduced in section 1.2.2, both States and Activities bear the feature [− event of change], while Accomplishments and Achievements have the feature [+ event of change]. Therefore, the former two types of verb cannot take time adverbials such as *zai yi fen zhong nei* 'in one minute' to indicate that a change has occurred within an interval, while the latter two can. States can hold at an instant, and Achievements are instantaneous changes of states,

---

① The disyllabic verb compound *chuxian* 'appear' is made up of two morphemes. A more precise gloss should be *chu-xian* 'exit-appear'. As the internal structure of this type of verb compounds does not affect our analysis in this study, they are glossed as monomorphemic words.

so they can be punctually located by expressions such as *zai na yi ke* 'at that moment'. Activities and Accomplishments hold at an interval, and thus normally do not go with punctually locating expressions.① The tests of 'in x time' and 'at x time' are widely used in the literature to diagnose event types in English (e.g. Dowty 1979, 56 – 59, 332 – 336; Rothstein 2004, 25 – 27, 177 – 182). Using the two diagnostics, we found the Mandarin verb *fang* 'put' in (77) an Accomplishment as it can take 'in x time' but not 'at x time', and in contrast, the verb *zhan* 'stand' in (78) a state because it can take 'at x time' instead of 'in x time'. More examples of the diagnostics will be provided in section 3.3.2.

(77) a. 在一分钟内，他在桌上放了一本书。

Zai yi feng zhong nei, ta zai zhuo shang fang-le yi-ben shu.

at one minute o'clock inside he at desk top put-Perf one-CL book

'In one minute, he put a book on the desk.'

b. #在那一刻,他在桌上放着/了一本书。

#Zai na yi ke, ta zai zhuoshang fang-zhe/-le yi-ben shu.

at that one moment he at desktop put-DUR/-Perf one-CL book

Intended meaning: 'At that moment, he put a book on the desk.'

(78) a. #在一分钟内，他站了。

#Zai yi feng zhong nei, ta zhan le.

at one minute o'clock inside he stand LE

Intended meaning: 'In one minute, he stood.'

---

① When an activity is forced to take a punctual adverb, the sentence expresses the idea that the activity began at the given temporal point as shown in (i) (Rothstein 2004, 25).

(i) John ran at 9 p.m.

b. 在那一刻,他站着。

   Zai na   yi   ke,   ta   zhan-zhe.

   at   that one moment he stand-DUR

   'At that moment, he stood.'

    The first type of verb that we examined is the locative verb, including the placement verb and the posture verb (see Li and Thompson 1981, 401 – 406; Huang 1987). These are verbs that most often take a locative argument or adjunct, and are our focus in this study. Placement verbs encode placement events, a basic part of the human experience, involving an Agent causing a Theme to move to a Goal cross-linguistically (Alferink and Gullberg 2014). Examples of placement verbs are shown in (79a). They are accomplishment verbs, and their event structures have a causing activity and a result state. Posture verbs as shown in (79b) specify the configuration of a Figure in relation to the Reference Entity. They are dynamic state verbs. Following Bach (1986), this study makes a distinction between static state and dynamic state. While Bach (1986) only provided some exemplars of the two types of State, we tried to make use of the following test to distinguish the two. Dynamic state verbs can shift into Achievements as discussed in section 2.2.2. When used as an achievement verb, the activity component in its event structure is still accessible, so we can say that one did the activity of standing for several times in (80a). By contrast, the activity component in the event structure of static state verbs such as *xing* 'awake' is not accessible, so it is unacceptable to say that one did the activity of being awake several times in (80b).

   (79) a. Placement verbs

        放 *fang* 'put, place', 种 *zhong* 'plant', 画 *hua* 'draw, paint', 吐 *tu* 'spit', 洒 *sa* 'spill', 藏 *cang* 'hide', 写 *xie* 'write', 抄 *chao* 'copy', 印 *yin* 'print', 刻 *ke* 'carve', 挂 *gua* 'hang', 贴 *tie* 'paste, stick'

b. Posture verbs

站 *zhan* 'stand', 睡 *shui* 'sleep', 趴 *pa* 'crouch', 蹲 *dun* 'squat', 浮 *fu* 'float', 漂 *piao* 'float', 停 *ting* 'stop', 坐 *zuo* 'sit', 躺 *tang* 'lie down', 跪 *gui* 'kneel', 倚 *yi* 'lean on', 住 *zhu* 'have residence'

(80) a. 他站了几次，可是没站起来。

Ta zhan-le   ji-ci,   keshi mei zhan-qi-lai.①
he stand-Perf several-CL but   not stand-rise-come

'He tried to stand for several times, but he did not stand up.'

b. #他醒了几次，可是没醒过来。

#Ta xing-le   ji-ci,   keshi mei xing-guo-lai.
he   awake-Perf several-CL but   not awake-cross-come

Intended meaning: 'He tried to be awake, but he failed.'

Locative verbs in Mandarin are usually associated with Location, but not necessarily so. One prominent difference between Mandarin and English is that English locative verbs require a Location argument as exemplified in (81), but they are optional in Mandarin as shown in (82). Location can be realized as a subject or object of the locative verb, or it can project into a *zai*-PP preceding or following the verb. These verbs are, therefore, found most frequently in locative subject sentences, and sentences with a postverbal *zai*-PP. Locative verbs should also include the state verb *zai* 'be at'. However, it is peculiar among locative verbs in not occurring in locative subject sentences, or taking postverbal *zai* phrases.

(81) He was at *(home).

(82) a. 他在家。

Ta zai jia.

---

① This example is from Ziyin Mai through personal communication.

he   be at   home

   'He is at home.'

b. 他在。

   Ta   zai.

   he   be at

   'He is here/there (at some place specified in the context).'

Motion verbs are the second type of verb examined closely in this study. There are at least two subclasses: manner-of-motion verbs and displacement verbs. Manner-of-motion verbs, or motional process verbs, are verbs such as *you* 'swim', and *pao* 'run'. They specify a manner—but not a specific direction—of motion, and they are Activities. Displacement verbs, also called directional verbs, can be further divided into two subtypes. The first subtype is verbs that describe an inherently downward direction, such as *tiao* 'jump', *reng* 'toss', *mo* 'spread, smear', *sa* 'sprinkle', *diao* 'drop, fall', *shuai* 'fall, trip', *die* 'fall', *dao* 'fall', and any resultative verb compound whose second verb is *dao* 'fall' and *fan* 'topple' (Li and Thompson 1981, 398 – 401; Fan 1982; Liu 2009).[①] The motion events denoted by these verbs or caused by the action conveyed by these verbs are inherently downward because of gravity, and the potential end location of these events is the ground if there is no other external force. These verbs are Accomplishments or Achievements. The second subtype is verbs of directed motion which specify a direction that is not downward such as *lai* 'come', *qu* 'go', *daoda* 'reach', *qianjin* 'move forward' and *shen* 'rise' (see Liu 2009). These are Accomplishments or Achievements. All the motional verbs can occur in the locative subject sentence, but only the downward displacement verbs can

---

① Section 4.2.2 will show that *tiao* 'jump' is like displacement verbs in the V-PP construction, but behaves differently from the rest of the group in the locative subject construction.

take postverbal *zai*-PPs productively. ①

The third focus of the current study is (dis) appearance verbs, including *fa-sheng* 'happen, occur', *chu-xian* 'appear', (*chu-*) *sheng* 'be born', *sheng-zhang* 'grow up', *chan-sheng* 'occur', *si* 'die', and *xiaoshi* 'disappear' (Li and Thompson 1981, 403 – 404; Liu 2009). They are achievement verbs, and they occur in locative subject sentences and sentences with postverbal *zai*-PPs.

The fourth and fifth areas of focus in the present study are verbs with posterior entailment and verbs with anterior entailment. Verbs with posterior entailment are best exemplified by *wang* 'forget', and *la* 'forget' (see Fong 1997, 16). Verbs which mean 'to forget something' entail that the thing being forgotten is located at the place after the forgetting. Verbs with anterior entailment include *zhao-dao* 'find', and *sou-dao* 'search-find' (see ibid.). Verbs expressing finding something entail that the thing being sought is located at a certain place before being found. Both types are Achievements. Verbs with posterior entailment can take the postverbal *zai*-PP, and verbs with anterior entailment can occur in locative subject sentences.

The sixth type is verbs of combining, such as *he* 'combine', *ju* 'get together', *hun* 'mix', and *ji-zhong* 'centralize' (Liu 2009). These verbs are Accomplishments, and take the postverbal *zai* to a limited extent.

The last type is non-motional process verbs such as *wan* 'play' and

---

① There are some exceptions. For instance, the resultative verb compound (RVC) *xia-jiang* 'descend-come down' denotes downward motion, but it cannot take postverbal *zai* phrases. There is a grammatical constraint that may provide an explanation for this exception: Mandarin RVCs cannot take postverbal *zai*-phrases unless the second verb (V2) in the compound subcategorizes for *zai*-phrases (Fan 1982). The V2 of *xia-jiang* is *jiang* 'come down'. When the verb *jiang* occurs independently (i.e. not as part of a compound), it does not subcategorize for *zai*-phrases. Consequently, the same restriction will apply when *jiang* is the V2 in a compound. In contrast, another RVC *jiang-luo* 'descend-land', which is similar to *xia-jiang* in meaning, can take postverbal *zai*, because its V2 *luo* 'land' subcategorizes for *zai* when it occurs independently.

xiao 'laugh'. These verbs are Activities that generally cannot occur in locative subject sentences and sentences with a postverbal *zai*-PP.

In this chapter and Chapter 4, it will be shown that the semantics of a verb, especially its aspectual properties or event type, is a fundamental determinant in the interpretation of sentences involving a locative argument/adjunct.

3.2　Classification of spatial prepositions

Mandarin spatial modifiers are realized by prepositional phrases (PPs). This section introduces the head of the spatial PP, namely the spatial preposition (P). There is a basic distinction between location and direction for spatial expressions across languages. Movement-directional spatial expressions involve change of location whereas stative-locational ones do not (Nam 2000; Cinque 2010). In Mandarin, this distinction is partly realized by the contrast between the locational preposition *zai* 'at', and directional ones such as *dao* 'to' (Li and Thompson 1981: 390, 409). Directional or Path Ps can be further divided into four types: those signifying Goal, Source, Direction, and Route as exemplified by the English Ps in (83) (see Jackendoff 1983; Cinque 2010). Goal specifies the end point of a path, while Source indicates the starting point of the path. As for Direction, the reference point does not fall on the path, but would if the path were to extend. Route elements such as *by* occur with verbs like *pass*. In terms of aspect, these prepositions can be divided into bounded and unbounded as introduced in section 2.1.3 (Verkuyl and Zwarts 1992; Nam 2000; Zwarts 2005). In the same vein, the spatial Ps in Mandarin can be classified as in (85) (see J. Li 1924, 198 – 202). Importantly, the Goal P *dao* 'to' and Source P *cong* 'from' are bounded while the locational P *zai* 'at' is not. The former two but not the latter make the whole predicate bounded. Among the Source Ps, *zi* 'from' and *you* 'from' are rarely used in spoken language. The directional Ps *wang* 'towards', *xiang* 'towards', and *chao* 'towards' are synonyms as shown by the glosses.①

(83) a. Location: at
　　 b. Direction/Path
　　　　 Goal: to
　　　　 Source: from
　　　　 Direction: away from, toward
　　　　 Routes: by, along, through, via
(84) Bounded: to, into, from, away from, past, via
　　 Unbounded: towards, along
(85) a. Location: 在 *zai* 'at'
　　 b. Direction/Path
　　　　 Source: 从 *cong* 'from', 自 *zi* 'from', 由 *you* 'from'
　　　　 Goal: 到 *dao* 'to'
　　　　 Direction: 往 *wang* 'towards', 向 *xiang* 'towards', 朝 *chao* 'towards'
　　　　 Route: 沿 *yan* 'along', 顺 *shun* 'along'

While the semantic classification of these Mandarin Ps seems clear enough, the categorical status of some of them is actually controversial. For instance, the syntactic category of *dao* 'reach, to' is contentious. The preverbal *dao* is generally considered a verb occurring in the serial verb construction (e.g. S. Huang 1978), but the postverbal *dao* is argued to be a directional verb (Y. Liu et al. 1998; Lü et al. 2010; Huang, Li, and Li 2009) or a preposition (J. Li 1924; Chen 2002).② The categorical

---

① But there are still subtle differences. For instance, *wang* but not *chao* and *xiang* can be followed by an abstract LP (Jin 1996, 49 – 51), *chao* and *xiang* are less grammaticalized than *wang* since they can be followed by the durative aspect marker *-zhe* as verbs.

② Postverbal *dao* 'reach' could also be the second verb in a resultative verb compound without spatial meaning, such as *dao* in *zhao-dao* 'find'. We disregard this non-spatial usage in this study.

status of spatial Ps in modern Chinese is debatable, because they have verbs as etymological precursors, and some of them can still be used as verbs in certain contexts. For instance, *zai* was a verb in Early Archaic Chinese, and was used in serial verb constructions during the Wei Jin Nan-Bei Chao (Wei, Jing, Southern and Northern Dynasties, 220 – 589 AD), until it was grammaticalized into a preposition in the 8th century (Peyraube 1994). In terms of grammaticalization, Mandarin spatial Ps in (85) are not homogenous: some of them have progressed further in the transition from verbs to prepositions than others. For instance, present-day *cong* 'from' is more grammaticalized than *zai* and *dao*, and is generally considered as having no verbal use (Li and Thompson 1981), while *dao* are arguably mainly used as a verb. *Zai* seems to be somewhere in between. Some argue that *zai* has multiple statuses—it is a verb when standing alone, and a preposition when occurring with a verb (Huang, Li, and Li 2009, 30; Mulder and Sybesma 1992; Huang 1994; Lü et al. 2010), or there are two *zai*'s, the verb *zai* 'be at' and the preposition *zai* 'at' being homophones (Lam 2013, 33 – 34). We found two more logical possibilities: *zai* is consistently verbal, or it is consistently prepositional even when it is used without a main verb. However, neither is feasible.

The first possibility that *zai* is always verbal is not tenable. There is strong evidence for treating preverbal and postverbal *zai* as prepositions. The object of a postverbal *zai* cannot be omitted as shown in (86). Since Chinese Ps cannot be stranded, it follows logically that postverbal *zai* should be a P (see Li 1990, 60). There is also evidence for the prepositional status of preverbal *zai*: preverbal prepositional *zai*, but not verbal *zai*, can be omitted in some special cases as shown in (87) (see Mai 2007, 7). Therefore, it is not plausible to analyze preverbal *zai* as a verb.

(86) 他睡在 * (地上)。
     Ta   shui-zai   * (di   shang).
     he   sleep-at   floor   top

'He slept on the ground.'

(87) a. 我们＊(在)飞机上。

Women ＊(zai) feiji shang.

we at plane top

'We are on a plane.'

b. 我们(在)飞机上聊。

Women (zai) feiji shang liao.

we at plane top talk

'Let's talk on the plane!'

The second possibility that zai is always prepositional is also not feasible. If zai is consistently a preposition, one cannot explain why zai sometimes can be used without an object, whereas other prepositions in Mandarin, for instance, cong 'from', cannot do so, as shown by the contrast between (88a) and (88b). Therefore, zai in (88a) is not a preposition but a verb. There is also a contrast between the verbal zai and the prepositional zai in their ability to license the ellipsis of the object, as exemplified by the contrast between (88a) and (88c) (see Lam 2013, 46–47).

(88) a. 那老房子还在(村里)。

Na lao fangzi hai zai (cun li).

that old house still be at village inside

'The old house is still (in the village).'

b. 我从＊(村里)来。

Wo cong ＊(cun li) lai.

I from village inside come

'I come from the village.'

c. 我在＊(家)睡觉。

Wo zai ＊(jia) shuijiao.

I at home sleep

'I sleep at home.'

Since this study is mainly concerned with the semantics of pre- and postverbal phrases introduced by *zai* and *dao* rather than their syntactic categories, the syntactic category of pre- and postverbal *zai* and *dao* will not be given extensive treatment. Given evidence above, we treat *zai* in the absence of a main verb as shown in (88a) as a verb. Other occurrences of *zai* are simply treated as prepositions unless further distinction is required. However, there is a caveat: in answering a question, a speaker may elide the main verb that co-occurs with the prepositional *zai* when the subject is dropped as shown in (89). Thus, the category of *zai* that stands alone without a subject must be decided after the previous context is checked.

(89) a. Question: 他在哪儿玩?

        Ta   zai   nar   wan?

        he   at   where play

        'Where did he play?'

b. Answer: (* 他)在学校(玩)。

        (* Ta)   zai   xuexiao   (wan).

        he   at   school   play

        '(He played) at school.'

Almost all Mandarin spatial Ps occur in the preverbal position, but *zai* and *dao* 'to' are two exceptions: both can be placed either before or after the verb (with some differences in meaning). The spatial Ps *zi* 'from', *wang* 'towards', and *xiang* 'towards' occasionally follow verbs. Such usages do not typically occur in spoken language, and are considered formal or archaic. The spatial Ps are used with different frequencies. Based on a 1.5-million-word corpus collected from five contemporary novels, W. Zhou (2011) identified the following ranking of frequency for Ps with *zai* being used most frequently. *Dao* 'reach, to' is absent from this ranking, because W. Zhou (2011) treated it as a verb rather than a preposition.

(90) 在 *zai* 'at' > 从 *cong* 'from' > 往 *wang* 'towards' > 向

xiang 'towards' > 沿 *yan* 'along' > 朝 *chao* 'towards' > 顺 *shun* 'along' > 自 *zi* 'from' > 由 *you* 'from'

3.3 Spatial prepositional phrases headed by *zai* (*zai*-PPs)

As introduced in section 1.1.2, while some languages use Cases to distinguish Goal and Location, Mandarin uses the word order of *zai*-PPs to encode the semantic distinction as exemplified in (5). Preverbal *zai*-PPs express the location of an action or a state of affairs, and postverbal ones denote the result location of a participant in an action (Wang 1957, 1980; Tai 1975; Zhu 1978). The semantics-to-syntax mapping is schematized in (91).

(91) a. Location-V
b. V-Goal

Some functional and syntactic accounts have been proposed to explain the word-order regularity. Tai (1985) invoked iconicity and proposed that the word order in (91) reflects the temporal sequence in reality: an event first takes place at a location and then ends at a goal, hence the word order Location, V, and Goal in describing the event. Syntacticians argue that the semantic contrast between (91a) and (91b) arises from the fact that syntactically, preverbal *zai*-PPs are adjuncts and postverbal ones complements (Mulder and Sybesma 1992; Huang 1994). Here adjunct is a structural notion used in the X-bar theory (Chomsky 1981), distinct from the traditional term 'adverbial' or 'modifier'. In Mandarin, time, locative, manner, and instrumental adverbials only occur before the verb, while resultative, duration, frequency and descriptive adverbials exclusively occur after the verb (Tai 1973; Huang 1994). Even though both groups are adverbials, they take different syntactic positions, with the first type in the preverbal adjunct position and the second in the postverbal complement position as shown in (92). *Zai*-PPs can occur both before and after the main verb with a contrast of meaning. The semantics-syntax mapping in (91) is a result of preverbal *zai*-PPs being adjuncts modifying the V-bar (V') and postverbal ones being complements of the V as in (92). Later, we will show that both the functional and the syntactic approaches cannot account for some systematic exceptions to the word order regularity in (91).

(92) a. Adjunct-V'

b. V-Complement

3.3.1 Distribution of *zai*-PPs

The Location-V and V-Goal word-order regularity has systematic exceptions (see Li and Thompson 1981; Fan 1982; Fong 1997). As discussed in Chapter 2, *zai*-PPs following posture verbs such as *zuo* 'sit' are ambiguous between a locational reading and a directional reading as in (93a). Under the locational reading, (93a) has the same meaning as (93b) which involves a preverbal *zai*-PP as the modifier. When placement verbs such as *tie* 'paste' are modified by a preverbal *zai*-PP, both the locational reading and the directional reading are available as in (94a). In contrast, the postverbal *zai*-PP with placement verbs unambiguously denotes Goal as shown in (94b) (Teng 1975). These examples with the posture verb and the placement verb clearly demonstrate that preverbal *zai*-PPs can denote Goal and postverbal ones Location as shown in (95). The 'posture V-Location' and 'Goal-placement V' word orders constitute exceptions to the word-order regularity in (91).

(93) a. 他坐在沙发上。

Ta zuo zai shafa shang.

he sit at sofa top

i. 'He sat on the sofa.' (location)

ii. 'He sat down on the sofa.' (direction)

b. 他在沙发上坐。

    Ta zai shafa shang zuo.
    he at   sofa   top   sit
    'He is/was sitting on the sofa.'

(94) a. 他在床上贴了两张相片。

    Ta zai chuang shang tie-le liang-zhang xiangpian.
    he at bed top paste-Perf two-CL photos
    i. 'He was in the bed and pasted two photos.' (location)
    ii. 'He pasted two photos onto the bed.' (direction)

b. 他贴了两张相片在床上。

    Ta tie-le liang-zhang xiangpian zai chuang shang.
    he paste-Perf two-CL photos at bed top
    'He pasted two photos onto the bed.'

(95) a. Posture V-Location/Goal

b. Goal/Location-placement V

    The grammatical aspect in (93) deserves an excursus here. The two sentences are natural without aspect markers. In absence of other aspect elements, *zai* in the preverbal position is both an aspect marker of the verb and a spatial preposition, and the surface form results from phonological deletion of one of the copies in haplology (C. Chen 1978; P. Li 1990, 118). As preverbal *zai* is a progressive aspect marker, (93b) is in the progress aspect with present or past time reference depending on the context. Sentence (93a) is also natural without overt aspect markers. C. Chen (1978) argues that here a zero aspect marker occurs with a postverbal *zai*-PP to convey a snapshot of the state of affairs at the termination of the action. We hold that only under the directional reading, such is the case as shown by (93a).

    The distributions of the preverbal and postverbal *zai*-PPs are not symmetrical in terms of frequency. The use of postverbal *zai*-PPs is more restricted than that of the preverbal ones. For instance, the non-motional process verbs such as *chi* 'eat' are incompatible with postverbal *zai*-PPs as in (96). Only a limited number of verb classes can take both preverbal and postverbal *zai*-PPs. Besides placement verbs and posture verbs, displacement verbs such as *tiao* 'jump', and (dis)appearing verbs such as *si* 'die' can take both types of *zai*-PPs (Li and Thompson 1981). Liu (2009) adds a few more to the list—manner-of-motion verbs such as *zou* 'walk', and verbs of combining such as *bing* 'combine'.

(96) *他吃在馆子里。

    *Ta   chi   zai   guanzi   li.

    he   eat   at   restaurant   inside

    Intended meaning: 'He ate in the restaurant'.

3.3.2 An event-semantic account of the use of *zai*-PPs

As mentioned above, the systematic mapping of Location and Goal onto the pre- versus postverbal positions is disrupted by some exceptions. In what follows, an event-semantic account of the syntax-semantics mismatch will be provided. Several classes of verbs will be examined in order to demonstrate that the aspectual features of a verb can help explain the word order and the interpretations of its co-occurring *zai*-PP. There are only a few classes of verbs that can take postverbal *zai*-PPs (Li and Thompson 1981; Fong 1997; Liu 2009; Hsieh 2010), and we find that all of them contain a State component in their event structures.

The first class of verb is (dis)appearance verbs introduced in section 3.1. The *zai*-PP following such a verb expresses stative location rather than change of location, as in (97). This group of verbs are achievement verbs, and in their event structure there is a change of state. For instance, in the event encoded by *si* 'die' in (97), there is a change of state from being alive to being dead. The postverbal *zai*-PP is used to modify the result state of being dead. As there is no change of location in the dying event, the postverbal *zai*-PP does not express Goal.

(97)他死在医院里。
　　Ta　si　zai　yiyuan　　li.
　　he　die　at　hospital　inside
　　'He died in the hospital.'

　　Posture verbs are dynamic state verbs (see Bach 1986). Both pre- and postverbal *zai*-PPs can express Location as shown in (93). As long as the posture verb is in its basic-level event type, the co-occurring *zai*-PP expresses Location regardless its syntactic position. However, when the verb shifts from State to Achievement as discussed in section 2.1.3, the postverbal *zai*-PP gets the directional reading as exemplified in (93a).① The ambiguity of postverbal *zai*-PPs with posture verbs is caused by aspect shift. One may ask why preverbal *zai*-PPs are not ambiguous. For instance, in (93b), the preverbal *zai*-PP unambiguously expresses Location. Why does aspect shift fail to occur in this sentence? As introduced in the previous section, preverbal *zai* is both a spatial P and a progressive aspect marker, in the absence of other aspect markers (C. Chen 1978; P. Li 1990). The presence of the progressive aspect marker blocks the aspect shift from State to Achievement, as Achievement is normally incompatible with the progressive aspect. Nevertheless, preverbal *zai*-PPs can express Goal, when the posture verbs combine with resultative complements as shown in (98). In this case, an external form *xia-lai* 'descend-come' coerces the aspect shift of the posture verb *zuo* 'sit'. With a Transition predicate, the preverbal *zai*-PP expresses Goal. Posture verbs are the only type of state verbs that take postverbal *zai*-PPs. Static

---

① Smith (1997, 295) treats posture verbs in the directional reading as Accomplishments. However, in the present study they are treated as Achievements because they can co-occur with the punctually locating expression 'at x time' which is a diagnostic of Achievement and State.
　　(i) Zai　na　yi　miao,　　ta　zuo　zai-le　　yizi　shang.
　　　　at　that　one　second　he　sit　at-Perf　chair　top
　　　'At that second, he sat down on the chair.'

state verbs generally are not allowed in the V-*zai* construction. They are mostly individual-level predicates lacking inherent temporality. Since they do not encode change of state, they are incompatible with postverbal *zai*-PPs. Some of them (e.g. *hao* 'good', *huai* 'bad', and *nan* 'difficult') take postverbal *zai*-PPs to a limited degree (Liu 2009), but such usage is rather idiomatic and lacks syntactic productivity.

(98) 他在椅子上坐了下来。

     Ta   zai   yizi   shang   zuo-le   xia-lia.

     he   at   chair top   sit-Perf   descend-come.

     'He sat down on the chair.'

Placement verbs in Mandarin are Accomplishments with two subevents in their event structures. As shown in section 2.2.1.3, Accomplishments can be decomposed into two underlying subevents and the spatial modifier may modify either of the two (Dowty 1979; Parsons 1990). In the case of a placement verb such as *tie* 'paste, stick', the preverbal *zai*-PP modifies either the causing subevent of sticking, leading to a locational reading, or the result state, giving rise to the directional reading as shown in (94a). A special use of placement verbs is worth mentioning. When the Agent of a placement verb is missing, the Accomplishment shifts into a State as shown in (99). Aspect shift has been shown to be prevalent in natural languages (see section 2.2.2). In the case of (99), *tie* 'stick' is originally an accomplishment verb, as it can go with 'in x time' expressions to express the completion of the event, but does not allow 'at x time' expressions, similar to *fang* 'put' in (77). However, when the Agent of the verb is deleted, the verb can co-occur with the punctual time adverbial 'at x time', but is incapable of being combined with 'in x time' to express the completion of the event as shown in (100). Therefore, we argue that *tie* 'stick' in (99) has undergone aspect shift from Accomplishment to State. The postverbal *zai*-PP following the stative placement verb in (99) thus expresses static location.

(99) 相片贴在床上。

    Xiangpian tie   zai   chuang   shang.
    photo   stick at   bed   top
    'Photos are/were stuck on the bed.'   (location)

(100) a. 在那一毫秒，相片贴在床上。

    Zai na   yi   haomiao, xiangpian tie   zai chuang shang.
    at   that one millisecond photo   stick at bed   top
    'At that millisecond, photos were stuck on the bed.'

b. #在一分钟内，相片贴在床上。

    #Zai yi feng zhong nei, xiangpian tie zai chuang shang.
    at   one minute o'clock inside photo stick at bed   top
    Intended meaning: 'In one minute, photos were stuck on the bed.'

Displacement verbs that denote downward motion are also Accomplishments or Achievements. Some of them, e. g. *tiao* 'jump' and *reng* 'toss', appear to be Activities at first glance, but the events encoded by these verbs have inherent end point, namely, the ground, due to gravity. Thus, they are telic. Downward displacement verbs readily take postverbal *zai*-PPs to express result location. For instance, the resultative verb compound (RVC) *shuai-dao* 'trip-fall' or the verb *dao* 'fall' in (101) is followed by a *zai*-PP which modifies the result state of being fallen. The sentence means that he fell and ended up on the ground.

(101) 他（摔）倒在地上。

    Ta   (shuai-) dao   zai   di   shang.
    he   (trip-) fall   at   ground   top
    'He fell down on the ground.'

The final two types of verbs are verbs with posterior/anterior entailment. According to Fong (1997, ch. 2), in the event structure of Finnish verbs with posterior/anterior entailment, there is a phase change which is defined as change from negation of p to p, p standing for one concrete or abstract phase. Parallel to their Finnish counterparts, Mandarin verbs with posterior entailment such as *wang* 'forget' in (102) encode a phase change from having the potential to move something to not having such potential. They are just like telic verbs. There is no movement through space when the postverbal *zai*-PP is used with this type of verb as in (102), as there is no change of location in a forgetting event. Mandarin verbs with anterior entailment, however, behave differently from their Finnish counterparts in disallowing postverbal *zai*-PPs as in (103a). This is due to a peculiar constraint that RVCs in Chinese do not take postverbal *zai*-PPs except when the second verb in the RVC subcategorizes for *zai*-PPs when used independently, such as *dao* 'fall' and *fan* 'topple' (Fan 1982). This constraint was a rather late development in the history of Chinese, emerging around the late Qing Dynasty (Liu 2009). In the case of (103a), *dao*4 'arrive' does not subcategorizes for *zai*-PPs, so the RVC that it forms with *zhao* 'find' cannot be followed by *zai*-PPs, either.① Similar to preverbal *zai*-PPs with placement verbs, the preverbal *zai*-PPs with this group of verbs have both a locational reading and a phase change reading as exemplified in (103b).

(102) 他把钥匙忘在家里了。

Ta   ba   yaoshi   wang   zai   jia   li   le.
he   BA   key   forget at   home   inside LE

'He forgot the key at home.'

(103) a. *那封信，他找到在书架上。

*Na-feng   xin,   ta   zhao-dao   zai   shujia   shang.
that-CL   letter he   find-arrive   at   shelf   top

Intended reading: 'He found that letter when it was on the shelf.'

---

① Note that 到 *dao* 'reach' is in Tone 4, different from 倒 *dao* 'fall' above which is in Tone 3.

b. 那封信，他在书架上找到了。

    Na-feng xin, ta zai shujia shang zhao-dao le.
    that-CL letter he at shelf top find-arrive LE

  i. 'He found that letter when he was on the shelf.'

                                                (location)

  ii. 'He found that letter on the shelf.'   (phase change)

Thus far, it has been shown that dynamic States and Accomplishments and Achievements can occur in the V-*zai* construction. Verbs in these event types all have a state component in their event structures. Importantly, verbs of other event types cannot occur in the V-*zai* construction. For instance, the non-motional Activity verbs such as *chi* 'eat' are incompatible with postverbal *zai*-PPs as in (96).

To recap, event structure can help to explain the interpretations of Mandarin *zai*-PPs, and describe the underlying pattern of the distribution of postverbal *zai*-PPs. There are systematic exceptions to the 'Location-V' and 'V-Goal' word-order regularity: preverbal *zai*-PPs occurring with placement verbs can denote Goal, and postverbal *zai*-PPs with posture verbs can convey Location. The exceptions pose problems for the functional and syntactic approaches introduced previously, but can be well explained by aspect shift of posture verbs and subevent modification with placement verbs. The postverbal *zai*-PPs are licensed by dynamic state and transition verbs, which all have a state component in their event structures.

3.3.3 Syntactic positions of *zai*-PPs

Previously, we provided an event-semantic account of the interpretation and distribution of *zai*-PPs. However, the theory cannot explain all the facts about *zai*-PPs. For instance, to explain the asymmetry of the preverbal and postverbal *zai*-PPs in terms of the availability of ambiguity, a syntactic account has to be invoked. In Mandarin, a spatial

PP can occur either before or after a placement verb such as *fang* 'put'. When it is preverbal, it can be interpreted ambiguously as subject- or object-oriented, but when it occurs postverbally, it is unambiguously object-oriented (Teng 1975). The contrast between (104a) and (104b) illustrates this point. Some native speakers feel that V-DP-PP sentences such as (104b) are not very natural and prefer to use the disposal construction marker *ba* to prepose the object *yi-ben shu* 'one book' as in (104c). Nevertheless, in both (104b) and (104c), the *zai*-PPs follow the verbs, and are unambiguous.

Adopting a *v*P-shell analysis (Larson 1988; Huang 1994), this section will discuss the influence of syntactic positions on the interpretation of *zai*-PPs. The *v*P-shell analysis posits that (104b) has the structure in (105). Following Lin (2001) and Huang (2007), the present study contends that the event structure of a main verb can be directly mapped onto different V heads in the syntactic structure of a Mandarin sentence. Thus the lexical item *fang* 'put' can be decomposed into two event predicates CAUSE and BECOME and mapped onto a small *v* and a big V in the tree diagram. Even though postverbal *zai*-PPs are spatial modifiers, they occupy the complement position of the verb (see Larson 2004; Huang 1994; Lin 2001, 2008). They predicate over the result state in the complex event, as embodied by the lowest VP in the tree (105), abstracting away from the aspect. The verb *fang* 'put' moves from BECOME to CAUSE, resulting in the surface word order. Since the postverbal *zai*-PP is within the scope of a BECOME predicate, it receives a result location or direction reading.

(104) a. 他在桌上放了一本书。
    Ta zai zhuo shang fang-le yi-ben shu.
    he at desk top put-Perf one-CL book
    i. 'He put a book on the desk.'
    ii. 'He was on the desk and put a book (somewhere).'

b. 他放了一本书在桌上。

 Ta fang-le yi-ben shu zai zhuo shang.
 he put-Perf one-CL book at desk top

 'He put one book on the desk.'

c. 他把一本书放在了桌上。

 Ta ba yi-ben shu fang-zai-le zhuo shang.
 he BA one-CL book put-at-Perf desk top

 'He put one book on the desk.'

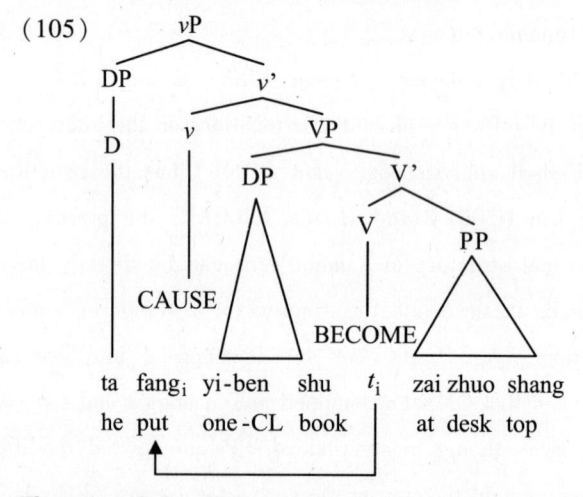

(105)

```
              vP
             /  \
           DP    v'
           |    /  \
           D   v    VP
               |   /  \
               |  DP   V'
               |  /\  /  \
               | /  \ V   PP
               |/    \|  /  \
             CAUSE   BECOME /  \
               |      |    /    \
              ta   fangᵢ yi-ben shu  tᵢ  zai zhuo shang
              he   put  one-CL book      at desk top
```

The preverbal *zai*-PP, on the other hand, is outside the scope of BECOME as shown in (106). It modifies *v*P, representing the whole event, and has scope over both CAUSE and BECOME. It thus can be associated with either the causing activity or the result state, leading to ambiguity. Verbs of other event types have only one event predicate in their syntactic representations as shown in (18) in section 1.2.2. As *zai*-PPs preceding these verbs have scope over only one event predicate, the type of ambiguity between a locational reading and a directional reading will not arise.

(106)

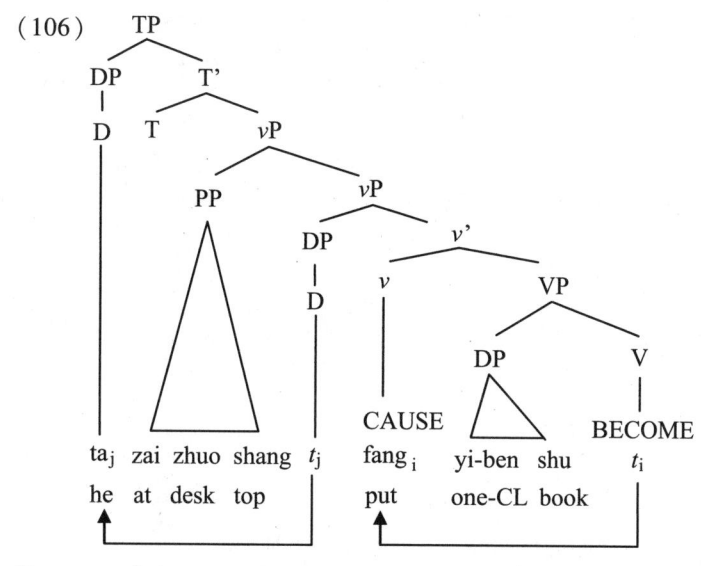

```
         TP
        /  \
      DP    T'
      |    /  \
      D   T    vP
                 \
                  vP
                 /  \
               PP    vP
              /\    /  \
                  DP    v'
                  |    /  \
                  D   v    VP
                          /  \
                        DP    V
                       /\     |
                 CAUSE        BECOME
      taⱼ zai zhuo shang tⱼ  fangᵢ  yi-ben shu  tᵢ
      he  at  desk  top      put    one-CL book
```

However, there is another logical possibility: the Goal-denoting *zai*-PP that precedes a placement verb may be base-generated in the postverbal position as one argument and complement of the V, and moves to the preverbal position via focus movement or topicalization (Lin 2001, 153).[①] In contrast, the Location-denoting *zai*-PP is base-generated preverbally as Mandarin adjuncts always precede the V (Mulder and Sybesma 1992). The present study does not go in this direction. In what follows, several diagnostics of adjuncts in Schütze (1995) and Hoffmann (2011, 67 – 71) will be used to demonstrate that the preverbal *zai*-PP, be it Goal-denoting

---

[①] Besides the analysis provided in the ensuing discussion, there are independent arguments for preverbal *zai*-PPs not being focuses (Haoze Li, personal communication). First, occurring before a verb is not sufficient for us to determine if this element is focus or not. In (i), the preverbal PP functions as contrastive focus only if it is stressed. Otherwise, it cannot be a focus.
 (i) Ta [zai zhuo shang]_Focus fang-le yi-ben shu, bu shi zai chuang shang.
   he at desk top   put-Perf one-CL book, not be on bed top
   'He put a book on the desk, not on the bed.'
In addition, it is also felicitous to have the focus on another constituent in the sentence.
 (ii) Ta zai zhuo shang fang-le [yi-ben shu]_Focus, bu shi yi-zhi bi.
   he at desk top   put-Perf one-CL book, not be one-CL pen
   'He put a book on the desk, not a pen.'

or Location-denoting, is adjunct rather than argument when they go with placement verbs. The first diagnostic is the test of optionality. Adjuncts are optional whereas arguments are obligatory in a sentence. For instance, the indispensability of the spatial PP *on the desk* in (107a) indicates that it is an argument occupying the complement position of the verb *put*. By contrast, the optionality of the Goal-denoting PP *zai zhuo shang* 'on the desk' in (107b) hints at its adjunct status in Mandarin.

(107) a. John put the book * (on the desk).

b. 张三（在桌上）放了一本书。

  Zhangsan （zai zhuo shang） fang-le yi-ben shu.
  Zhangsan at desk top put-Perf one-CL book
  'Zhangsan put a book (on the desk).'

The second is the test of iterativity. Adjuncts but not arguments can be stacked on one side of a verb. Again, both types of PPs seem to be equally able to be iterated in Mandarin sentences. The two sentences in (108) are marginally accepted by native speakers to the same extent. (108a) involves two Goal-denoting *zai*-PPs while (108b) has two stacked Location-denoting ones. As both types of *zai*-PP pass the test of iterativity, they should both be adjuncts rather than arguments.

(108) a. ? 他在桌上在那张纸上写了一封信。

  ? Ta zai zhuo shang zai na-zhang zhi shang xie-le yi-feng xin. ①
  he at desk top at that-CL paper top write-Perf one-CL letter
  'He wrote a letter on that piece of paper on the table.'

---

 ① Native speakers feel that (108a) is questionable, because there is a succinct way to say it as in (i).
 (i) Ta zai zhuo shang de na-zhang zhi shang xie-le yi-feng xin.
  He at desk top DE that-CL paper top write-Perf one-CL letter
  'He wrote a letter on that piece of paper that was on the desk.'

b. ? 他在屋里在桌子旁边跳舞。

? Ta zai wu li zai zhuozi pang-bian tiaowu.
he at room inside at desk side-side dance
'He danced by the table in the room.'

The third test is pseudo-clefting. In English, adjuncts such as *at home* in (109a), but not arguments such as *on the shelf* in (109b), can be cleaved from the verb. Both locational PPs and directional PPs allow pseudo-clefting in Mandarin. As shown in (110a), the locational PP *zai wuding shang* 'on the roof' can be cleaved from the verb *chang* 'sing'. The same is true for the directional PP *zai heiban shang* 'on the blackboard' in (110b). The test result suggests that both locational PPs and directional PPs in Mandarin are adjuncts.

(109) a. What John did at home was meet Mary.

b. * What John did on the shelf was put the book.

(110) a. 李四在屋顶上做得是唱了一首歌。

Lisi zai wuding shang zuo-de shi chang-le yi-shou ge.
Lisi at roof top do-DE be sing-Perf one-CL song
'What Lisi did on the roof was sing a song.'

b. 李四在黑板上做得是写了一个字。

Lisi zai heiban shang zuo-de shi xie-le yi-ge zi.
Lisi at blackboard top do-DE be write-Perf one-CL character
'What Lisi did on the blackboard was write a character.'

The fourth test is the *do-so* pro-form test. Arguments but not adjuncts are included in the pro-form as shown by the contrast in (111). *Under the chair* in (111a) is an argument of *put* covertly included in the pro-form *did so*, so the second clause is underlyingly *Tom put a book under the chair on the desk* which is ungrammatical. *At home* in (111b) is an adjunct which is not included in the pro-form *did so*, so the sentence is well-formed. In

Mandarin, neither the directional *zai*-PP nor the locational one is included in the pro-form, as shown by the grammaticality of both sentences in (112). Therefore, they are both adjuncts.

(111) a. * John put a book under the chair but Tom did so on the desk.

b. John read a book at home but Tom did so at school.

(112) a. 张三在桌上放了一本书。李四在书架上也是。

Zhangsan zai zhuo shang fang-le yi-ben shu.
Lisi zai shujia shang ye shi.
Zhangsan at desk top put-Perf one-CL book.
Lisi at bookshelf top also be

'Zhangsan put a book on the desk. Lisi put a book on the shelf.'

b. 张三在家里读书。李四在学校里也是。

Zhangsan zai jia li dushu. Lisi zai xuexiao li ye shi.
Zhangsan at home inside read. Lisi at school inside also be

'Zhangsan read at home. Lisi did so at school.'

The last test involves ordering. In English, an argument is closer to a verb than an adjunct. Reversing the positions of an argument and an adjunct gives rise to degraded grammaticality. In (113a), for instance, the Goal *Mary* must be closer to the verb than the time adjunct *three times* and reversing the two leads to degraded grammaticality in (113b). In Mandarin, directional *zai*-PPs must follow locational *zai*-PPs and reversing the two leads to ungrammaticality as shown by the contrast in (114). The parallel between (113) and (114) might lead to the conclusion that directional PPs are arguments, and locational PPs are adjuncts. However, the unacceptability of (114b) may have other causes. As observed by Gruber (1965, 112), it is preferable to order successive spatial PPs from the general to the specific. For example, the first sentence of the pair in

(115) is preferred to the second, as *New York* is more general than *Bill*. Another possible constraint is that locative expressions must occur outside the verb-Path complex (Gruber 1965, 89). For instance, in (116), the locational PP *in New York* must occur outside the V-Source complex *jump off of the train*. The ordering test is the only test that points to argument status of directional PPs, but there might be other reasons. The fixed order 'Location-Goal-V' in (114a) may be caused by some conceptual constraints that dictate that spatial PPs are arranged from the general to the specific, or that the locational PP must occur outside the V-Goal complex. As a locational PP of a verb refer to an area normally larger than that conveyed by the directional PP of the same verb, the former goes before the latter. Summarizing all the test results, we argue that preverbal *zai*-PPs are all adjuncts, be they directional or locational.

(113) a. John offered the gift to Mary three times.

b. ? John offered the gift three times to Mary. ①

(114) a. ? 张三在屋里在桌子上写字。

? Zhangsan zai wu li zai zhuozi shang xie-zi.

Zhangsan at room inside at desk top write

'Zhangsan wrote on the desk in the room.'

b. * 张三在桌子上在屋里写字。

* Zhangsan zai zhuozi shang zai wu li xie-zi.

Zhangsan at desk top at room inside write

Intended meaning: 'Zhangsan wrote on the desk in the room.'

(115) a. John sent the book to New York to Bill.

b. * John sent the book to Bill to New York.

(116) a. John jumped off of the train in New York.

b. * John jumped in New York off of the train.

---

① This sentence is marginally acceptable when 'three times' is focused.

There is still another logical possibility: even though both types of preverbal *zai*-PPs are base-generated, they occupy different syntactic positions—directional *zai*-PPs are internal to VP whereas locational ones are external to VP. The *ba* construction can be used to test the syntactic position of the two types of *zai*-PP. It contains the morpheme *ba* (originally meaning 'to take, hold') which follows the sentence subject and precedes a DP that is the object or Theme of the subsequent verb phrase (Sybesma 1999, 131). The object marker *ba* in this construction is structurally higher than *v*P (Huang, Li and Li 2009, 177 – 178). In (117), the Goal-denoting *zai*-PP is obviously structurally higher than *ba* which in turn is higher than *v*P and VP. Therefore, the Goal-denoting *zai*-PP is external to the VP. This example indicates that the VP-external *zai*-PP can also express result location. Therefore, directional preverbal *zai*-PPs and locational ones do not differ in syntactic position.

(117)我在合同上把字签了。

Wo   zai   hetong shang ba   zi   qian le.
I   at   contract top   BA   character sign LE
'I signed my name on the contract.'

Preverbal *zai*-PPs can be adjuncts of *v*P, tense phrase (TP) or complementizer phrase (CP). The locational and directional readings are not confined to any of the syntactic positions. Both readings are accessible in all the three positions. The modal verb *hui* 'will' can serve as future tense marker, occupying the T position (Li 1990, 21 – 22). In (118a), *zai zhuo shang*$_3$ (abbreviated as z. z. s$_3$ in 119) 'on the desk' lies between the modal verb *hui* 'will' and the *v*P, so it is the adjunct of the *v*P. In (118b), however, the spatial modifier *zai zhuo shang*$_2$ occurs between the subject and the modal verb *hui* 'will', so it adjoins to the TP. In (118c), *zai zhuo shang*$_1$ is the topic, occupying the Specifier position of CP (see Radford 2004, ch. 9). In all the adjunction sites as in (119), the *zai*-PP denotes Goal. Similarly, *zai*-PPs in the three preverbal adjunction sites can also have locational readings. In other words, regardless of the position that they occupy, preverbal *zai*-PPs modify the whole event and are potentially ambiguous.

(118) a. 他会在桌上放一本书。
　　　　Ta　hui　zai　zhuo　shang　fang　yi-ben　shu.
　　　　he　will　at　desk　top　　put　one-CL　book
　　　　'He will put one book on the desk.'

b. 他在桌上会放一本书。
　　　　Ta　zai　zhuo　shang　hui　fang　yi-ben　shu.
　　　　he　at　desk　top　　will　put　one-CL　book
　　　　'He will put one book on the desk.'

c. 在桌上，他会放一本书。
　　　　Zai　zhuo　shang,　ta　hui　fang　yi-ben　shu.
　　　　at　desk　top　　he　will　put　one-CL　book
　　　　'On the desk, he will put one book.'

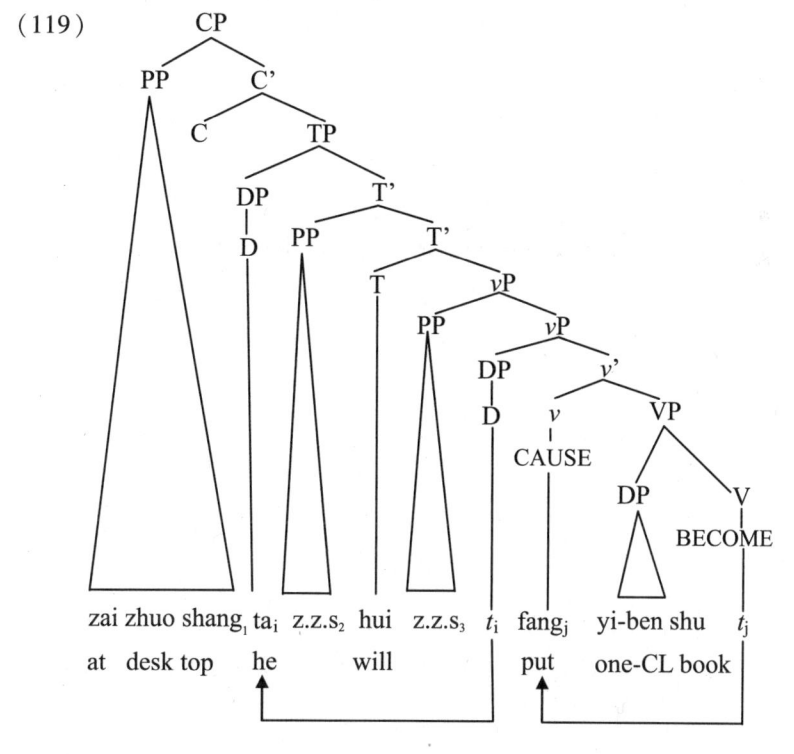

(119)

[Tree diagram: CP dominating PP and C'; C' dominating C and TP; TP dominating DP and T'; DP dominating D; T' dominating PP and T'; T' dominating T and vP; vP dominating PP and vP; PP dominating DP and v'; v' dominating v and VP; v = CAUSE; VP dominating DP and V; V = BECOME.

Terminal string: zai zhuo shang$_1$　ta$_i$　z.z.s$_2$　hui　z.z.s$_3$　t_i　fang$_j$　yi-ben shu　t_j
at desk top　he　　　　　　will　　　　　　put　one-CL book]

To summarize, the syntactic position of a *zai*-PP contributes to its interpretation. The preverbal *zai*-PPs with the placement verb are ambiguous but postverbal ones are not, due to the structural relation between the spatial modifier and the event-denoting predicate. However, syntactic position cannot explain why the ambiguity arises in Mandarin. They also cannot explain why *zai*-PPs in different syntactic positions may have the same interpretation: the preverbal *zai*-PP and the postverbal *zai*-PP with the placement verb can both denote Goal; in the preverbal position, *zai*-PPs can modify the vP, TP or CP—no matter where is the adjunction site, they can express Goal or Location. Syntactic positions also cannot explain why *zai*-PPs in the same syntactic position may have different interpretations: in the postverbal position, *zai*-PPs can express either Location or Goal. One way out is to say that postverbal Location with posture verbs occupies the adjunct position whereas Goal occupies the complement position. However, such an assumption bears the burden of proof since it overthrows the generalization that Mandarin adjuncts are always on the left of the verb (see Mulder and Sybesma 1992; Huang 1994).

3.4.3 Cognitive constraints on the use of *zai*-PPs

Besides semantic and syntactic principles, some extra-linguistic cognitive constraints are also found to influence the way *zai*-PPs are used. For instance, a large place tends to be encoded as Location where an event takes place, whilst a small place is more likely to be conceived as the Goal of an event. The two sentences in (120), for instance, share the same syntactic structure V-*zai*, but vary in the extent to which they are accepted. (120b) is semantically odd. The contrast in (120) can only be explained by the cognitive constraint. The result location of the placement verb *xie* 'write' can be *gezi*, a small cell, but cannot be *shufang*, a large study.

(120) a. 把字写在格子里。

  Ba zi   xie zai gezi li.

  BA character write at cell inside

  'Write the character in the cell!'

b. #把字写在书房里。

  #Ba zi   xie zai shufang li.

  BA character write at study inside

  Intended meaning: 'Write the character in the study!'

(adapted from Fan 1982)

Moreover, some events are conceived by native speakers as happening in a small location rather than in a large one. In (121), the preverbal Location could be a small location *jiaoshi li* 'inside the classroom' but not Beijing: it is very odd to consider a person's writing characters as happening in a large metropolis, hence the reduced acceptability of (121b).

(121) a. 我在教室里写了字。

  Wo zai jiaoshi li xie-le zi.

  I at classroom inside write-Perf character

  'I wrote characters in the classroom.'

b. ? 我在北京写了字。

  ? Wo zai Beijing xie-le zi.

   I at Beijing write-Perf character

  'I wrote characters in Beijing. (adapted from Fan 1982)

Another important field showing constraint from our cognition is the capacity of displacement verbs and some placement verbs to take postverbal *zai*-PPs. The Goal conveyed by the postverbal *zai*-PPs with the displacement verb must be lower than the starting point of the event. For instance, the verb *tiao* 'jump' can be followed by *zai mabei shang* 'on the horseback' in (122a) only if he jumped from a higher place to the horseback. If he started from a place lower than the horseback, then *zai* must be replaced by the directional *dao* 'reach, to'. In addition, the Goal of jumping in the horizontal direction also cannot be encoded by a *zai*-PP as shown in (122b). Here *zai* must be replaced by *dao* 'reach, to'. The sentences in (122) suggest that only when the displacement event is conceived as downward, can the postverbal *zai* be used. The 'wear' subclass of the placement verbs, including *chuan* 'wear', *dai* 'wear', *dai* 'carry' and *na* 'carry' (Liu 2009; Hsieh 2010), also demonstrates some peculiarities. The *zai*-PPs following these verbs could only denote the inherent end point of the action encoded by these verbs. For instance, the inherent end point of the action *na* 'take' is one's hand, so the verb can take the LP *shou li* 'inside hand' in (123a). LPs that denote other places are not allowed as shown in (123b).

(122) a. 他跳在马背上。

   Ta tiao zai mabei shang.

   he jump at horseback top

   'He jumped to the horseback.'

 b. *他跳在屋子里。

   *Ta tiao zai wuzi li.

   he jump at room inside

   Intended meaning:'He jumped into the room.'

(123) a. 钱，你最好拿在手里。

   Qian, ni zuihao na zai shouli. ①

   money, you best take at handinside

   'You'd better hold the money in your hand.' (Teng 1975)

 b. *维尼熊，你最好拿在腿上。

---

① The most natural reading of this sentence is shown in the gloss where the postverbal *zai*-PP denotes Location rather than Goal, in contrast to (123b). Under this reading, *na* 'take' is an Activity verb. Its combination with postverbal *zai*-PPs may be relics of an earlier grammar, comparable to the case of manner-of-motion verbs to be discussed in the next section. Our intuition, however, is that a directional reading is also available for this sentence.

* Weinixiong,　　　ni　zuihao　na　zai　tui　shang.
Winnie the Pooh,　you　best　　take　at　leg　top
'You'd better take Winnie the Pooh on your lap.'

To summarize, a large place tends to project into Location whereas a small place is often used as the Goal. Some events, such as writing a character, are conceived as happening in a small location rather than in a large one. Only when a displacement verb denotes a downward movement, can it take postverbal *zai*-PPs. Only *zai*-PPs that denote the inherent end point of the action encoded by the 'wear' subclass of placement verbs can follow these verbs. These constraints on spatial PPs are not from syntax or the physical world, but are governed by cognitive principles.

The ungrammatical sentences in (122b) and (123b) can be saved by substituting the directional *dao* 'reach, to' for the locational preposition *zai*. There is actually a language change in which postverbal *zai* gradually gives way to *dao* if Goal is to be expressed. The next section will discuss the division of labor between the two prepositions in the postverbal position in modern Mandarin, and the language change that brought about the current situation.

3.3.5 Diachronic changes of *zai*

The distribution of *zai* is a very complex phenomenon. Even though there are generally no constraints on the *zai*-V word order, there are many constraints on the V-*zai* word order. Apart from the aspectual constraint discussed in section 3.3.2, there are some others: *zai*-PPs cannot occur after VO compounds such as *xie-zi* 'write-character = write' (Tai 1975; Li and Thompson 1981; Fan 1982); most resultative verb compounds (RVCs) cannot take postverbal *zai*-PPs except for those with *dao* 'fall' and *fan* 'turn' as their second verb (Fan 1982). The restriction on VO compounds and RVCs may be caused by the fact that Mandarin verbs are normally restricted to take only one complement (Huang 1982, 1994). A postverbal *zai*-PP competes with the second morpheme in the VO compounds or RVCs for the complement position: only one can appear after the verb. It remains a mystery, however, why morphemes in the compound words are accessible for syntactic operations, contrary to the Lexical Integrity Hypothesis which states that 'no phrase-level rule may affect a proper subpart of a word', as discussed in Huang (1984, 60). The proportion of disyllabic verbs that occur in the V-*zai* structure is rather constrained compared with that of monosyllabic ones (Fan 1982). Based on a corpus study, Fan (1982) found that 84% of the monosyllabic verbs occur in the V-PP word order, but the percentage is only 15% for disyllabic verbs. The asymmetry between disyllabic verbs and monosyllabic ones is explained by constraints on disyllabic VO compound and RVCs. Other factors include prosody and register. Some constraints on postverbal *zai*-PP are not caused by syntax, but are constrained by prosody (Feng 2003, 2008).① Some usages of *zai*-PPs are found only in formal written language, as formal written Chinese has relics of ancient Chinese and thus differs from informal spoken Chinese in some aspects (Feng 2008).

This section deals with the constraint on the verbs that can appear in the V-*zai* structure, which is under historical change. Since Early Archaic Chinese, the preverbal and postverbal *zai* have been used with little difference in meaning, so it is natural that modern Chinese has cases of

---

① For instance, the V-PP-DP sequence shown in (ia) is ruled out because the Mandarin verb normally only takes one complement (Huang 1982, 1994). However, this sequence is licit when the nominal phrase in the PP is a pronoun which is prosodically light as in (ib). The contrast in (i) can be explained by prosodic constraints Nuclear Stress Rule and Structural Removing Condition (Feng 2003).

(i) a. *Ta   fang zai hao   ji   zhang zhuozi shang le   hen   duo   ben   shu.
       he   put   at   good some CL   table   top   Perf very many CL   book
       'He put many books on many tables.'

   b. Ta   fang (zai) nar   le   hao   ji-ben   shu.
      he   put   at   there Perf good   some-CL   book
      'He put there many books.'

pre- and postverbal *zai* continuing to show semantic overlaps (S. Huang 1978). On the other hand, PPs, including spatial PPs, began to move from postverbal position to preverbal position since the Han Dynasty (202 BC – 220 AD). By comparing *Zuo Zhuan* 'Chronicle of Zuo' and *Shiji* 'Records of the Grand Historian', He (1985) observed that most PPs moved from postverbal to preverbal position in the 300 years between *Zuo Zhuan* and *Shiji*.① C. Zhang (2002) observed that the trend was prominent in Wei Jin Nan-Bei Chao (220 – 589 AD), and reached equilibrium in the Song, Yuan, and Ming Dynasties (960 – 1644 AD). In a corpus study on *Hongloumen* 'Dream of the Red Mansions' written in the Qing Dynasty (1644 – 1911 AD), the transition period from pre-Modern Chinese to Modern Chinese, Deng (2011) identified some postverbal *zai*-PPs that are only allowed before the verb in Modern Chinese.② The findings from these studies suggest that from the Han Dynasty to modern times, postverbal *zai*-PPs continue to move forward to before the verb. This is equivalent to saying that the types of verbs that can take postverbal *zai*-PPs become more and more restricted. As for the reason of the fronting of spatial PPs, C. Zhang (2002) argued that it was caused by the emergence of a syntactic constraint that a verb can only take one complement, and a semantic constraint that only Goal is mapped to the postverbal position.

Due to the scope of the present study, only a few verb classes that do not fit well into the aspectual analysis in section 3.3.2 will be discussed from the perspective of language change. We will first elaborate on some verb types that lack syntactic productivity in taking postverbal *zai*-PPs to

---

① It was estimated that *Zuo Zhuan* was compiled not later than 389 BC, and *Shiji* was written from 109 to 91 BC in the Han Dynasty.

② *Hongloumen* was written in the early Qing Dynasty. One example of postverbal *zai*-PPs that should be put in preverbal position nowadays is shown below.

(i) ···Xiren he yi shui-zhe zai na li.
    Xiren with clothes sleep-DUR at that inside
    'Xiren is sleeping there without taking clothes off.'

form V-*zai* sequences, and then discuss the division of labor between *zai* 'at' and *dao* 'reach, to' in the postverbal position.

The verb types that take postverbal *zai*-PPs are broader than those discussed in section 3.3.2, but the additional types take postverbal *zai*-PPs to a very limited extent. For instance, the verb of combining like *bing* 'combine' only occurs with *zai yikuai* 'at together', and *zai yiqi* 'at together' as in example (124a) (see Liu 2009). It cannot be followed by other *zai*-PPs as shown in (124b). The V-*zai* structure with the verb *bing* 'combine' lacks syntactic productivity, as there is only a limited number of lexical items that can occur after *zai*. This usage is thus considered idiomatic.

(124) a. 并在一块啊。

    Bing   zai   yikuair   a.

    combine   at   together   sfp

    'Combine together!'

b. *并在纸上。

    * Bing   zai   zhi   shang.

    combine   at   paper   top

    Intended meaning: 'Combine onto the paper.'

Manner-of-motion verbs, e.g. *fei* 'fly', *fu* 'float', and *piao* 'float in the air', can take postverbal *zai* to express general location rather than result location, as shown in (125a) (Fan 1982; Fong 1997). Such sentences run counter to the V-Goal word-order regularity. They are possibly fossils in modern Mandarin, keeping the property of an earlier grammar. They mostly appear in formal written language which embodies different layers of grammars diachronically. In addition, the LPs following *zai* are also restricted (see Hsieh 2010). The verb *fei* can take the LP *tian shang* 'on the sky' which is the prototypical location for flying in (125a), but it cannot go with another LP *shu shang* 'on the tree' as shown in (125b).

(125) a. 鸟儿飞在天上。
　　　　Niao'er　fei　zai　tian　shang.
　　　　bird　　fly　at　sky　top
　　　　'Birds fly on the sky.'
　　b. *鸟儿飞在树上。
　　　　*Niao'er　fei　zai　shu　shang.
　　　　bird　　fly　at　tree　top
　　　　Intended meaning: 'Birds fly on the tree.'

　　In what follows, the division of labor between zai 'at' and dao 'reach, to' in the postverbal position will be discussed. It has been shown that zai can follow several classes of verbs to express Location, or Goal. All the Goal-denoting zai-PPs actually are interchangeable with phrases headed by dao, and the classes of verbs that can take postverbal dao are broader than those that take zai. For instance, with non-motional process verbs such as wan 'play', dao rather than zai is used by Mandarin speakers to express Goal. Moreover, Liu (2009) observes that the postverbal zai does not occur with directional verbs or displacement verbs, unless the direction is downward. For instance, the directional verb sheng 'rise' in (126) does not encode downward motion, so it cannot be followed by zai, but has to take dao to express Goal. The division of labor between zai and dao can be tentatively formulated as follows: while dao marks non-motional process verbs, directional or displacement verbs, zai marks downward directional or displacement verbs. The use of dao is actually very broad. Posture verbs and placement verbs, for instance, can occur with dao as exemplified in (127). (Dis)appearance verbs and verbs of posterior/anterior entailment, however, cannot take dao as shown in (128), as there is no change of location involved in sentences with these verbs. A more precise generalization, therefore, is that any verb involving change of location can take dao.

(126) 月亮升到/*在天上。

Yueliang sheng dao/ * zai tian shang.
moon   rise   to/ * at   sky   top
'The moon rose onto the sky.'

(127) a. 张三坐在/到椅子上。

Zhangsan zuo zai/dao yizi   shang.
Zhangsan sit at/to   chair   top
'Zhangsan sat down on the chair.'

b. 张三放了一本书在/到桌上。

Zhangsan fang-le   yi-ben   shu   zai/dao zhuo shang.
Zhangsan put-Perf   one-CL   book at/to   desk top
'Zhangsan put one book on the desk.'

(128) a. 张三死在/ * 到医院里。

Zhangsan si   zai/ * dao   yiyuan   li.
Zhangsan die at/ * to   hospital inside
'Zhangsan died in the hospital.'

b. 张三把钥匙忘在/ * 到家里了。

Zhangsan ba   yaoshi wang zai/ * dao jia   li   le.
Zhangsan BA   key   forget at/ * to   home inside LE
'Zhangsan forgot the key at home.'

From Archaic Chinese to Contemporary Chinese, the verb classes that occurred with postverbal *zai* expanded greatly (Liu 2009). Meanwhile, from the late Tang Dynasty (618 – 907 AD), the locative marker following directional verbs which specify a non-downward direction changed from *zai* to *dao*. It is important to note, however, that different dialects of Chinese proceed at different rates in this language change. In the Guiyang and Chongqing dialects (varieties of Southwest Mandarin dialects), *zai* still occurs with directional verbs (non-downward) such as *lai* 'come' as in (129), which is ruled out in standard Mandarin (Wu 1996, cited in Liu 2009).

(129) 天黑才来在城里头。

Tian hei cai lai   zai cheng li-tou.
sky   dark only come at   town   inside
'(He) didn't come to town until it was dark.'

(Liu 2009)

Based on the discussion so far, we can see a language change from marking postverbal locatives with *zai* into marking them with *dao* if there is a change of location. The change is still in progress. Some southern dialects are more permissive of postverbal *zai* than standard Mandarin Chinese. The idiosyncrasy of the use of postverbal *zai* and the contact of various Chinese dialects in big cities in China may give rise to ambiguous input for children growing up in this environment, which, in turn, gives rise to language change.

3.4 Summary and discussion

This chapter has shown that the interpretation of the *zai*-PP depends on the event type of the verb it co-occurs with. Both pre- and postverbal *zai*-PPs are event modifiers, with the latter occupying the complement position of the main verb. The postverbal *zai*-PP that is within the scope of the event predicate BECOME can modify the result state of a complex event, and the directional meaning arises. Only verbs that have a (dynamic) state component in their event structures can take postverbal *zai*-PPs.

We have mainly discussed seven groups of verbs based on their event types, and their interactions with *zai*-PPs are summarized in Table 3 – 1. The general pattern is that postverbal *zai*-PPs denote Goal and preverbal ones Location. Exceptions to the 'Location-V' and 'V-Goal' word-order regularity can be explained by principles of event semantics. When *zai*-PPs occur after posture verbs (in their state use) and manner-of-motion verbs, they do not denote result location, because the event structure of these verbs contains no result state for the *zai*-PPs to modify. Conversely, placement verbs can take preverbal *zai*-PPs to express Goal because the event structure of these verbs contains a result subpart, and this subpart can be modified by a *zai*-PP which has the whole event within its scope. In other words, regardless of the syntactic positions, *zai*-PPs signify Goal if they modify the result state in the event structure of verbs that involve change of location. Otherwise, they signify Location. Postverbal *zai*-PPs are licensed by verbs that are dynamic State, or have a state component in their event structures. Some idiosyncrasies in the use of postverbal *zai*-PPs can be explained by historical relics and cognitive constraints. For instance, manner-of-motion verbs do not have a state component in their event structures, but they can take postverbal *zai*-PPs. This phenomenon only occurs in formal written language and may be a fossil of an earlier grammar historically. Lastly, the use of *zai* '(be) at' is more restricted than *dao* 'reach, to' in the postverbal position.

Table 3–1   The semantics of *zai*-PPs with different verb classes

Verb classes	Event type	Example	Preverbal *zai* Location	Preverbal *zai* Goal	Postverbal *zai* Location	Postverbal *zai* Goal
Posture	Achievement	*shui* 'sleep'				✓
	state	*zuo* 'sit'	✓		✓	
Placement	Accomplishment	*fang* 'put'	✓	✓		✓
	State	*hua* 'draw'	✓		✓	
Downward displacement	Transition	*diao* 'drop' *reng* 'toss'	✓			✓
Manner-of-motion	Activity	*fei* 'fly'	✓		✓	
(Dis)appearing	Achievement	*si* 'die'	✓		✓	
Posterior entailment	Achievement	*wang* 'forget'			✓	
Anterior entailment	Achievement	*zhao-zhao*① 'find'	✓			

---

① *Zhao3-zhao2* 找着 'find' is a resultative verb compound.

This chapter adhered to the paradigm of event semantics rather than a syntactic account because a great deal of data cannot be accounted for by the latter. The syntactic account equates the syntactic position of complement with a directional reading. However, there are two systematic exceptions to this account. First, it cannot explain the locational reading of the *zai*-PPs occurring after posture verbs. One might argue that the PPs with a directional reading are complements of the posture verb while the locational PPs are adjuncts. The problem with this analysis is that all other Mandarin adjuncts occur preverbally, and it is strange why the adjuncts formed by locational *zai*-PPs should appear postverbally. Second, it cannot explain why the locative object, being the complement of the verb, can have a locational reading. Section 4.3 will show in detail that some locative objects express Location. Another major problem with the syntactic account is that it cannot explain the ambiguity of preverbal *zai*-PPs with placement verbs. To capture the locational and directional readings of the preverbal *zai*-PP, the syntactic analysis would have to prove that the directional *zai*-PP and the locational one actually occupy two different syntactic positions, with the former being internal to the VP, as it contains an argument of the verb. However, the directional reading is freely available in any preverbal position, VP-internal or VP-external. Therefore, the VP-internal analysis of the directional PP is untenable.

Our account based on event semantics also fares better than that of Tai (1975, 1985) which is based on the role of iconicity in grammar. The iconicity account cannot explain why the Goal element, which happens last in a motion event, can occur before the placement verb. It also cannot explain why the locational element, which is the general location of the event, can appear after the posture verb. The mismatch between temporal sequence and word order poses a serious problem for a functional theory based on iconicity, but is well captured by our event-semantic account.

The analysis proposed in the present study also improves on previous attempts based on event semantics. In contrast to Fan's (1982) contention that topic PPs that precede subjects modify events whereas preverbal PPs that follow subjects modify the action or state, the present study argues that spatial PPs, as topic or as preverbal adjunct, always modify the event. Topic PPs are potentially ambiguous, just as PPs between the subject and the main verb. In contrast to Li (1990, 119) and Liu (2009) who claimed that the zai-PP serves as a telic point that makes the event bounded, we propose that the locational PP headed by zai is not bounded on its own, and so cannot make the event bounded. The word zai does not have the BECOME meaning, be it a verb or a preposition in any position of a sentence (Fong 1997). Liu's account cannot explain why sometimes the postverbal zai-PP makes an event bounded, but sometimes it does not as in the case of posture verbs and manner-of-motion verbs. The change of state reading is given by the verb *per se*, rather than by the zai-PP. Besides, an event has only one culmination point (Rothstein 2004, 79). Liu (2009) used the single culmination constraint to explain the incompatibility of RVCs with postverbal zai. She argues that both the second verb of the RVC and the postverbal zai-PP provide an event boundary, which results in an unacceptable doubly delimited event. Her argument has obvious counterexamples, as RVCs whose second verb subcategorizes for zai-PPs, such as *dao* 'fall' and *fan* 'topple', can take postverbal zai-PPs (see Fan 1982). We argue that postverbal zai-PPs do not bring an event boundary and thus do not violate the single culmination constraint. They can occur with Accomplishments or Achievements such as *fang yi-ben shu* 'place one book' or *si* 'die' whose culmination is already specified. As spatial modifiers, they only add a property of the culmination, namely the location where the culmination takes place.

Lastly, event semantics only helps to describe the underlying pattern of the distribution of Mandarin zai-PPs, but does not explain why there is such a pattern. So far, it remains unclear why Mandarin has the idiosyncratic restriction on postverbal *zai*-PPs that only verbs with a state component can take postverbal *zai*-PPs. C. Zhang (2002) argued that the restriction on postverbal *zai*-PPs was caused by the emergence of a syntactic constraint that a verb can only take one complement, as well as a semantic constraint that only Goal is mapped to the postverbal position in the historical development of Mandarin. This account has obvious counterexamples from placement verbs in the 'placement V-O-PP' structure which takes two complements, and posture verbs in the 'posture V-Location' structure. The two exceptions can be explained by the *v*P-shell analysis as shown in section 3.3.3, and principles of event semantics as discussed in section 3.3.2, respectively.

3.5 Acquisition of *zai*

As an important morpheme to express spatial relation, *zai* '(be) at' figures prominently in the early lexicon of Mandarin-speaking children (see Song 2009, 105), and has attracted many researchers working on language acquisition in Chinese. In what follows, we will review the distribution of *zai* and *zai*-PPs in child Mandarin. But before that, let us discuss the nature of input, an important factor that needs to be considered in language acquisition, and we then examine the acquisition of *zai* and *zai*-PPs from the perspective of input.

In the field of child language acquisition, it is well recognized that input from the environment plays a role. Input can be further divided into positive evidence, direct negative evidence, and indirect negative evidence (Chomsky 1981, 8 – 9). Direct evidence is what children hear in their environment. It is the main, or even the only source that children invoke to generalize a rule or learn a lexical item. Direct negative evidence refers to correction by adults, which is generally believed to be absent and unnecessary for first language acquisition (Chomsky 1981, 9; Pinker

1989, 10 – 14; Goodluck 1991/2000, 142). Children are not systematically corrected by adults, and they do not pay attention to the negative evidence even if available. Indirect negative evidence is negative evidence without corrections: "If certain structures or rules fail to be exemplified in relatively simple expressions, where they would be expected to be found", then it is inferred that they are ungrammatical and they are excluded from children's grammar (Chomsky 1981, 9). It is the least studied, because it is not fleshed out according to a particular theory, and no theoretical arguments rest crucially on it (Pinker 1989, 15; Gass 2003, 249). If "positive input" is defined as all that children hear, then "cues", which may also be termed "triggers", are the elements that children actively search for in the positive input (see Lightfoot 1999, 149). Some studies have shown that even infants actively scan their input and seek the distribution pattern of a structure. Marcus et al. (1999), for instance, tested 7-month-olds with the familiarization preference procedure. The infants were randomly assigned to either an 'ABA' condition, in which they were familiarized with sentences like 'ga ti ga' or 'li na li', or an 'ABB' condition, in which they heard sentences like 'ga ti ti' or 'li na na'. In the test phase, the infants attended longer to sentences with unfamiliar structures than to sentences with familiar structures. Evidently, they are sensitive to the distribution pattern, and build abstract ABB or ABA representations accordingly.

When cues exemplify a consistent pattern such as a constant distribution pattern of a structure, it provides unambiguous evidence that the structure is used in a certain way in adult grammar. Slobin (1997a, 1997b) suggests that as long as there are consistent cues, children have no difficulty in grasping a language-specific property. Conversely, inconsistent cues lead to ambiguous evidence which may confuse children. For instance, as reviewed in Slobin (1997a), Russian and Polish case inflectional paradigms look almost identical on paper: except for irregulars, masculine nouns end in a consonant, feminine nouns end in -*a*, and neuter nouns end in -*o*. However, unstressed vowels are reduced to schwa in Russian, but not in Polish. Therefore, Polish children have consistent cues to identify the gender of a noun, because masculine, feminine, and neuter nouns have different endings, but Russian children have inconsistent cues as feminine and neuter nouns are often not phonologically distinguished. Consequently, Polish children use the correct inflection from the very beginning, but Russian children produce many non-target forms. If inconsistent cues really slow down language acquisition, we expect to see, in the case of *zai* and *zai*-PPs, that 1) the placement of *zai*-PPs and 2) the division of labor between *zai* and *dao* 'reach, to' in the postverbal position pose problems for first language acquisition, as there are different types of verbs which interact with *zai*-PPs inconsistently. The two predictions are borne out by empirical studies.

First, experimental and longitudinal findings with learners of Chinese show that the word order of *zai*-PPs is difficult for learners. In Mandarin Chinese, preverbal *zai*-PPs generally encode Location, and postverbal *zai*-PPs generally encode Path. The mappings of these two notions to the two syntactic positions in adult input have some inconsistencies, mainly due to posture verbs and placement verbs. It is predicted that the inconsistent cues from language input will make the acquisition task difficult for language learners. Studies on bilingual children, first language (L1), and second language (L2) learners of Chinese all confirm the prediction. Yip and Matthews (2007, 190 - 199) show that Cantonese-English bilingual children have difficulty with the placement of locative PPs headed by *hai* '(be) at', the Cantonese counterpart of Mandarin *zai*, Cantonese being another dialect of Chinese. Among the V-PP utterances produced by six Cantonese-English bilingual children aged between 1;3 and 4;6, 11.8% are non-target. For instance, they allow V-PP word order with activity verbs like *sik*6 'eat', *waan*2 'play', and *fan*3-*gaau*3 'sleep'. The non-target forms are attributed to ambiguous input: both PP-V and V-PP orders are productive and some verbs allow both orders in Cantonese. The ambiguous input in Cantonese opens the door for language transfer from English to Cantonese. These bilingual children have acquired the notions of Goal and Location as they could express such meanings in English, but the word-order complexity in Cantonese slows down their acquisition. Cheung's (1991) experiments show that Cantonese-speaking children younger than 2;6 have not acquired the word order contrast between Goal and Location, whereas children older than 3;0 have acquired it. Non-target locational postverbal *zai*-PPs are also found in L2 learners of Mandarin from France, Korea, Vietnam, USA, Mongolia, Indonesia, Japan and Thailand (W. Zhou 2011, 96 – 99). Deng (2014) linked the distributional properties of the input and child acquisition of the word order of *zai*-PPs. Her experiment showed that four-year-old Mandarin-speaking children significantly differed from adults in tolerating non-target V-*zai* sentences. In the experiment, if Mandarin-speaking children had acquired the word order in expressing Location and Goal, they should be able to reject postverbal locational phrases headed by *zai* (* V-Location) such as *wan zai hai li* 'play in the sea', and preverbal directional phrases headed by *zai* (* Goal-V) such as *zai chuang shang diao* 'drop on the bed'. There was significant difference between four-year-olds and adults in rejecting *V-Location, but no significant difference between children and adults in rejecting *Goal-V. The results clearly suggest that children have trouble in rejecting non-target postverbal Location, especially under the age of five, but at a very early age, they are aware of the distribution pattern that Goal should not be in the preverbal position. The difficulty with the word order of *zai*-PPs or its dialectal equivalents in learners can be explained by cue inconsistency in input. In other words, inconsistent cues slow down language acquisition. The placement of Goal-denoting *zai*-PPs and locational ones in Mandarin is inconsistent. The otherwise consistent pattern of Location-V and V-Goal is disrupted by preverbal Goal-denoting *zai*-PPs with placement verbs and postverbal locational *zai*-PPs with posture verbs. As shown in Deng and Yip (2015), at least 11.3% of preverbal *zai*-PPs and 19.2% of postverbal ones in the adult input are exceptions to the word-order regularity. Besides, *zai*-PPs follow verbs from a restricted set: only verb classes that have a dynamic/resultative state component in the event structure can take them. The inconsistency of the word order of *zai* explains the late acquisition of the placement of locational *zai*-PPs. Children have difficulty in rejecting postverbal Location, while rejecting noncanonical preverbal Goal is easier for them. The difference can be attributed to the difference in the amount of inconsistent cues in the preverbal and postverbal positions: there are more postverbal locational *zai*-PPs than preverbal Goal-denoting *zai*-PPs in adult input (19.2% vs. 11.3%) as shown by Deng and Yip (2015); apart from Goal-denoting *zai*-PPs, other result elements in Mandarin are generally excluded from the preverbal position, whereas the postverbal position accommodates a variety of elements, including Result, Frequency, Duration, and Manner (see Huang 1994). As Result elements most frequently occur postverbally, children are good at rejecting preverbal result location, namely, Goal.

Second, experimental and longitudinal findings with monolingual Chinese-speaking children also suggest the division of labor between *zai* 'at' and *dao* 'reach, to' in the postverbal position is difficult to acquire, owing to inconsistent cues in input. Hsieh (2010) found the non-target use of postverbal *zai* in a Mandarin-speaking child's naturalistic speech as in (130). The child correctly put the Goal element after the verb, but the verb *na* 'take' normally does not take postverbal *zai*-PPs as discussed in section 3.3.4. *Zai* 'at' should be replaced by *dao* 'reach, to' in this case. Even at 5;8, the child attached *zai* to verbs that cannot take postverbal *zai*.

(130) *我是拿在你房间里,我确定。

* Wo shi na zai ni fangjian li, wo queding. (Sean 5;8)
I　be take at　your room　inside I　sure
'I took it to your room, I'm sure.'

This pattern is echoed by the naturalistic production data by children aged around 4;6 in a corpus study by Deng and Yip (2015). Non-target postverbal *zai* is also found in an elicited production experiment in P. Li (1990 ch. 5) who tested 99 children from Beijing between the ages of 2;9 and 6;4. Based on child utterances, he concluded that children's use of the V-PP word order is associated with telic verbs as in (131b) and (131c), while their PP-V word order is associated with process verbs as in (131a). However, the two sentences in (131b) and (131c) are judged as ungrammatical by us and they could be saved by substituting *dao* for *zai*.① We argue that *zuan* 'burrow, move' and *pa* 'crawl' are activity verbs which cannot be followed by *zai*. These children did not fully acquire the division of labor between *zai* and *dao* in the postverbal position. Their non-target forms boil down to insensitivity to the aspectual requirement of V-*zai* constructions, or unfamiliarity with the aspectual properties of the verbs *zuan* 'burrow, move' and *pa* 'crawl'.

(131) a. 鸭子在水里游呢。

Yazi　zai　shui　li　　　you　ne. (CHH 4;0)
duck　at　water　inside　swim　sfp
The duck is swimming in the water.

b. *小汽车钻在那小屋子里去了。

*Xiao qiche zuan zai nei xiao wuzi li　　qu le.

(LIB 3;11)

small　car　move at　that　little　room inside go　LE
'The small car moved into that room.'

---

① The verb *qu* 'go' in (131b) and (131c) collocates with *dao* 'to' in the postverbal position (Y. Liu et al. 1998).

c. *乌龟爬在床底下去了。

　　*Wugui　pa　　zai　chuang　di-xia　qu　le. (LIY 5;0)
　　 turtle　crawl　at　　bed　　bottom　go　LE
　　'The turtle crawled under the bed.'

In Deng's (2014) experiment designed to find out whether participants accepted an incorrect V-*zai* sentence in the presence of a correct V-*dao* one, those who chose the latter rather than the former were deemed able to distinguish between *zai* and *dao* in the postverbal position. Some children as old as six were not able to do so. The differences in accepting non-target postverbal *zai* were statistically significant between adults and three-, four-, five-, and six-year-olds. As introduced above, only verbs with a state component in their event structures can take a postverbal *zai*-phrase, and other verbs have to take a postverbal *dao*-phrase to express Goal. Evidently, the children in Deng (2014) overextended the use of the postverbal *zai* to verb classes that do not allow it. Children up to six have not fully acquired the division of labor between *zai* and *dao*. Taken together, these studies suggest that it takes time for Mandarin-speaking children to fully grasp the constraint that only a restricted set of verbs can take postverbal *zai*-PPs, and others must take *dao* 'reach, to' to express Goal. Again, the late acquisition can be explained by the fact that the division of labor between *zai* 'at' and *dao* 'reach, to' in postverbal position is not transparent in input.

　　The distribution of *zai*-PPs and division of labor between *zai* 'at' and *dao* 'reach, to' are difficult to learn also because they are determined by their co-occurring verbs, and learners have to master knowledge of the semantics of each verb and its membership in a verb class through experience. Postverbal *zai* follows a limited number of verb classes, and children have to learn whether a verb belongs to these classes or not. This task is difficult for at least two reasons. First of all, children have to learn through experience the semantics and syntax of each verb. Different languages may have different mappings from lexical semantics to syntax: for instance, the verb *sneeze* is unergative in Italian and Dutch, unaccusative in Eastern Pomo, and flexible in Choctaw (Rosen 1984). A further source of complexity is frequent aspect shift in Mandarin, which makes it difficult for learners to pin down some verbs' event types (see Chapter 2).

In sum, child data concerning word order of *zai*-PPs confirm the importance of input in language acquisition. In addition, learning the syntax and semantics of each verb through experience is an indispensable part of language acquisition.

There are more issues related to the acquisition of *zai*, *zai*-PPs, and other spatial PPs. As for the syntactic category of *zai* '(be) at' in early child Mandarin, it is found that *zai* is first acquired as a verb, and the prepositional usage develops later. Zhou and Wang (2001), based on a corpus of 376 locative sentences from 90 Mandarin-speaking children aged between 1;0 and 5;0, argued that before 2;0, *zai* is a verb that occurs only in the '*zai*-Location' structure, and the prepositional usage of *zai* appears later in the '*zai*-Location-V' structure. Cheung's (1991) production task on 33 Cantonese-speaking children shows that two-year-old Cantonese-speaking children rarely produced the locative coverb *hai* 'at', the Cantonese counterpart of Mandarin *zai* 'at', and the older children used it inconsistently.

Also of interest is children's preference for any particular word order of *zai*-PPs. There is evidence to show that in Cantonese, the PP-V word order is used more frequently than the V-PP word order, and the V-DP-PP word order is used more often than the PP-V-DP for the placement verb to express Goal. Based on two spoken Cantonese corpora CRC and HKCAC, both consisting of natural conversations of adult Cantonese speakers on radio in Hong Kong, Kwan (2005) observed that PP-V word order of *hai2* 'at', the counterpart of Mandarin *zai* 'at', is the dominant one between the two word orders of PP-V and V-PP (53% vs. 8% in CRC, and 40%

vs. 16% in HKCAC). The placement verb *baai2* 'put' occurs 100% in the V-DP-PP construction as in (132a) instead of the PP-V-DP sequence in (132b). Cheung's (1991) elicited production data also indicate that Cantonese children and adults prefer to express Goal in postverbal position with verbs of placement. The pattern suggests that Cantonese speakers, influenced by the prominent V-Goal word order, tend to map the goal of a placement event to the postverbal position, even though preverbal Goal is one option for placement verbs. Apart from these word orders, Kwan (2005) observed that *hai2* 'at' was also used in the topic PPs and the right-dislocated PPs, with the former occurring more frequently than the latter (39% vs. 0% in CRC and 43% vs. 1% in HKCAC).

(132) a. Keoi5 baai2zo2 bun2 syu1 hai2 gwai6 soeng6-min6.
       S/he   put Perf   CL   book at   cabinet top-face
       'S/he put a/the book on the shelf.'   (Preferred order)
     b. Keoi5 hai2 gwai6 soeng6-min6   baai2zo2 bun2 syu1.
       S/he   at   cabinet top-face   put Perf   CL   book
       'S/he put a book on the shelf.'   (Kwan 2005, 72)

Previous literature points to the inconspicuousness of Source in children's conception of a motion event. Some studies show that children have trouble in expressing Source. Landau and Lakusta (2006) performed spatial-linguistic tests on two groups: subjects who had Williams Syndrome (WS) and those who did not have it. All participants were asked to describe events in which the Figure underwent motion over a variety of Paths including Goal and Source. In the WS subjects' descriptions, the Source element was often omitted. This phenomenon is called 'Source vulnerability'. Fragility in representing Source may be a fundamental characteristic of our event representation, since it was found in all groups in this study: WS children, WS adults, as well as normal children and adults. Landau and Lakusta (2006) provided a processing-demands account for this fragility. In a motion event, the Figure moves from some origin (Source), along a path, and then ends up at some destination (Goal). The Figure coincides with the Goal at the time when the observer is required to produce a description. Thus the Figure and Goal are the foci of attention at the moment. On the other hand, expressing the origin of the Figure places large demands on memory and attention. Hence, Source is less salient to the observer. Fragility in representing Source has also been observed in Chinese children. Cheung (1991) tested 33 Cantonese-speaking children aged between 2;1 to 5;9, and found that they hardly talked about Source in a production task involving description of pictures or action sequences.

However, there seem to be some contradictory findings. Clark and Carpenter (1989) showed that children overextended the Source marker *from* to mark other elements, such as Agent and Cause. Some examples are shown in (133), where children used *from* to introduce Agents. Adults, instead, would use *by* in passives to introduce Agents. These children might have identified Agent as a kind of Source—the starting point of the action.

(133) a. These fall down from me.   (2;2)

b. I was caught from you.   (5;11)

The concept of Source may not be a late development, as the findings by Clark and Carpenter (1989) show that children do express such a concept and even overgeneralize, using the Source marker in other semantic fields. In event representation, however, Source may be left out due to some general cognitive constraints, such as the limit of attention and working memory. Given a reminder before children's production, for instance, the repetition of the Source after showing the event, would children be able to express Source in a motion event? If not, attention and memory cannot explain 'Source vulnerability'. This hypothesis was tested in Deng (2014). In an elicited production task with hints given at the time when the subject was required to produce a motion event, 52 out of 98 children (53%) failed to describe Source of the motion event with the preposition *cong* 'from', and the correct response rates for 2-, 3-, 4-, 5- and 6-year-olds and adults (N = 4, 29, 26, 30, 9, 20, respectively) were 0%, 14%, 58%, 73%, 67% and 90%, respectively. Many young children either did not express Source, or did not use a PP headed by *cong* 'from' to encode Source. Deng (2014) thus argued that the processing-demand account proposed by Landau and Lakusta (2006) is not supported; instead, Source is vulnerable at the representational level for young children.

In contrast to Source, the conceptual category of Goal or result location has been proven to be prominent in children's perception and conception of motion events. Cheung (1991) tested 33 Cantonese children aged between 2;1 to 5;9, and found that among Location, Source, Goal, children were most likely to talk about Goal. She hypothesized that the prominence of Goal is attributed to the cognitive salience of Result. So she tested how children expressed the notion of Result in describing picture sequences depicting causal events. Two-year-olds were more likely to comment on the result of the event than on the causal action. Over 80% of their production were Result-only. Older children produced more 'V + Result' tokens than Result-only ones. The cognitive salience of Result is confirmed by a number of studies. Erbaugh (1982) shows that two-year-olds sometimes used stative verbs causatively in her longitudinal study, as illustrated in (134). It suggests that children pay more attention to the result subpart in a complex event while overlooking the subevent that causes this result. In a novel verb experiment conducted on 32 children aged from 2;9 to 4;0, Deng (2010) found that Mandarin-speaking children relied heavily on the result-denoting verb in a resultative verb compound (RVC), such as *po* 'broken' in *da-po* 'hit-broken', to process and produce the RVC. P. Li (1990, ch. 4) tested 4- to 6-year-old Mandarin speakers to gauge their comprehension of the perfective aspect marker -*le* and the progressive marker *zai* in Mandarin. He found that children understood perfective -*le* better with telic verbs, or verbs with complex event structure, than with process verbs. He also found that they understood the progressive *zai* better with process verbs than with telic verbs. He argues that the semantic notions Result and Process are salient to Chinese children. Because Result is salient in the representation of event, it is predicted that Goal, which is one type of Result, will be acquired early by children. That is exactly what is found in Cheung (1991).

(134) *我喜欢碎。

*Wo　xihuan　sui. (Pang 2;10)

I　like　fragmentary

'I like to fragmentary.'

(meaning *wo xihuan nong-sui* 'I like to make (things) fragmentary'.)

Chapter 4 Localizer Phrases, Locative Subjects, and Locative Object

Apart from spatial PPs discussed in the previous chapter, localizer phrases (LPs) are also pivotal in investigating the linguistic encoding of space in Mandarin. This chapter discusses the formation of LPs and their grammatical functions. Besides being the complement of spatial Ps such as *zai*, Mandarin LPs can serve as locative subjects and locative objects. The Mandarin locative subject construction will be compared with locative inversion constructions in English and Chichewa. It will be argued that Mandarin has both locative topics as in English and locative subjects as in Chichewa. Furthermore, we distinguish two types of Mandarin locative subject sentences: one-argument and two-argument. Only dynamic state verbs and verbs containing a result state can enter into the two-argument locative subject construction. Mandarin differs from English in that Mandarin locative objects formed by LPs can follow verbs directly. There is some overlap between postverbal spatial PPs and locative objects, but the latter cannot be analyzed as the elliptical form of the former.

In this chapter, section 4.1 introduces Mandarin localizers (Ls) and their distributions, and discusses the syntactic category and function of Ls. The internal structure of LPs will also be touched upon. Section 4.2 provides a detailed analysis of the locative subject construction from the perspective of event semantics. Verb types that occur in this construction will be examined based on event type and event structure. Section 4.3 revolves around the locative object construction. Section 4.4 summarizes the theoretical analyses in previous sections, and the last section discusses relevant acquisition issues.

4.1 Syntax and semantics of localizers and localizer phrases

A prominent characteristic of Chinese is its use of Ls. There are less than 20 monosyllabic Ls which could be suffixed by -*bian* 'side', -*mian* 'face', -*tou* 'end' or -*fang* 'position' to form disyllabic ones, as introduced in section 1.1.2 (Ding et al. 1961; Chao 1968; Zhu 1982). Ls add spatial information to noun phrases (NPs) that they attach to. For instance, *zhuo pang* 'desk side = beside the desk' refers to the area that extends along the left-right axis of the table. However, due to different grammaticalization paths and rates, Ls do not perform uniformly in terms of their semantics. Some have evolved to lose their specific meaning under some circumstances (see Chappell and Peyraube 2008). For example, consider *di xia* 'ground bottom'. These two syllables could be a phrase meaning 'under the ground', but most of the time it seems to be a word meaning 'on the ground' in which the localizer *xia* has lost its original meaning. The boundary between a word and a phrase in Mandarin is notoriously unclear, and the boundary between an LP and a word is also not that clear-cut sometimes (see Fang 2004). This study treats all N(P)-L clusters, disyllabic or multisyllabic, as phrases, because, whether a word or a phrase, it does not affect our analysis. Ls could have other usages, but this study is only concerned with the prototypical usage of Ls, namely those that are used

Chapter 4　Localizer Phrases, Locative Subjects, and Locative Object　119

after an NP and make reference to space. ①

It is difficult to pin down the exact function of Ls at the first glance. Chu (2004) argued that besides converting things to places, Ls also convert mass to discrete entities as in (135a), and abstractness to concreteness as in (136a), and they also serve as plural makers as in (137a). These assertions do not provide an accurate description of Ls: *li* 'inside' in (135b) does not convert *sha* 'sand', a type of mass, into entities; in (136b) *zhong* 'middle' does not turn the abstract laugh into a concrete thing; and in (137b), the localizer *li* 'inside' does not mark *ren* 'people' as plural.

(135) a. 水里

　　　　shui　　li
　　　　water　　inside
　　　　'in the water'

　　　b. *沙滩有很多沙里。

　　　　*Shatan　you　hen　duo　sha　li.
　　　　 beach　have　very　much　sand　inside
　　　　Intended meaning: 'The beach has a lot of sand.'

(136) a. 笑声中

　　　　xiaosheng　zhong
　　　　laughter　　middle

---

① Localizers can also be used as adjectives as in (ia), as verbs as in (ib), or attached to another functional word in order to form new words that may not have spatial meaning as in (ic) (Fang 2004).
(i) a. hou　　　ban-ben
　　　back　　half-CL
　　　'the second half of a book'
　　b. shang　　lou
　　　ascend　　building
　　　'go upstairs'
　　c. yi　　　qian
　　　YI　　　front
　　　'in the past'

'in the laughter'

b. *我喜欢他的笑声中。

　　*Wo　xihuan　ta　de　xiaosheng　zhong.

　　I　like　he　DE　laughter　middle

　　'I like his laughter.'

(137) a. 十二个人里

　　shi'er-ge　ren　li

　　twelve-CL　people　inside

　　'in twelve people'

b. *我们班有十二个人里。

　　*Women　ban　you　shi'er-ge　ren　li.

　　our　class　have　twelve-CL　people　inside

　　'Our class has 12 people.'

Sun (2008) observed that LPs function as definite NPs. For instance, the demonstrative quantifier phrase *zhe-ben* has an explicit definite marking *zhe* 'this' which renders the localizer-less sentence (138a) licit as compared with (138b). Sentence (138a) is equally good as (138c) with a localizer. Sun thus argued that the L functions as definiteness marker. Sentence (139), however, shows that Ls do not mark definiteness, because the LP *mei-zhang zhuo shang* 'on every desk' does not refer to the top of a definite desk, but to area on any desk in a set defined by certain context. That is to say, Ls do not have the function of definiteness.

(138) a. 我在这本书做了记号。

　　Wo　zai　zhe-ben　shu　zuo-le　jihao.

　　I　at　this-CL　book　make-Perf　mark

　　'I made marks in this book.'

b. *我在书做了记号。

　　*Wo　zai　shu　zuo-le　jihao.

　　I　at　book　make-Perf　mark

　　Intended meaning: 'I made marks in the book.'

c. 我在书里做了记号。
　　Wo　zai　shu　li　　zuo-le　　jihao.
　　I　　at　 book inside make-Perf mark
　　'I made marks in the book.' (Sun 2008)

(139) 他在每张桌上放了一本书。
　　Ta　zai　mei-zhang　zhuo　shang　fang le　yi-ben　shu.
　　he　at　every-CL　 desk　 top　　put-Perf one-CL book
　　'He put one book on every desk.' (Audrey Li, personal communication)

Following Li (1990), and Huang, Li and Li (2009), the present study contends that the most essential function of Ls is to convert common NPs into locative NPs or LPs. Mandarin word order for LPs is thought to result from Complement-to-Spec(ifier) movement as in (140) (N. Zhang 2002; Huang 2009; Wu 2015). Huang (2009) proposes that *zhuozi* 'table' is moved to Spec of LP to get Case from V or P as shown in (140). As *de* can function as a genitive case marker, and occur optionally between the DP and L in an LP, N. Zhang (2002) posits that the Complement-to-Specifier movement is related to genitive Case.

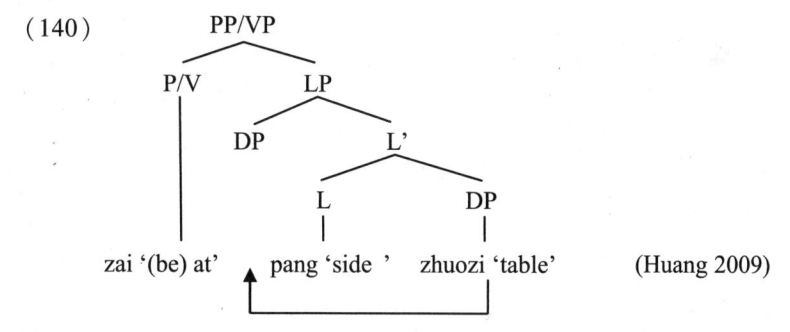

(140)
```
            PP/VP
           /     \
         P/V      LP
          |      /  \
                DP   L'
                    /  \
                   L    DP
                   |    |
    zai '(be) at'  pang 'side'  zhuozi 'table'    (Huang 2009)
```

The categorical status of the L has been a source of controversy in Chinese linguistics. In traditional descriptions, the L was simply called particle (Li and Thompson 1981). With the development of linguistic theories, some argue that Ls belong to a subclass of nouns (Li 1990; N. Zhang 2002; Huang, Li, and Li 2009) or they are light nouns parallel to light verbs in a verb phrase (Huang 2009). Ls also have properties of postpositions, and combinations such as *cong*⋯*li* 'from⋯inside' can be viewed as circumpositions (preposition⋯postposition) (D. Liu, 2008; Lam 2013, 30 – 31). Huang, Li, and Li (2009, 16 – 18) admitted that Ls have some distinct features not shared by typical Ns. Despite this, they argued that the deviations are not random but predictable by some language-specific properties. Following Li (1990) and Huang, Li, and Li (2009), Mandarin Ls are treated as a subclass of Ns in this book.

After discussing the function and syntactic category of Ls, we move to the distribution of Ls in Mandarin. The situation is complicated. On the one hand, they are obligatorily required by NPs formed by common nouns. As shown by the contrast in (141a) and (141b), *zai* '(be) at', which subcategorizes a locative phrase, cannot take a common noun *zhuozi* 'desk' without an L.① On the other hand, Ls are optional with some types of NP, including NPs formed by Ns with inherent locative meaning such as *xuexiao* 'school', demonstrative locative pronouns like *zher* 'here', NPs with a quasi-localizer like *lu-kou* 'road-mouth', and definite NPs such as *zhe-zhang chuang* 'this-CL bed' (Chao 1968; Chu 2004; Sun 2008). Chu (2004) noticed a restriction on the optionality: one can omit the L with an NP when the reference entity denoted by the NP contains or touches the Figure; otherwise Ls cannot be omitted.② For example, one can omit

---

① It is through language change that Ls have become obligatory in this condition in Modern Chinese. In Archaic Chinese (11th – 2nd centuries BC), there is no fundamental difference between common nouns and place words and the use of Ls is much less frequent (Guo 2002; Chappell and Peyraube 2008).

② There are only three possible relationships between Figure and reference entity (RE): the Figure is outside, inside, or touching the RE. There is an asymmetry between presenting a situation where Figure is inside the RE and presenting a situation where it is outside or touching the RE. Herskovits (1986, 164) observes that when the Figure is outside the RE, the RE is usually conceived as a point, whereas when the Figure is inside or touching the RE, it is necessary to put the origin of the base axes at the center of the RE or at some salient point. For example, in 'the house is to the right of the tree', the RE 'the tree' is viewed as a point, but in 'the seats in the front of the classroom', the origin must be placed on the center of the room.

the localizer *li* 'inside' in *xuexiao li* 'school inside = in the school', but cannot omit *wai* 'outside' in *xuexiao wai* 'school outside = outside the school'. Mandarin nouns that have locative implications fall into three major classes—nouns for areas such as *sheng* 'province' and *shi* 'city', nouns for institutions, e.g. *xuexiao* 'school' and *yiyuan* 'hospital', and those for various buildings, e.g. *tushuguan* 'library' and *keting* 'living room' (M. Wang 1990). Moreover, the localizer *li* 'inside' and its derived forms are forbidden with proper names for places such as countries, provinces, cities, and towns as exemplified in (142) (M. Wang 1990; Guo 2002).① The present study holds that the constraint that forbids *li*' inside' from accompanying proper names is a conceptual one rather than a grammatical one, as other Ls such as *zuo-bian* 'left-side' and *shang-mian* 'top-face' can co-occur with proper names of places.② A proper place names is conceptualized by Mandarin speakers as a point instead of a container that has the inside, therefore *li* 'inside' is forbidden with this type of NP (Ziyin Mai, personal communication). This is a special property of Mandarin, because *in China* is good in English, as shown in the gloss of (142).

(141) a. *在桌子

　　　 * zai　 zhuozi

　　　　 at 　 desk

b. 在桌子上

---

①　With proper names for organizations such as *Xianggang Zhongwen Daxue* 'the Chinese University of Hong Kong', the localizer *li* is optional (Guo 2002).

②　Huang (2009) provided a grammatical account of the situation that a location-denoting DP can license a phonetically defective L. In (i), the uninterpretable L finds in its minimal search domain an element with interpretable [+L] feature such as New York. By the relation Agree, L can inherit the interpretable feature and get licensed. This analysis explains why place names can go without Ls, but it does not explain why *li* 'inside' cannot co-occur with place names.

(i) [PP/VP　zai　[LP　L　[DP　Niuyue]]]

　　　　　 at　　　　　　　 New York

zai   zhuozi   shang
at   desk   top
'on the desk'

(142) 他在中国(＊里)学中文。
Ta   zai   Zhongguo   (＊li)   xue   Zhongwen.
he   at   China   inside   study   Chinese
'He studies Chinese in China.'

Languages differ in which concepts are lexicalized as nouns with inherent locative meaning. Such differences are reported between Mandarin and Shanghainese, another Chinese dialect, by D. Liu (2008). As shown by (143), the concepts of school and playground are lexicalized as locative nouns in Mandarin and thus are optionally marked by Ls, but in Shanghainese they are conceived as common nouns and obligatorily require Ls.

(143) a. Mandarin
zai   xuexiao   (li)   dao   caochang   (shang)
at   school   inside to   playground top

b. Shanghainese
laq   uqdong   ＊(li)   to   tshozang   ＊(long)
at   school   inside   to   playground top

(D. Liu 2008)

From a cross-linguistic perspective, one may ask why localizers are necessary in turning non-spatial phrases to spatial phrases (SPs) in Mandarin, while such a condition is not required in languages like English, as shown by the contrast between (141a) and its English counterpart *at the desk*. We argue that this is only a superficial difference. At a deep level, Mandarin shares with other languages the same structure within SPs (see Cinque 2010). English Axial Part (AxPart) expressions such as *front* and *behind*, the corresponding forms to Mandarin Ls, are also normally required in forming SPs such as *in front of the desk*, and *from behind the desk*. Only in some special cases, the semantic ingredients Path/Place and AxPart are lexicalized into one preposition as shown by *in* in the SP *in the box*. In the cases where some English common nouns form SPs without Axial Part expressions, as in *at the desk*, we argue that the common noun *desk* is conceived to have locative meaning and does not obligatorily need an Axial Part expression, hence the grammaticality of *at the desk*. Other common nouns in English, such as *bird*, behave just like Mandarin common nouns, in requiring an Axial Part expression to become SPs, as shown by the contrast in (144). It seems that in English more common nouns are considered to have inherent locative meanings than in Mandarin. In other words, common nouns without inherent locative meanings must merge with AxPart or localizer to become SPs cross-linguistically, but languages differ in which noun is conceptualized as having the locative meaning. As discussed above, even the two dialects of Chinese—Mandarin and Shanghainese differ in this aspect.

(144) a. * at bird

b. in front of the bird

The deictic pronouns *zher* 'here' and *nar* 'there', also called demonstrative locative pronouns, can be used either alone as place words, or after a common noun as shown in (145) (Chappell and Peyraube 2008). The deictic pronoun, together with the preceding NP, forms a phrase that functions as an LP. However, there are some differences between a phrase with deictic pronoun and a real LP. Syntactically, the combination as in (145) is of coordinate structure, with the pronoun serving as an appositive of the DP, while in an LP, the L chooses a DP as its complement. Semantically, the reference of the DP in the LP is pictured as an area or volume with axial part information, whereas that before the deictic pronoun is conceived as a 'point' location.

(145) [$_{LP}$[$_{DP}$ zhuozi] [$_{DP}$ zher/nar]]

desk   here/there

Lastly, some interesting facts about the lexical semantics of Ls in comparison with Axial Part expressions in other languages are worth mentioning. Mandarin disyllabic Ls such as *shang-mian* 'top', and *qian-bian* 'front' convey both the meaning of contact and that of adjacency. The spatial configurations for Mandarin *shang-mian* 'top-face = top', for instance, is broken down for linguistic encoding into two different categories in English, expressed by *on*, and *above* or *over*. Mandarin patterns with Korean, Japanese, and Mixtec in this regard, in contrast to English, German and Dutch (see Bowerman 1989, Guo 2008). The monosyllabic Ls, however, only express the spatial relationship of contact. The relationships between *shang* 'on', *shang-mian* 'on, above', and *shang-fang* 'above' can be schematized in Fig. 4.1. The denotation of *shang* forms a set A, which is the subset of the set C formed by the denotation of *shang-mian*, and the non-overlapping area B is covered by the denotation of *shang-fang* 'top-position = above', which is another derived form of *shang*. Another interesting difference between Mandarin and English is that Mandarin localizer *pang* 'side' or *pang-bian* 'side' only refers to left or right side of an entity, in contrast to English *beside* which refers to front, back, left and right sides of an entity (Jia 2010).

A	B
shang 'on'	shang-fang 'above'
C: shang-mian 'on, above'=A+B	

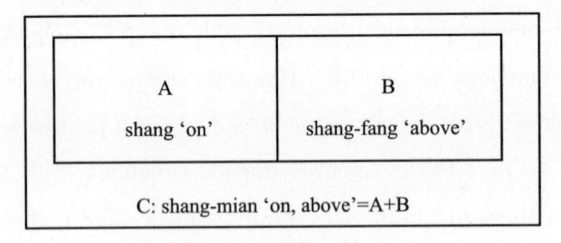

Fig. 4.1 The semantic relationship between *shang* 'on',
shang-fang '**above**' **and** *shang-mian* '**on, above**'

To summarize, semantically, an L provides spatial information about the RE. Syntactically, it trails an NP to form an LP, converting the NP into a locative phrase. As LPs have the same syntactic behaviors as NPs, Ls should be treated as a subclass of Ns with some special properties not shared by prototypical Ns. The LP-formation rule is complicated in Mandarin: Ls are obligatorily required by common nouns to form LPs; they are optional with NPs with inherently locative meaning; and the localizer *li* 'inside' and its derived forms are forbidden with places names.

4.2 Locative subjects

Localizer phrases can function as subjects, and locative subjects are very productive in Mandarin (Lin 2008). The locative subject sentence (abbreviated as LSS hereafter) discussed here with the structure in (146a) is a subset of the existential sentence (Huang 1987) or the presentative sentence (Li and Thompson 1981, ch. 17; Afarli and Jin 2010) which has the structure in (146b). Crucially, an existential sentence, as in (147c), can go without an initial LP, but an LSS must be initiated by an LP, as in (147a) and (147b). The sentence in (147b), having only one argument *di shang* 'on the ground' (Location), represents a type of LSS which is called 'one-argument LSS', in contrast to 'two-argument LSS' as in (147a), the two arguments being *zhuo shang* 'on the desk' (Location) and *shu* 'book' (Theme).

(146) a. LP V (DP)

b. (LP) V DP (XP)①

(147) a. 桌上有书。

---

① The structure formalized in Huang (1987) is actually '(NP) V NP (XP)'. He discussed sentences whose sentence-initial position may be a locative NP, LP in our terminology, or an NP assuming the role of a possessor as *wo* 'I' as in the following sentence. Therefore, the locative subject sentences that we discuss are a subset of these sentences.

(i) Wo you yi-ben shu hen you qu.
　　I 　 have one-CL book very have fun
'I have a book that is very interesting.'

Zhuo shang you shu.

desk top have book

'On the desk is a book/books.'

b. 地上湿了。

Di shang shi le.

ground top wet LE

'The ground became wet.'

c. 有鬼。

You gui.

have ghost

'There are ghosts (here).'

The Mandarin two-argument locative subject construction is parallel to the locative inversion construction in English as in (148a). Locative subjects in English can go with unaccusative verbs and passivized transitive verbs (Bresnan 1994, Levin and Rappaport Hovav 1995). The subject can be 'restored' to its predicate-internal position, as *into the hole* in (148b). According to Bresnan (1994), English locative inversion demonstrates mismatches across the levels of argument structure and grammatical relations—since in this construction there is no structural subject, the logical subject such as *the rabbit* in (148a) is a focused object, and the functional subject such as *into the hole* in (148a) is an oblique PP that does not show any subject properties. She pointed out that this construction poses a learnability problem as evidence of these inner relations is subtle and indirect, coming from interactions of syntactic processes that the language learner is not explicitly taught.

(148) a. Into the hole jumped the rabbit.

b. The rabbit jumped into the hole. (Bresnan 1994)

4.2.1 Information structure of locative subject sentences

Mandarin two-argument LSSs also demonstrate syntax-semantics mismatch in the same manner as English locative inversion. This mismatch results from the interaction between argument structure, and information structure. In the following discussion, 'LSSs' will be used to refer exclusively to two-argument LSSs, unless otherwise indicated.

Chapter 1 has shown the ways in which argument structure is influenced by the thematic hierarchy. In this hierarchy, arguments with theta-roles that are more prominent in the thematic hierarchy occupy the syntactically more prominent positions. Subject position, for instance, is more prominent than the object position. In English, locative inversion can occur with verbs that have the argument structure < Theme Location > (Bresnan 1994). The verb must have a Location, and a Theme in the narrowest sense of Gruber (1965) and Jackendoff (1972), on which the location, or change of location is predicated. In expressing an event of the tax collector coming back to the village, the canonical word order is to map the Theme 'the tax collector' onto the subject position and the Location 'the village' to the object position as in (149a), since Theme is more prominent than Location in the thematic hierarchy (Bresnan and Kanerva 1992; Lin 2001, 23). Thematic hierarchy is not, however, the only determinant of syntactic prominence. In fact, thematic hierarchy will yield to aspectual hierarchy when the two clash, as discussed in section 1.2.1. Besides thematic structure and aspectual structure, a third dimension in determining argument structure is information structure. According to Bresnan (1994), speakers forming sentences sometimes need to set a scene with a location, and then introduce a referent into the scene to be the focus of attention. Subject is the unmarked discourse topic. This conflicts with the need to focus on the Theme. To solve the problem, the speaker needs to make the Location the subject and realize the Theme as the object. For instance, the derivation of (149b) results from the interaction between different levels of structures as shown in (150).

(149) a. The tax collector came back to the village.

b. Back to the village came the tax collector.

(150) Argument structure   <Theme Location>
                                         | |
     Function structure   object subject
                                          |
     Information structure   focus

(Bresnan 1994)

  Besides the Location-V-Theme word order as in (149b), Mandarin also has the Theme-V-Location word order as in (149a). The determinant of the word order alternation is information structure: the argument which is the topic precedes the verb and the argument which is the focus follows the verb (LaPolla 2009). In the LSS in (151a), the Location *qiang shang* 'on the wall' sets the scene, and the Theme *yi-fu hua* 'one painting' which is hung on the wall is the focus. In other words, Mandarin LSSs also involve complex interaction between argument structure, functional structure, and information structure. Sentences (151b) and (151c) have the same truth value as (151a). The permutation of the three elements Location, Theme and Verb is caused by the need to focus on different elements (Qi 1998, 76). The focuses are elements presented last in the sentence, namely the Location *qiang-shang* 'on the wall' in (151b) and the locative verb *gua* 'hang' in (151c), respectively. In sum, the information structure explains the word order of the LSS in (151a) and the contrast in (151).

(151) a. 墙上挂着一幅画。   (Location-V-Theme)
   Qiang shang gua-zhe yi-fu hua.
   wall top hang-DUR one-CL painting
   'On the wall hangs a painting.'

  b. 那副画挂在墙上。   (Theme-V-Location)
   Na-fu hua gua zai qiang shang.
   That-CL painting hang at wall top
   'That painting is hanging on the wall.'

  c. 那幅画在墙上挂着。   (Theme-Location-V)

Na-fu   hua   zai   qiang   shang   gua-zhe.
that-CL painting at   wall   top   hang-DUR
'That painting is hanging on the wall.'

(adapted from Qi 1998, 76)

To summarize this section, similar to English locative inversion, the surface word order Location-V-Theme of Mandarin LSSs is derived because the need to focus on the Theme overrides thematic hierarchy. Thematically less prominent Location is projected to the subject position functioning as the discourse topic, while the thematically more prominent Theme is projected to the object position serving as the focus.

4.2.2 Aspectual properties of locative subject sentences

Mandarin has three aspect markers suffixed on the verb: the perfective *-le*, the experiential *-guo* and the durative *-zhe*. LSSs are closely related to these aspect markers. In many Mandarin sentences, aspect is neutral, and no aspectual suffix is required; however, aspect is mandatorily marked in most LSSs. There seem to be an exceptional case as shown in (152).①

---

① Besides the exception given by the neutral aspect discussed in this paragraph, there seems to be another exception exemplified in (i). At the surface level, (i) seems to be an aspectless LSS, but underlyingly it is not an LSS, because it is an elliptic form of (ii). The evidence for *zhe li* 'this inside' being an adjunct rather than a subject is that it can be negated by a negator (*bu* 'not' or *mei* 'not') while Mandarin subjects cannot be negated (Ziyin Mai, personal communication). The contrast is shown between (iii) and (iv). Therefore, (i) is not an aspectless LSS.

(i) Zhe li   xie   ge   yi,   hao-bu-hao?
    this inside write CL one, good-not-good
    '(Let's) write *one* here, OK?'   (Beijing corpus, Tardif 1993, 1996)

(ii) (Wo-men zai) zhe li   xie   ge   yi,   hao-bu-hao?
     I-PLU   at   this inside write CL one, good-not-good
     '(Let's) write *one* here, OK?'

(iii) Bu zai zhe li   xie   ge   yi.
      not at   this inside write CL one
      'Don't write *one* here!'

(iv) *Bu/mei zai tai   shang zuo-zhe   laoshi-men.
      not   at   stage top   sit-DUR   teacher-PLU
      Intended meaning: 'There are no teachers on the stage.'

This LSS goes without an aspect marker. However, we can easily feel that historical present tense is used here in the narration and an underlying perfective aspect marker -le has been omitted. The strong association between LSSs and aspectual markers may be explained by this construction's function to express an episodic, stage-level eventuality. Individual-level predicates such as *xihuan* 'like' and *zhidao* 'know' are not allowed in this construction as shown in (153) (Lin 2001, 160 – 161).

(152) 屋子里飞进来（了）一只蜜蜂。
    Wuzi li   fei-jin-lai(-le)   yi-zhi   mifeng.
    room inside fly-enter-come(-Perf) one-CL bee
    'Into the room flew a bee.'   (X. Wu 2006, 2)

(153) *教室里知道（着/了）一个答案。
    *Jiaoshi li   zhidao(-zhe/-le)   ji-ge   da'an.
    classroom inside know(-DUR/-Perf) several-CL answer
    Intended meaning: 'In the classroom are knowing/were known several answers.'   (adapted from Lin 2001, 160)

The present study will focus on the interaction between LSSs and aspect markers, especially the durative -*zhe*. *Zhe* describes a homogeneous eventuality lasting over an interval larger than an instant, and is used to mark Activities, States and resultative states (P. Li 1990, 35; J. Wu 2007). More to the point, it plays a very important role in forming LSSs. According to Pan (1996), -*zhe* operates on an accomplishment verb with the thematic structure < Agent Theme Location > and transforms it into a verb with the thematic structure < Theme Location > that can occur in LSSs. Pan argued that after the deletion of the Agent, an accomplishment verb becomes a resulting state verb, and -*zhe* brings the focus to the result state in the event structure of the Accomplishment. In (154), for instance, after the activity of carving, a word came into existence, and -*zhe* brings this property of 'the desk' into focus.

(154) 桌上刻着一个字。
　　　　Zhuo　shang　ke-zhe　　　yi-ge　　zi.
　　　　desk　top　　carve-DUR　one-CL　character
　　　　'On the desk was carved one character.'　　　(Pan 1996)

While the present study partly agrees with the intuition of Pan (1996) for accomplishment verbs, it is also important to notice that *-zhe* applies to activity verbs, too. In examples like (155a), *ji-ge ren* 'several people' is both Agent and Theme of the intransitive activity verb *pao* 'run', following Jackendoff (1972). *Ji-ge ren* here has Agent property as agent-oriented adverbs such as *xiaoxinyiyi-de* 'carefully' can be added. The aspect marker *-zhe* does not delete the Agent. *Zhe* also applies to the transitive activity verb *he* 'drink' in (155b). In this case, the Agent is dethematized, but there is no result state. If the *-zhe* operation applies only to accomplishment verb, then it is *ad hoc*.

(155) a. 路上（小心翼翼地）跑着几个人。
　　　　Lu　shang　(xiaoxinyiyi-de)　pao-zhe　　ji-ge　　　ren.
　　　　road　top　　(carefully)　　　run-DUR　several-CL　people
　　　　'On the road arerunning several people.'

　　　b. 屋里（正）喝着酒。
　　　　Wu　li　　　(zheng)　　　he-zhe　　　　jiu.
　　　　room　inside　(right now)　drink-DUR　wine
　　　　'Wine is being drunk in the living room.'

Different from Pan (1996), the present study will approach this phenomenon from the perspective of aspect shift. It will be argued that there are mainly three event types that can enter into the two-argument locative subject construction: dynamic States, Accomplishments, and Achievements. In addition, Activity verbs that have a Theme can also appear in this construction, because *-zhe* can trigger the activity verbs to undergo aspect shift to States. The function of this construction is to present a state, or a result state. Thus, sentence (155a) is possible because *-zhe* triggers the aspect shift of *pao* 'run' from Activity to State. Sentence (156a) is ungrammatical under the Activity reading, as the perfective aspect marker *-le* cannot trigger the aspect shift from Activity to State. It presents a terminated activity, which is in conflict with the aspectual requirements of this construction, and, therefore, the sentence is ruled out. One point of clarification is that this constraint disappears in (156b), the same as (156a) in form, because the verb *pao* has undergone a semantic-class shift, and actually means 'to escape' in (156b). When used in this sense, the verb *pao* is an Achievement. With perfective *-le* added, it can shift into result state. Thus, (156b) also fulfils the aspectual requirements of the locative subject construction and is grammatical.

(156) a. *路上跑了几个人。

   * Lu shang pao-le ji-ge ren.

   road top run-Perf several-CL people

   Intended meaning: 'On the roadwere running several people.'

b. 路上跑了几个人。

  Lu shang pao-le ji-ge ren.

  road top escape-Perf several-CL people

 'From the road escaped several people.'

What are the verb types that are allowed in the locative subject construction? Pan (1996) observed that unaccusative verbs, passivized verbs and accomplishment verbs followed by *-zhe* can enter this construction. However, the set of verbs that take locative subjects is larger than these. Activity verbs such as *dun* 'stew' and *xiu* 'repair' are also allowed in this construction (Lin 2001, 137). Wu (2012) claimed that verbs that take locative subjects are generally those that can occur with postverbal *zai*-PPs. Nevertheless, the former is a superset of the latter (see Liu 2009). Lin (2001, 2008) held that the verbs allowed in

Mandarin LSSs are more diversified than verbs in English locative inversion. It is claimed that 'all kinds of action verbs in Mandarin can take locative subject in an unselective way' (Lin 2001, 143). There are counterexamples to this generalization. Unergative verbs, or intransitive activity verbs, such as *xiao* 'laugh' and *chao* 'quarrel', are actional, but are generally incompatible with the locative subject construction as shown in (157).

(157) *屋里笑着几个人。

  *Wu li xiao-zhe ji-ge ren. [1]

  room inside laugh-DUR some-CL person

  Intended meaning: 'Inside the room some people are laughing.'

In what follows, verb types that can enter the locative subject construction will be discussed one by one from the perspective of event semantics. The first type of verbs includes existential verbs *you* 'have', its negated form *mei (you)* 'not have', and *shi* 'be' as exemplified in (158) (see Li and Thompson 1981, ch. 7; Lü et al. 2010, 497). They denote a pure state of (non) existence in this construction. LSSs with existential verbs generally go without aspect markers. When LSSs with *you* 'have' are suffixed with the perfective aspect markers *-le* and *-guo*, a change of state is highlighted: with the perfective *-le*, they convey a contrast between a previous state of nonexistence and the present state of existence (X. Wu 2006, 91); with the experiential *-guo*, they imply a contrast between a previous state of existence and the present state of nonexistence. Under such interpretations, they are no longer existential verbs, but undergo semantic-class shift to be verbs of appearance (see Liu 2007). In some special cases, the durative *-zhe* can be attached to *you*

---

[1] Changing *-zhe* into the perfective aspect suffix *-le* or the experiential *-guo* does not make the sentence better.

'have' (Liu 2007).① However, such uses only appear in written language. Therefore, it is generally safe to say that in spoken language, existential verbs in LSSs appear without aspect markers. They are always aspectless, presenting on-going states at the speech time, or at the reference time encoded by the co-occurring time adverbial. Since LSSs with existential verbs are generally aspectless, different from the types of LSSs discussed below, they are considered to belong to a separate group, called proto-existentials in Yang and Pan (2001). As shown in (158), *you* 'have' and *shi* 'be' are roughly interchangeable in this construction, but there is a difference: *shi* 'be', but not *you* 'have', presupposes that something is there (Li and Thompson 1981, 515). In asking *wai-mian shi shenme* 'what is outside', the speaker presupposes that there is something outside, but for its counterpart with *you* 'have', the speaker does not know if there is anything outside.

(158) 外面有/是一只狗。

   Wai-mian you/shi yi-zhi gou.
   outside-fac ehave/be one-CL dog
   'Outside is a dog.'

The second type is posture verbs such as *zuo* 'sit', *zhan* 'stand', and *tang* 'lie'. They are dynamic state verbs and can shift into Achievement when followed by the perfective aspect marker *-le*. As shown by (159), no matter whether perfective *-le* or durative *-zhe* is used, this sentence presents a state. There is a very subtle difference, however, which many native speakers are not aware of. If the aspect marker is *-le*, the sentence conveys a result state following the action of *zuo* 'sit'. If the aspect marker is *-zhe*, the sentence depicts a pure state of sitting. One

---

① Liu's (2007) example is shown below.
(i) Ta duzili you-zhe shuo bu wan de gushi.
  he stomach have-DUR tell not finish DE story
  'In his stomach are endless stories.'

thing to add is that except for posture verbs, other state verbs cannot follow locative subjects. As discussed in the case of (153), States that are individual-level, namely, lacking temporality, are incompatible with the locative subject construction which is used to present a state with current relevance.

(159)桌上坐了/着一只猫。

   Zhuo shang zuo-le/-zhe yi-zhi mao.
   desk top sit-Perf/-DUR one-CL cat
   'On the desk is sitting a cat.'

  The third type is Agentless placement verbs. They are Accomplishments, but shift into States when the Agent is dethematized. In (160), if *-zhe* is used, the sentence conveys the state of a book lying on the desk that lasts over a period covering the speech time or the reference time encoded by a time adverbial, but if *-le* is used, it portrays a result state following the action of *fang* 'put, place'. In this respect, we differ from Pan (1996): *-zhe* does not bring the focus to the result state; rather, it is *-le* that does the job in LSSs. As observed in Pan (1996), the sentence-initial LP in LSSs must predicate on the Theme as in (161a) where the Theme *yuan* 'circle' is located on *zhi shang* 'on the paper'. As the Theme of the placement verb is associated with the result state, we push the generalization further, and claim that all the LPs in LSSs with placement verbs express Goal. Places normally not conceived as result locations of placement events cannot be realized as locative subjects in LSSs. For instance, *wu li* 'inside room' in (161b) cannot be the Goal of the event of drawing a circle according to our real world knowledge, so the sentence is unacceptable.

(160)桌上放着/了一本书。

   Zhuo shang fang-zhe/-le yi-ben shu.
   desk top place-DUR/-Perf one-CL book
   'On the desk is lying/was placed a book.'

(161) a. 纸上画着/了圆。

  Zhi shang hua-zhe/-le   yuan.
  paper top draw-DUR/-Perf circle
  'On the paper is drawing/was drawn a circle.'

b. #屋里画着/了圆。

  #Wu li hua-zhe/-le   yuan.
  room inside draw-DUR/-Perf circle
  Intended meaning: 'In the room is drawing/was drawn a circle.'

  The fourth type is transitive process verbs with agent being dethematized, such as *he* 'drink', *chang* 'sing', *tiao* (*wu*) 'dance'. Cooccurring with *-zhe*, these agentless Activity verbs shift into States, but with *-le*, aspect shift is not possible as shown in (162a). As *-le* combines with the Activity verb to express a terminated activity, and the locative subject construction does not present a terminated activity, (162a) with *-le* is ungrammatical. Agents of transitive process verbs cannot appear in this construction. For instance, in (162b), the Agent of singing *liang-ge xiaopengyou* 'two kids' is not allowed. Agent is associated with a causing activity, but not with the state or result state, so it is incompatible with the locative subject construction which serves to present a state or a result state. One may ask why Agent of the manner-of-motion verbs such as *pao* 'run' in (155a) is allowed in the construction. As we mentioned earlier that the only argument of the manner-of-motion verb is both Agent and Theme following Gruber (1965) and Jackendoff (1972). Because the Agent phrase also has the properties of Theme, it is acceptable in the locative subject construction. An alternative account for the ban on the Agent of the transitive process verb is that syntactically Agent never occurs after transitive verbs in Mandarin, so it cannot follow transitive process verbs in the locative subject construction. We, however, found that Agents of posture verbs and manner-of-motion verbs also never appear after these verbs in other structures, but they can follow verbs in LSSs. So the ban on the Agent of the transitive process verb is not a syntactic constraint, but a semantic one.

(162) a. 台上唱着/*了歌。

    Tai   shang   chang-zhe/*-le   ge.
    stage   top   sing-DUR/*-Perf   song
    'On the stage is being sung a song.'

b. *台上唱着两个小朋友。

    *Tai   shang   chang-zhe   liang-ge   xiaopengyou.
    stage   top   sing-DUR   two-CL   kid
    Intended meaning: 'On the stage are singing two kids.'

The fifth type is manner-of-motion verbs such as *you* 'swim' and *fei* 'fly'. Similar to agentless process verbs, they are Activities which shift into States with *-zhe*, but are incompatible with *-le* as shown in (163a). As discussed in section 2.1.3, the progressive aspect can induce aspect shift at sentential level as shown in (58), and the aspect shift from Activity to State is found in English as exemplified in (59). Mandarin durative *-zhe* is also a progressive aspect marker marking a homogenous eventuality (Y. Wang 2011). In LSSs with manner-of-motion verbs, *-zhe* works on the aspectual value of the activity verbs, and changes the interpretation of these verbs at the sentential level. In choosing the progress perspective for this type of LSSs, the speaker presents an activity as an on-going state. The test of 'at x time' lends support to the aspect shift: under the activity meaning, the manner-of-motion verb *fei* 'fly' cannot be modified by a punctual time adverbial 'at x time' as shown in (163b), because the shortest possible activity cannot hold at an instant; but under the state use, the verb can be modified by the punctual time adverbial as shown in (163a), as the shortest possible state can hold at an instant.

(163) a. 在那一毫秒天上飞着/*了几只鸟。

Zai na yi haomiao,　　tian shang fei-zhe/∗-le ji-zhi　　niao.

at　　that one millisecond　　sky　　top　　fly-DUR/∗-Perf several-CL　bird

'At that millisecond, on the sky are flying several birds.'

b. #在那一毫秒,鸟飞了。

#Zai　na　yi　haomiao,　　niao　fei　le.

at　　that one millisecond,　bird　fly　LE

Intended meaning: 'At that millisecond, the bird flew.'

The sixth type is (dis)appearance verbs, which are Achievements. As they denote instantaneous change of state, they are incompatible with the durative *-zhe*. When they are used with *-le* in LSSs, they express a result state. For instance, (164) with the achievement verb *si* 'die' suffixed with *-le* expresses the state of the cat lying on the desk after its death.

(164) 桌上死了/∗着一只猫。

Zhuo　shang　si-le/∗-zhe　　yi-zhi　mao.

desk　top　　die-Perf/∗-DUR　one-CL　cat

'On the desk died a cat.'

The last type is displacement verbs. This group is not homogeneous. Most displacement verbs, such as *sa* 'sprinkle' and *diao* 'drop, fall', are Accomplishment/Achievement. They take perfective *-le* to present a result state in the locative subject construction. For instance, the action of sprinkling happened in the past in (165), but the speaker uses (165) to present a currently relevant state that results from the activity. On the other hand, for the displacement verb *tiao* 'jump' (Li and Thompson 1981, 398 – 401), even if it can shift into an Accomplishment in the V-PP construction, it behaves as an Activity in the LSSs. It cannot go with *-le* to occur in an LSS. Rather, it undergoes aspect shift to be State in the presence of *-zhe* as in (166), just like manner-of-motion verbs. *Tiao* 'jump' is special among displacement verbs, and is called a derived directional/displacement verb in Liu (2009).

(165) 面包上洒了/*着一点糖。

    Mianbao shang sa-le/*-zhe   yi-dian tang.
    bread   top   sprinkle-Perf/*-DUR one-CL sugar
    'On the bread was sprinkled some sugar.'

(166) 塔松下跳着/*了一只小鸟。

    Tasong xia   tiao-zhe/*-le   yi-zhi xiao niao.[①]
    pine   bottom jump-DUR/*-Perf one-CL little bird
    'Under the pine is jumping a little bird.'

To conclude, the function of the two-argument LSS is to present a dynamic state or a result state that is relevant to the speech time. States, Accomplishments and Achievements can enter into LSSs, because they all have a state component in their event structures. Some activity verbs, for instance, manner-of-motion verbs, can also shift into State in the presence of *-zhe* and enter this construction. Agent is associated with a causing activity, but not with the state or result state, so it is not allowed in LSSs. An unergative verb such as *xiao* 'laugh' does not appear in the LSS because its only argument is an Agent. Transitive verbs must have their Agent dethematized before occurring in this construction. The perfective *-le* helps verbs with complex event structure shift into result state verbs.

The present analysis has several advantages that make it preferable to previous accounts. It improves on the syntactic approach based on the light verb theory developed in Lin (2001, 2008). In his analysis, the locative subject is base-generated in the Spec position of the *v*P projected by the

---

[①] Liu (2007, 192 – 193) treated *tiao* 'jump' as intransitive process/activity verb and claimed that it cannot occur in LSSs. We, however, found that *tiao* 'jump' can occur in LSSs with *-zhe*. The example shown here is from http://blog.sina.com.cn/s/blog_4e8bff550100nzc5.html (accessed September 6, 2017). There is a comma between the localizer phrase and the rest of the sentence in the original example. As we will discuss in section 4.2.4, a comma following a constituent does not necessarily mark it as a topic (see Jiang 1991, 54 – 55), so the localizer phrase in this example could be a locative subject.

light verb EXIST, OCCUR and PROGRESS, which then rises to the subject position of the sentence. The last type of light verb is called PROGRESS because LSSs with this light verb must have the durative aspectual marker *-zhe* or the progressive aspectual adverb *zheng* 'right now'. There is no mechanism in Lin's system, however, to rule out the ungrammatical sentences exemplified in (162b), in which the object position is occupied by the Agent of a transitive verb. His system cannot rule out unergative verbs from the LSS, either. To account for these two facts, the present study contends that the presence of Agent is incompatible with the function of LSSs to present states or result states. Second, Lin (2001, 2008) does not make it explicit why some verbs enter into sentences involving some light verb and other verbs do not. Although the verb *fang* 'put' can enter into both an EXIST sentence with the durative aspect marker and an OCCUR sentence with the perfective marker in (160), the same alternation is not possible with the verb *fei* 'fly', as exemplified in (163a). We argue that it is the different aspectual properties of the two verbs that explain their different syntactic behaviors. Moreover, OCCUR is not an appropriate label for the light verb, as it has been shown that LSSs cannot present an activity that occurred in the past.

　　Moreover, we drew a better generalization than X. Wu (2006) which approached this issue in the light of grammatical aspect. X. Wu (2006, ch. 4) presented a typology of two-argument LSSs: there are durative and non-durative LSSs; the durative ones are either static or dynamic, and the non-durative ones involve temporal process or spatial process. His classification is based on the LSSs' interaction with the aspect markers *-le*, *-zhe* and *-guo*: durative LSSs are marked with durative *-zhe* while the non-durative ones contain perfective *-le* and experiential *-guo*. However, X. Wu (2006) did not look into verb classes and the aspectual properties of the verbs in these sentences. His static durative LSSs actually are those involving posture verbs and placement verbs, his dynamic durative LSSs involve manner-of-motion verbs and some other Activity verbs, his spatial non-durative LSSs contain Accomplishment/Achievement verbs which are directional resultative verb compounds, e. g. *fei-jin-lai* 'fly-enter-come' as in (152), and his temporal non-durative LSSs contain other Accomplishment/Achievement verbs. The first two subtypes are better characterized as involving state verbs or verbs that can shift into States, while the latter two involve verbs that have a phase change in their event structures—the change can be a change of location, or a change of state. The use of aspect markers is affected and constrained by the event type of the verb (Smith 1997, 62). Therefore, the aspectual properties of verbs are more essential in the discussion of LSSs than their co-occurring aspect markers. In this way, our generalization captures the deeper pattern compared with X. Wu's (2006).

Before proceeding to the next section, the role of real-world knowledge in the acceptability of an LSS will be discussed. Wu (2012) distinguished between inner locatives (arguments) and outer locatives (adjuncts) following Baker's (1988, 244 – 245) treatment of English and Kinyarwanda locatives. This distinction was used to explain the contrast between the minimal pair in (167): the inner locative *lüguan* 'inn' but not the outer locative *Xianggang* 'Hong Kong' can be locative subject. We argue, however, that both locatives occupy the same syntactic position, and the contrast has nothing to do with the argument vs. adjunct distinction. Instead, real-world knowledge explains the difference in acceptability: Hong Kong is such a large location which could not have only a dozen of people sleeping in it. Changing *shi-ji-ge ren* 'more than ten people' into *liu-bai-wan ren* 'six million people' makes (167b) acceptable. ①

---

① Suppose two speakers are discussing how many people sleep in Hong Kong given the situation that some people work in Hong Kong in the daytime but go back home in Shenzhen, a neighboring city, in the evening. It is felicitous under this situation to make the statement that six million people sleep in Hong Kong.

(167) a. 旅馆里晚上睡了十几个人。

　　Lüguan li　　wanshang　shui-le　　shi-ji-ge　　ren.
　　inn　　inside　evening　　sleep-Perf　ten-several-CL　people
　　'In the inn slept more than ten people in the evening.'

b. #香港晚上睡了十几个人。

　　#Xianggang　wanshang　shui-le　　shi-ji-ge　　ren.
　　Hong Kong　evening　　sleep-Perf　ten-several-CL　people
　　Intended meaning: 'In Hong Kong slept more than ten people in the evening.'　　　　　　　　　　（Wu 2012）

Another case showing the effect of real-world knowledge is the idiosyncrasies of some transitive verbs. Previously, we have reached the generalization that a transitive verb with its Agent dethematized can enter into the locative inversion construction as long as it goes with the durative *-zhe*. However, there seem to be some exceptions as in (168a) and (169a). It turns out that there are grammatical sentences with this type of verbs as in (168b) and (169b). Why are (168b) and (169b) acceptable while (168a) and (169a) are out? The minimal pairs in (168) and (169) demonstrate that real-world knowledge influences our judgments of LSSs: people tend to associate the instruments *xiyiji* 'washing machine' and *kaoxiang* 'oven' with the activities of washing and baking, which explains the acceptability of (168b) and (169b), in contrast to (168a) and (169a).

(168) a. *水池里洗着衣服。

　　*Shuichi　li　　xi-zhe　　yifu.
　　sink　　inside　wash-DUR　clothes
　　Intended meaning: 'In the sink some clothes were washed.'　　　　　　　　　　　　　　　　　（Wu 2012）

b. 洗衣机里洗着衣服。

　　Xiyiji　　　　li　　xi-zhe　　　yifu.
　　washing machine　inside　wash-DUR　clothes

'In the washing machine some clothes were washed.'

(169) a. ?? 屋里烤着面包。

?? Wu   li   kao-zhe   mianbao.
room   inside   bake-DUR   bread

'In the room bread is being baked.'

b. 烤箱里烤着面包。

Kaoxiang   li   kao-zhe   mianbao.
oven   inside   bake-DUR   bread

'In the oven bread is being baked.'

4.2.3 One-argument locative subject sentences

A Mandarin LSS consists of an LP, a verb, and an optional DP, as shown in (170). When the DP is absent, the sentence has only one argument, and is called one-argument LSS, as exemplified in (171). In these sentences, the initial LP is followed by an adjective. In Chinese linguistics, adjectives are also called stative verbs because they possess many verbal properties. For instance, they can serve as predicate directly without a copular verb. The adjectives denote static State as in (171a) and (171b), or result state as in (171c).

(170) LP V (DP)

(171) a. 脸上有点肿。

Lian   shang   youdian   zhong.
face   top   somewhat   swollen

'The face is somewhat swollen.'

b. 城外很美丽。

Cheng   wai   hen   meili.
City   outside   very   beautiful

'Outside of the city it is beautiful.'

c. 地下湿了。

Di   xia   shi   le.

ground　　bottom　wet　LE

'The ground became wet.'

　　There is another type of one-argument LSSs. In (172), there is an empty argument in each sentence. They are not true one-argument LSSs: true one-argument LSSs cannot be changed into sentences initiated by PPs, as in (173a), but this type of sentence can, as shown in (173b). These one-argument LSSs are derived from two-argument ones through ellipsis. The omitted object can be recovered from discourse.

(172) a. 床上还有。

　　　　　Chuang　shang　hai　you.

　　　　　bed　　　top　　still　have

　　　　　'On the bed still has (something mentioned in the previous discourse).'

　　　b. 黑板上写着呢。

　　　　　Heiban　　shang　xie-zhe　　ne.

　　　　　blackboard　top　　write-DUR　sfp

　　　　　'On the blackboard were written (something mentioned in the previous discourse).'

(173) a. *在地下湿了。

　　　　　*Zai　di　　xia　　shi　le.

　　　　　at　ground　bottom　wet　LE

　　　　　Intended meaning: 'The ground became wet.'

　　　b. 在床上还有。

　　　　　Zai　chuang　shang　hai　you.

　　　　　at　bed　　　top　　still　have

　　　　　'On the bed still has (something mentioned earlier).'

4.2.4　Nature of locative subjects: subject or topic?

　　By comparing locative inversion constructions in English and those in Chichewa, Bresnan (1994) concluded that the former has the PP as the topicalized subject while the latter has the NP as the real subject. Her arguments are shown below. In English locative inversion, the Locative PP seems to occupy the surface subject position, but it does not have properties of canonical subjects. First, it does not have subject-verb agreement as shown in (174). The copular verb *be* does not agree with *in the room*, but with the surface object *many children*. Locative PPs also cannot undergo subject-auxiliary inversion like other NP subjects, as shown by the contrast in (175). However, since the topicalized locative PP is a subject at an abstract level of representation, it has some subject properties as it can undergo subject raising. For example, the locative PP in (176a) *over my window* is raised from a position lower than the raising verb *seem*, patterning like a real subject as in (176b).

(174) In the room were/ * was found many children.

(175) a. Do you remember?

　　　b. * Did on the wall hang a picture?

(176) a. Over my windowsill seems _ to have crawled an entire army of ants.　　　　　　　　　　　　　(Bresnan 1994, 96)

　　　b. Mary seems _ to like you.

The locative inversion construction in Chichewa, an African language, however, clearly has the Location argument as the subject, because there is subject-verb agreement between Location and the verb as shown in (177). The locative class marker *ku* on the subject 'village' agrees with the locative class marker *ku* on the verb. The agreement relationship clearly shows that *village* is the subject of the verb. In other words, Location in Chichewa locative inversion is real subject, while Location in English locative inversion mainly has the characteristics of topic.

(177) Ku mu-dzi　　ku na-bwer-a　　　　　　a-lendo. ①

---

① The number 17 indicates a locative class marker on nouns. The following abbreviations are used: SUBJ = subject, REC. PST = recent past, and FV = final vowel.

17 3-village　　17. SUBJ-REC. PST-come-FV　2-visitor

'To the village came visitors.'　　　　　(Bresnan 1994, 93)

There is a controversy as to whether Mandarin locative subject is subject or topic. To address this issue, we need to distinguish between Mandarin subject and topic, two concepts still under debate in the field. There are three different views about subject and topic in Chinese. Some hold that Chinese is a topic-comment language (Chao 1968; LaPolla 2009). LaPolla (2009) even argued that an information structure analysis can explain all clause patterns in Chinese, and there is no need to posit the grammatical relation 'subject'. Some argue that Mandarin has subjects, and refer to Chinese as a Subject-Verb-Object (SVO) language, just as English. A third view is that Chinese is a topic-prominent language which has both topic and subject. The topic is the definite or generic noun phrase that establishes what the sentence is about, and the subject is the noun phrase that has a 'doing' or 'being' relationship with the verb (Li and Thompson 1981, 93). A topic is sometimes indistinguishable from a subject as both occupy the sentence-initial position. Li and Thompson (1981, 86) suggested that if there is a pause or a pause particle between the sentence-initial constituent and the rest of the sentence, the constituent is treated as a topic.[①] Nonetheless, we found that Li and Thompson's (1981) approach does not give us clear criteria for identifying topic: all sentence-initial NPs that meet their criteria of subject can be separated from the sentences with a pause or a pause particle. That will lead to the conclusion that all subjects are topics, hence the impossibility to tease

---

[①] It is difficult to decide whether *wo* 'I' is subject or topic in (i). It could be both if there is no pause between *wo* 'I' and the predicate. If there is a pause or a pause particle, *a*, *ba* and so on, *wo* 'I' is treated as the topic by Li and Thompson (1981).

(i) Wo　xihuan　pingguo.
　　I　like　apple
　'I like apples.'

apart the two. Actually, as pointed out by Jiang (1991, 55), a pause, graphically represented by a comma, or a particle does not necessarily mark topic. For instance, an adverb, which is not a topic, can be separated from the rest of the sentence by a comma or a particle as shown in (178).

(178)慢慢地（啊），你就会知道。
    Manman de (a), ni jiu hui zhidao.
    slow DE PARTICLE you as-soon will know
    'Gradually, you will find out.' (Jiang 1991, 54 – 55)

According to Jiang (1991), a subject combines with a predicate, or, simply put, a VP, to form a sentence, while a topic combines with a comment, which can be a sentence on its own, to form a sentence. He adopted a syntactic definition of topics and subjects as in (179) which utilizes the syntactic notion of 'sister' based on hierarchical structure in a syntactic tree diagram. Some syntactic tests, which rest crucially on the distinction between predicate and comment, can be used to distinguish topic and subject. Jiang (1991, ch. 2) provided a series of such tests: VP modifiers such as *guyi* 'intentionally' can appear before predicates but not comments; negation items, comparative PPs introduced by *bi* 'than', and auxiliary verbs such as *hui* 'will' precede predicates but not comments; A-not-A questions can be formed with predicates but not with comments. Shi (2000) integrated discourse factors into the syntactic definition of topic. He defined topic as an NP (or its equivalent) that precedes a clause, is related to a position inside the clause, and represents an entity that has been mentioned in the previous discourse.

(179) a. Topics are preverbal NPs that are sisters of sentences.
  b. Subjects are preverbal NPs that are sisters of VPs.
            (based on Jiang 1991, 46)

Getting back to LSSs, we find in the literature some arguments for sentence-initial LPs being topics in LSSs (Li and Thompson 1981; J.

Wang 2003). Firstly, subjects must go with predicates formed by verbs, but the verb in the locative subject construction is sometimes omitted (X. Fan 1998, 208). After omission of the verb, the LSS retains its meaning—presenting a Theme with the Location as the background as in (180). Therefore, the locative subject construction does not have a subject. Secondly, it is unnatural to have other elements before the locative topic in an LSS. Thirdly, the initial LP may be followed by a pause or pause particle. However, even though (180) is verbless, the DP in (180) serves as predicate for itself. The initial LP can be preceded by a topic. For example, in (181) the LP *guo li* 'in the cooker' is preceded by another element *niurou* 'beef', so it cannot be a topic which should be at sentence-initial position. Moreover, pause particles do not necessarily mark topic as shown in (178). All in all, these arguments are not strong enough to argue for the topic status of sentence-initial LPs in LSSs.

(180) 屋外（是）一片草地。
Wu   wai   (shi)   yi-pian   caodi.
room   outside be   one-CL   lawn
'Outside the room is a lawn.'

(181) 牛肉（啊）锅里炖着。
[Niurou]_Topic (a)   guo   li   dun-zhe.
beef   TOP   cooker inside   stew-DUR
'In the cooker is stewing the beef.'   (Wu 2015)

On the other hand, there is much evidence supporting LPs in LSSs as true subjects. By comparing English and Mandarin, Wu (2015) found that Mandarin LPs in LSSs can occur after another topic as in (181), but English topic PPs in locative inversion sentences cannot. Mandarin locative subjects can serve as the complements of Exceptional Case Marking verbs such as *dang* 'consider' in (182b), in contrast to English topic PPs as in (182a). These are two pieces of evidence for sentence-initial LPs being subjects rather than topics.

(182) a. ?? John considers [_TP_ in that room$_i$ to have sat a frog t$_i$].

b. 张三当地上躺了一只死老鼠。

　　Zhangsan dang [_TP_ di　　shang　tang-le　yi-zhi　si laoshu].

　　Zhangsan consider ground top　　lie-Perf　one-CL dead rat

　　Lit. 'Zhangsan considers the ground to lie a dead rat.'

(Wu 2010)

　　In addition, LPs in LSSs pass the syntactic tests for subjects provided in Jiang (1991).① Due to limit of space, we only show two tests here. First, VP modifiers such as *xiaoxinyiyi-de* 'carefully' can appear before predicates but not comments. For instance, they can occur between the sentence-initial LP *lu shang* 'on the road' and the rest of the LSS as in (183a), but cannot occur between a topic such as *ji* 'chicken' and a comment (the rest of the sentence) as in (183b), suggesting that the LP in (183a) is a subject rather than topic, and the rest of the sentence is the predicate. Second, no negative elements can appear as sisters of comments, but they can be sisters of predicates. It turns out that the negative element *mei* 'not' can occur before the part of LSS that follows the LP as shown in (184a), in contrast to (184b), indicating that the part of LSS that follows the LP is the predicate, and the LP is the subject. Based on evidence above, the present study treats sentence-initial LPs in LSSs as subjects.

(183) a. 路上小心翼翼地跑着几个人。

　　Lu　　shang　xiaoxinyiyi-de　pao-zhe　　ji-ge　　　ren.

　　road　top　　carefully　　　run-DUR　several-CL people

---

　　① Among all the syntactic tests for subjects in Jiang (1991), there are a few tests that sentence-initial LPs in LSSs do not pass. However, we find that the failure is not caused by syntactic reasons, but due to semantic incompatibity of the locative subject construction and the elements used in those tests.

'On the road arerunning several people.'

b. *鸡，小心翼翼地我吃了。

　*Ji,　　　　xiaoxinyiyi-de　wo　chi　le.

　chicken　carefully　　　 I　　eat　LE

　Intended meaning: 'Chicken, I ate carefully.'

(184) a. 牛背上没坐着两个小孩。

　Niu-bei　　shang　mei　zuo-zhe　liang-ge　xiaohai.

　cow-back　top　　not　sit-DUR　two-CL　child

　'On the cow's backdid not sit two children.'

b. *鸡，没我吃。

　*Ji,　　　mei　wo　chi.

　chicken　not　I　　eat

　Intended meaning: 'Chicken, I did not eat.'

At the level of argument structure, locative inversions in English and Chichewa are identical. However, at the level of syntactic category, inverted locatives are PPs in English but NPs in Chichewa, and at the level of functional structure, inverted locatives are subjects in Chichewa but topics in English. Now, it has been shown that the nominal LPs in Mandarin LSSs are real subjects, patterning in the same way as Chichewa locative subjects. Does Mandarin also have the English type of locative topics? The corresponding Mandarin construction can actually be found as shown in (185a), which has the structure in (185b). The construction in (185a) is judged as unacceptable by some researchers who speak Taiwan Mandarin, or is not native speaker of Mandarin (Huang 1987; Wu 2012; Djamouri et al. 2013). It has been noted, however, that Taiwan Mandarin is divergent from Mandarin spoken in mainland China in terms of some grammatical structures (see Lin 2001, 15). In mainland China, locative sentences with PP topics as in (185) are generally accepted. J. Wang (2003, 99) also found such sentences in his diachronic data of Chinese. Chu (1996) observes that the majority of *zai*-PPs in the structure of

Chapter 4   Localizer Phrases, Locative Subjects, and Locative Object

(185a) are interchangeable with the corresponding LPs without *zai* 'at'. They differ only in discourse function.

(185) a. 在山下盖了很多房子。

    Zai shan xia gai-le henduo fangzi.
    at mountain bottom build-Perf many house
    'At the foot of the mountain (someone) builds many houses.'

  b. PP-V-DP[①]

One might argue that the *zai*-PP is not a topic, but an adjunct following an empty *pro* (nominal) referring to an identifiable person or persons in the discourse or an arbitrary person as shown in (186) (see Afarli and Jin 2010). In the case of intransitive verbs, however, the sentence-initial *zai*-PP is unlikely to be an adjunct following an unpronounced subject. For instance, in (187), there could not be a *pro* as the only argument of the intransitive verb *tang* 'lie' is present in the sentence.

(186) 在山下盖了很多房子。

    (pro) Zai shan xia gai-le henduo fangzi.
    (pro) at mountain bottom build-Perf many house
    i. 'At the foot of the mountain builds many houses.'
    ii. '(Someone) built many houses at the foot of the mountain.'

(187) 在桌上躺着一只猫。

    (*pro) Zai zhuo shang tang-zhe yi-zhi mao.
    (*pro) at desk top lie-DUR one-CL cat
    'On the desk lies a cat.'

Under Jiang's (1991) definition, subjects are restricted to NPs.

---

  ① In the PP-DP-VP construction as exemplified in (118c) in section 3.3.3, the sentence-initial PP is also a locative topic, but we only discuss locative topic constructions as in (186) in this chapter.

English locative inversion, however, suggests the possibility of PPs functioning as subjects in natural language. It is possible that Mandarin *zai*-PPs in (185a), (186) and (187) are subjects rather than topics. There seems to be mixed evidence. Following Bresnan's (1994) method of identifying subject with the raising construction, we find that this type of *zai*-PP can undergo subject raising. In (188a), for instance, the *zai*-PP seems to move from a position below *sihu* 'seem', the translational equivalent of the English raising verb *seem*, to the sentential subject position. However, the raising construction is not a good diagnostic test of Mandarin subjects. For instance, the VP *chi shousi* 'eat sushi' precedes *sihu* 'seem' in (188b), but obviously it is a topic rather than a subject. The different patterns in English and Mandarin can be ascribed to the fact that Mandarin expressions like *haoxiang* 'seemingly' and *sihu* 'seemly' are not raising verbs, but adverbs, and elements before them are topics (see Jiang 1991, 75). The parallel between (188a) and (188b) actually suggests that the sentence-initial *zai*-PP is a topic. However, this type of *zai*-PPs also has some properties of subject, as some of them can pass Jiang's (1991) tests for subjects. If the verb in this construction is posture verb or manner-of-motion verb, VP modifiers such as *xiaoxinyiyi-de* 'carefully' can appear between the sentence-initial *zai*-PP and the rest of the sentence as shown in (189a), and negative elements can occur before the part that follows the *zai*-PP as shown in (189b).① The two tests point to the *zai*-PP in (189) being a subject, because the rest of the sentence is the predicate.

(188) a. 在桌上似乎躺着一只猫。
   Zai zhuo shang sihu tang-zhe yi-zhi mao.
   at desk top seem lie-DUR one-CL cat

---

① In this construction, some verbs such as *gai* 'build' can pass the negation test, but cannot be modified by VP modifiers. That's why we say that some, but not all *zai*-PPs, can pass Jiang's (1991) tests for subjects.

'On the desk seems to lie a cat.'

b. 吃寿司似乎他不太喜欢。

Chi shousi sihu ta bu tai xihuan.
eat sushi seem he not very like

'He does not seem to like to eat sushi very much.'

(189) a. 在路上小心翼翼地跑着几个人。

Zai lu shang xiaoxinyiyi-de pao-zhe ji-ge ren.
at road top carefully run-DUR several-CL people

'On the road are running several people.'

b. 在牛背上没坐着两个小孩。

Zai niu-bei shang mei zuo-zhe liang-ge xiaohai.
at cow-back top not sit-DUR two-CL child

'On the cow's back did not sit two children.'

To summarize so far, the *zai*-PP in the sentence type as in (185) has properties of both topic and subject, as shown by the syntactic tests. Since it is distinct from the locative subject in the locative subject construction discussed above in that it cannot serve as the subject in one-argument sentences as shown in (190), we call it locative topics to differentiate the two. Sentence-initial *zai*-PPs are simply dubbed locative topics in this study, but we admit that they also have some subject properties, just like the topicalized subjects in English locative inversion.

(190) (*在) 台上脏了。

(*Zai) tai shang zang le.
at stage top dirty LE

Intended meaning: 'On the stage, it is dirty.'

Mandarin and English are alike in using LPs or AxPartPs as the locative subject and PPs as the locative topic. In English, the AxPartP can be locative subject as in (191a), but cannot occur in the initial position of a locative inversion sentence as in (191b) in contrast to (191c). This demonstrates once again that the English locative inversion construction involves topic but not subject.

(191) a. [$_{\text{AxPartP}}$ The front of the room] is dirty.

b. * The front of the table ran a mouse.

c. In front of the table ran a mouse.

English locative topics subsume a broad range of spatial relations, including Location, Source, and Goal;① a similar breadth of range is covered by Mandarin locative subjects. However, there is a gap: phrases headed by *dao* 'reach, to' (abbreviated as *dao*-phrases) cannot be used as locative topics. When expressing Goal, LPs rather than *dao*-phrases must be used as shown by the contrast between *wu li* 'inside the room' (192a) and *dao wu li* 'into the room' (192b). This is exceptional as PPs headed by *zai* 'at' and *cong* 'from' both can be used as locative topics as shown in (187) and (192c). It is hypothesized that the difference between *dao* and the other two is caused by their different levels of grammaticalization: *zai* and *cong* have been fully grammaticalized from verbs into prepositions whereas *dao* has not. It is still a verb. As only PPs can serve as locative topics, VPs headed by *dao* 'reach' is ruled out in this position.

(192) a. 屋里来了一个人。

Wu   li   lai-le   yi-ge   ren.
room   inside come-Perf   one-CL   person

'Into the room came a man.'

b. *到屋里来了一个人。

*Dao   wu   li   lai-le   yi-ge   ren.
to   room   inside come-Perf   one-CL   person

Intended meaning: 'Into the room came a man.'

c. 从屋里来了一个人。

---

① Some researchers hold that sentence-initial Goals are odd in English. But examples in (148a) and (149b) clearly show that Goal topics are possible in English.

Cong   wu   li   lai-le   yi-ge   ren.
from   room   inside   come-Perf   one-CL   person
'Out of the room came a person.'

Mandarin locative subjects and locative topics both occur in the sentence-initial position, and they have semantic overlap. For instance, both locative subjects and locative topics headed by *cong* can express Source. The presence or absence of *cong* in (193) does not change the meaning of the sentence. Some locative subjects are ambiguous between a Source reading and a Goal reading as shown in (194). When the speaker is in Zhangsan's home, Zhangsan's home is the Goal of the motion, but when the speaker is at another place, Zhangsan's home is the Source. In brief, LPs in the locative subject construction can express Goal, Source and Location. They have semantic overlap with locative topic PPs, but sentence-initial Goal cannot be encoded by *dao*-phrases, as schematized in (195).

(193) (从) 桌上跳下来一只猫。

    (Cong)   zhuo   shang   tiao-xia-lai   yi-zhi   mao.
    (from)   desk   top   jump-descend-come   one-CL   cat
    'From the desk jumped down a cat.'

(194) 张三家来了一个人。

    Zhangsan   jia   lai-le   yi-ge   ren.
    Zhangsan   home   come-Perf   one-CL   person
    i. 'A person came to Zhangsan's home.'   (Goal)
    ii. 'From Zhangsan's home came a person.'   (Source)

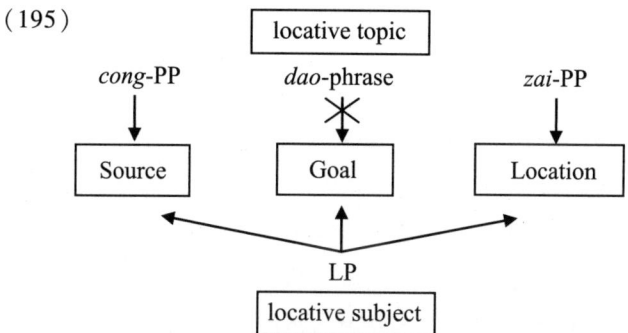

(195)

	locative topic	
cong-PP	*dao*-phrase	*zai*-PP
↓	✳	↓
Source	Goal	Location

LP

locative subject

To summarize this section, the LPs in Mandarin LSSs are true subjects, just like Chichewa locative subjects. There are also locative topics in Mandarin, which have properties of topic and subject, just as the topicalized subject in the English locative inversion construction.

4.3 Syntax and semantics of locative objects

In English, Location and Goal are realized as oblique, such as *in the room* or *to the park*. In Chinese, however, they can immediately follow the verb, serving as the direct object. In the present study, LPs that serve as the direct objects of verbs are called 'locative objects'. It is necessary to distinguish ordinary NPs and spatial LPs after verbs (X. Fan 1998, 48 – 49; D. Liu 2008). There are some important differences between the two types as shown by the contrast in (196) and (197a) (D. Liu 2008). In (196), *xiao chuang* 'little bed' is an NP formed by a common noun with no spatial meaning. It is incompatible with the preposition *zai* 'at', because *zai* subcategorizes for an LP. On the other hand, the LP *xiao chuang shang* 'on the little bed' in (197a) can co-occur with *zai*. The NP *xiao chuang* 'little bed' in (196) is a type of non-canonical object (Barrie and Li 2012), whereas LPs that directly follow verbs, such as *xiao chuang shang* 'on the little bed' in (197a), are regarded as real locative objects in our study. Both intransitive and transitive verbs, as exemplified by *shui* 'sleep' in (197a) and *ge* 'put' in (197b) respectively, can take locative objects.

(196) 你睡（*在）小床。

    Ni　　shui　　(*zai)　　xiao　　chuang.

    you　　sleep　　(*at)　　little　　bed

    'You sleep on a little bed.'

(197) a. 你睡（在）小床上吧。

    Ni　　shui　　(zai)　　xiao　　chuang　　shang　　ba.

    you　　sleep　　(at)　　little　　bed　　top　　sfp

'You sleep on the little bed.'

b. 行李搁（在）房间里了。

Xingli ge (zai) fangjian li le.
luggage put (at) room inside LE

'The luggage has been put in the room.' (D. Liu 2008)

It is interesting to see that in the preverbal position, omission of the spatial preposition is hardly grammatical as shown in (198), but in the postverbal position, the omission is quite free as shown in (197). The contrast can be explained by a linguistic theory—Case theory. There are two possible explanations based on Case theory. First, the Case of the LP in the postverbal position is assigned by an empty preposition as represented by [e] in (200a). D. Liu (2008) contended that locative objects formed by LPs are adverbials rather than real objects. He found that the perfective aspect marker -le can be inserted between the verb and its non-canonical object in (199a), but not between the verb and a locative object in (199b). In Mandarin, the verb followed by a preposition cannot take any aspect marker as in (199c), unless the aspect marker follows the preposition as in (199d). (199b) is out because the aspect marker follows the verb directly. It thus can be inferred that the verb in (199b) is underlyingly followed by a preposition as in (199c). This analysis leads to the generalization that locative objects are PPs underlyingly and are the result of ellipsis of spatial prepositions. The second explanation is that the verb directly assigns Case to an LP that follows it as in (200b). The preverbal position is not a Case position, so an LP needs a preposition in order to be assigned a Case, but the postverbal position is a Case position, in which an LP is governed and case-marked by the verb. Mandarin differs from English in Case assignment: English has overt morphological case and the Accusative Case is assigned to the direct object, but Mandarin lacks morphological Case, and undifferentiated Case is assigned by the verb to any argument that occupies the object position and requires Case (Barrie and Li 2012). The locative object of an intransitive verbs can get undifferentiated Case and be licensed as well.

(198) 你??（在）椅子上坐一会。

Ni ?? (zai) yizi shang zuo yi-huir.

you ?? (at) chair top sit one-while.

'You sit in the chair for a while.'

(adapted from D. Liu 2008)

(199) a. 他睡了小床。

Ta shui-le xiao chuang.

he sleep-Perf little bed

'He slept on a little bed.'

b. *他睡了小床上。

*Ta shui-le xiao chuang shang.

He sleep-Perf little bed top

Intended meaning: 'He slept on a little bed.'

c. *他睡了在小床上。

*Ta shui-le zai xiao chuang shang.

He sleep-Perf at little bed top

Intended meaning: 'He slept on a little bed.'

d. 他睡在了小床上。

Ta shui zai-le xiao chuang shang.

He sleep at-Perf little bed top

'He slept on a little bed.' (adapted from D. Liu 2008)

(200) a. Case assigned by an empty preposition

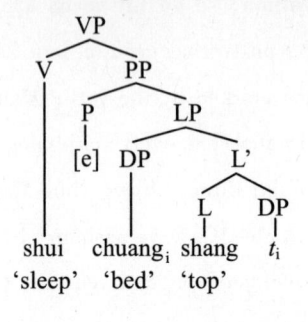

```
              VP
             /  \
            V    PP
                /  \
               P    LP
               |   /  \
              [e] DP   L'
                      / \
                     L   DP
                     |   |
        shui  chuang_i  shang  t_i
        'sleep' 'bed'   'top'
```

b. undifferentiated Case assigned by a verb

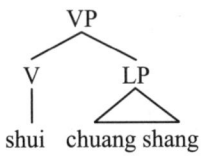

```
        VP
       /  \
      V    LP
      |    /\
    shui chuang shang
```

The present study opts for the second possibility, namely, locative objects not being the result of ellipsis. Admittedly, there are instances where prepositions can be inserted between the locative objects and their verbs, supporting the ellipsis analysis. For instance, *zai* '(be) at' or *dao* 'reach, to' can be inserted between the Goal-denoting locative objects and posture, placement, or displacement verbs as in (197b), and *zai* can be inserted between the Location-denoting locative objects and posture verbs as in (197a). These locative objects could be the result of omission of preposition. However, there is compelling evidence for the non-ellipsis analysis. Locative objects with some verbs cannot be derived from spatial PPs. The verbs include non-motional process verbs *kan* 'look', *he* 'drink', *kou* 'scratch' and *qiao* 'look', as exemplified in (201a), existential verbs *shi* 'be' and *zai* 'be at', and other verbs like *jian* 'pick up'. The locative object of verbs of directed motion such as *hui* 'return', *jin* 'enter', and *lai* 'come' could result from omission of *dao* 'reach, to', but with some locative objects, they could not as in (201b). Moreover, some postverbal *zai*-PPs do not have the corresponding locative object form, for instance, with verbs of (dis)appearance as in (201c). Based on evidence above, we argue that the locative object construction and the V-PP construction overlap in some respects, but they are two independent constructions: the former is not derived from the latter through ellipsis.

(201) a. 看(* 到/在)这里!

    Kan   (* dao/zai)   zhe   li!

    look   (* to/at)   this   inside

'Look here!'

b. 来(＊到/在)床上！

Lai （＊dao/zai） chuang shang!

come （＊to/at） bed top

'Come onto the bed!'

c. 他死＊(在)医院里。

Ta si ＊(zai) yiyuan li.

he die ＊(at) hospital inside

'He died in the hospital.'

Examples above demonstrate that locative objects can express Location and Goal. Source elements, however, cannot be locative objects, as shown in (202), as Mandarin consistently maps Source onto the preverbal position.

(202)＊他跳台上。

＊Ta tiao tai shang.

he jump stage top

Intended meaning: 'He jumped from the stage.'

To summarize, in Mandarin, Location and Goal, but not Source, can be realized as direct objects. They receive undifferentiated Case from the preceding verbs, and get licensed. Even though prepositions can be inserted between the locative objects and their verbs in many cases, they cannot in other cases, indicating that the locative object construction does not result from ellipsis from the V-PP construction.

4.4 Summary

In this chapter, we have shown that Mandarin Ls have complex distributions and pose a learnability problem. Mandarin LPs can function as locative subjects, locative objects, and objects of spatial prepositions, and this chapter focuses on the first two. Verbs that can occur in the locative subject constructions must have a (dynamic) state component in their event structures, as the function of the construction is to present a dynamic state or a result state. Besides the Chichewa-type locative subjects, Mandarin also has the English-type locative topics. The Mandarin locative object construction is not the elliptical form of the V-PP construction. Locative objects are not case-marked by an empty preposition, but receive undifferentiated Case from the preceding verbs. In what follows, we review some studies that probe into the acquisition of LPs and the locative subject construction.

4.5 Acquisition of the localizer phrase and the locative subject construction

Mandarin localizers have some language-specific properties not shared by their English counterparts. The complexity of the distribution of LPs poses problems for language acquisition. We wonder how first language (L1) and second language (L2) learners of Mandarin acquire the LP-formation rule, and use the LPs in the locative subject construction. In this section, we will introduce some acquisition studies.

The Mandarin LP-formation rule does not apply to all NPs in an across-the-board manner: for NPs formed by common nouns, Localizers (Ls) are obligatorily required; for NPs formed by proper names, the localizer *li* 'inside' and its derived forms are disallowed; and for NPs with inherent locative meaning, L is optional. The difficulty in acquiring the LP-formation rule was reported for L2 learners. Based on 435 utterances elicited from 71 L2 learners of Mandarin in a picture description task, F. Chen (2008) finds that L2 learners omitted Ls, especially in V-*zai* sentences. Her subjects were from different linguistic backgrounds, speaking English, Indonesian, Russian, Vietnamese, Tai, Japanese and Korean. They were classified into 5 levels ranging from the beginner level to the advanced level. The omission rate for the Ls in the V-*zai* structure for the beginner level is 20% and the average for all the levels is 15%. Moreover, the omission rate of Ls in the V-*zai* construction is much higher than that in the locative subject sentences with *you* 'have'.

The LP-formation rule also proves to be difficult for L1 acquisition. Deng and Yip (2015) found in their corpus study that 2% of the LPs following *zai* '(be) at' in child speech are common nouns without a localizer as shown in (203). Such a nontarget pattern persists until 6 years of age as indicated by (203b). Omissions of Ls are unacceptable in these examples, as *jiaoche* 'car' and *chuanglian* 'curtain' are conceptualized by Mandarin speakers as common nouns which obligatorily require Ls when following *zai* '(be) at'. The complexity of the LP-formation rule may explain the difficulty in acquisition. Or, children may have acquired the rule that common nouns must be followed by Ls, but they have to learn through experience which noun phrases are formed by common nouns that do not have inherent locative meaning, and which encode locative meaning. They need to distinguish different types of NP through experience to fully acquire the rule. With presence in at least 90% of all obligatory contexts for three successive samples as a criterion of acquisition, Brown (1973, 314) found that the three English-speaking children that he investigated longitudinally acquired *in* and *on* before or around 2;10. The findings were confirmed by experiments on more than 20 English-speaking children (Brown and Fraser 1963; de Villiers and de Villiers 1973, cited in Brown 1973, 316 – 324). However, by examining the 259 child utterances containing *zai* from the Zhou2 corpus (Zhou and Chang 2009), Deng and Yip (2015) found that the Mandarin-speaking children did not reach the criterion by 3 years of age: 3- and 4-year-olds supplied localizers for common nouns 83% of the time, and 5- and 6-year-olds did so 93% of the time, the omitted localizers including *li* 'inside' and *shang* 'top', the counterparts of *in* and *on*. English-speaking children systematically provide locative prepositions, the counterparts of Mandarin localizers, earlier than Mandarin-speaking children, suggesting that the language-specific LP-formation rule poses a challenge for Mandarin-speaking children.

(203) a. *放在轿车。

  *Fang zai jiaoche.
  put at car
  '(It was) put at the car.'   (WX 1;11)

b. *还有一只躲在窗帘。

  *Hai you yi-zhi duo zai chuanglian.
  still have one-CL hide at curtain
  'There is still another one hiding at the curtain.'

              (SRQ 6;0)

  How do children use LPs as subjects and form locative subject sentences (LSSs)? Song's (2009) detailed longitudinal study on 3 children aged between 0;10 and 2;6 (28, 53, and 55 sessions of data for each child) provides a clue. Song (2009, ch. 5) found that children's sentences in the form of 'Location-V-Theme' were predominantly those with the verb *you* 'have', which emerged around 1;8, and accounted for 70.54% to 84.44% of the total tokens of the 'Location-V-Theme' sentences produced by each of the three children. His data suggest that early LSSs are very limited in terms of verb type. His data also points to the difficulty of this construction: children produced *you* sentences in the form of 'Location-V-Theme' less frequently than adults (10.16% vs. 34.91% for one child's data, and 14.79% vs. 32.79% for another). However, his definition of Location is not restricted to LPs, but also includes NPs with inherent locative meaning, and NPs that are not conceived as having locative meaning, e.g. *wo* 'I' in *wo you pingguo* 'I have apples' (Song 2009, 30). Therefore, his data included sentences without spatial meanings which are somehow different from LSSs defined in this study.

Among various types of locative subject sentences, F. Chen (2008) found that the types frequently used by L2 learners of Mandarin are those with *you* 'have' (50%), those with *shi* 'be' (2%), and those with V-*zhe* (24%).[①] The order of frequencies of the sentence types in L2 learners' production from the highest to the lowest is: *you* sentences > V-*zhe* sentences with placement verbs > *shi* sentences > V-*zhe* sentences with posture verbs. Locative subject sentences with V-*le* did not occur in L2 learners' utterances, in contrast to what was found for 15 native speakers in the control group (V-*le* accounting for 13% of their production).

[①] The percentages do not add up to 100% because F. Chen (2008) also tested the locative sentences other than the locative subject sentences, e. g. , sentences with *zai* as the main verb.

Chapter 5   Linguistic Space, Perception, and Cognition

In this chapter, we go beyond spatial words and constructions in Mandarin, and address a broader issue—the relationship between L-space, perception and cognition.[①] Two interesting phenomena in spatial language—choice of frames of reference and asymmetrical representations of Figure and Ground—will be discussed to unveil the interaction between language, perception and cognition in the domain of space. Language and perception are generally considered subsystems of cognition. In what follows, the term cognition is used exclusively to refer to non-linguistic and non-perceptual cognition, including memory, attention, reasoning, problem solving, and so on. The fundamental questions to bear in mind are as follows: what does natural language reveal about the nature of perception and cognition? How is communication about the world affected by the perception of it? Is thought dominant in its interaction with language or the other way around? Are there any language universals given by human beings' shared perception and cognition? There are also related questions in child language acquisition. Do child data confirm the proposed language universals? What is the relationship between cognitive development and language development? We will provide our answers to these questions in

---

[①] An abridged version of this chapter appeared as sections 1 and 2 (pp. 288 – 296) of the following article: Deng, Xiangjun and Virginia Yip. 2016. Cognition and perception in the linguistic encoding of space in child Mandarin. *Journal of Chinese Linguistics* 44 (2): 287 – 325.

sections 5.1 and 5.2.

5.1 Frames of reference, reference strategies and Figure-Ground asymmetry

Owing to the legacy of Gestalt psychology, it is generally understood that perception is the result of an interaction between environmental input and active principles in the mind (see Piaget and Inhelder 1948; Jackendoff 1983). In the extreme cases of dream and hallucination, vividly perceived scenarios do not come from environmental input but from one's own mind. Perception is shaped by our cognition—the real world cannot be perceived immediately, but only through the 'lens' of general cognition. The boundary between perception and conception is claimed to be artificial by Miller and Johnson-Laird (1976).

Perception is generally conceived of as being relatively independent of language. The reasoning is that linguistic skills were acquired later than perceptual skills in the evolution of human beings (Miller and Johnson-Laird 1976, 2). On the other hand, various languages may share something in common due to human beings' common perceptual processes. H. Clark (1973) contended that languages around the world are basically similar in expressing spatial information: properties of P-space are preserved in the L-space of English; many languages are similar to English in this regard; and a child's P-space is also directly reflected in his L-space. The universality in language may arise from a shared perceptual apparatus. However, this view is only based on well-studied Western languages, and was criticized by Levinson (1996a, 1996b, 2003) and Levinson and Wilkins (2006) who revealed great variation in choosing frames of reference across cultural groups. English people, for instance, tend to use the viewer-centered frame of reference involving words like *left*, *right*, *front* and *back*,[1] while Tzeltal or Arrernte rely heavily on an environment-centered system using cardinal directions like *uphill* or *north*. People may adopt different strategies within the viewer-centered system. When the reference entity (RE) has no intrinsic orientation, a larger field of orientation will be established to locate the objects. The field is either aligned with the speaker's field, or faces the speaker's field. The former is called the aligned strategy, and the latter the facing strategy. Hill (1982) reported that there are cross-cultural differences in the choice of reference strategies. For instance, Hausa speakers prefer the aligned strategy while English speakers prefer the facing strategy in normal cases.

Nevertheless, under some special perceptual conditions, the cross-cultural differences are neutralized. For instance, when people ride in a vehicle and are in motion, they tend to describe a further object as in front of a nearer one. English speakers, similar to Hausa speakers, show such a tendency in adopting the aligned strategy. Moreover, when the Figure is covered by the RE as shown by the relationship between the ball and the tree in Fig. 5.1, the Hausa speaker will shift from the aligned strategy to a facing strategy, and say sentences like (204), just like English speakers. The shift for Hausa speakers has been experimentally confirmed (Isma'il 1979, cited from Hill 1982), and that for English speakers is supported by impressionistic data.

(204) There is a ball behind the tree.

The two perceptual conditions above lead to similar responses from Mandarin speakers. By testing 99 adult Mandarin speakers, Guo (2008) found that Mandarin speakers had no preference for either of these reference strategies when they are static and the Figure is not covered by the RE. However, when the subject was set in motion in an imagined scenario (indicated by the [+Motion] feature), for instance, if a sentence

---

[1] English speakers also use the object-centered system to a lesser degree.

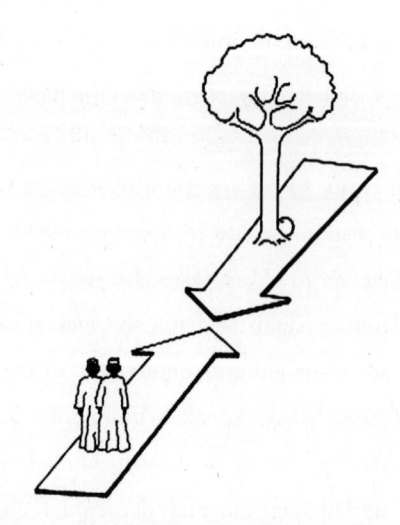

**Fig. 5.1 The perceptual condition that the
Figure is covered by the RE (Hill 1982)**

like (205) was asked, the majority of the subjects chose the aligned strategy. When faced with a situation where the target object was covered by the reference object (indicated by the [+Cover] feature) and thus not easily perceived, the majority of the Mandarin-speaking subjects used the facing strategy, similar to English and Hausa speakers. His results are summarized in Table 5-1. The cross-linguistic similarities in interpreting *front* and *back* under some special perceptual conditions may be triggered by constraints placed by perception, and ultimately by cognition.

(205)从深圳大学出发，罗湖口岸在福田口岸的前面还是后面？①
   Cong Shenzhen Daxue   chufa,   Luohu Kou'an zai
   Futian Kou'an de qian-mian haishi hou-mian?
   from Shenzhen University depart, Luohu Port at
   Futian Port   DE front-face or   back-face
  'Is Luohu Port in front of or behind Futian Port if you start from

---

① We converted the original test sentence with locations in Beijing into a case in Shenzhen.

Shenzhen University?'

Table 5 – 1   Choice of reference strategies under different perceptual conditions in Guo (2008)

Perceptual condition	Aligned strategy	Facing strategy
[– Motion] [– Cover]	58%	42%
[+ Motion] [– Cover]	78.7%	21.3%
[– Motion] [+ Cover]	3 – 29%	71 – 97%

There is another case showing that perceptual cues from the environment influence people's choice of reference frames. Experiments by Levinson and his colleagues show that people from different linguistic backgrounds choose different frames of reference in the same condition (cited from Li and Gleitman 2002). The main paradigm employed in these studies is the 'animals in a row' test. The experimenter sets up three animals on one table as the subject watches. Then the subject turns 180 degrees to face another table. He is required to 'make it the same' with the same three animals on the new table. It is found that people from linguistic communities that rely heavily on expressions with the viewer-centered frame of reference, for instance, Dutch, strongly favored the viewer-centered perspective in solving the problem, while the majority of people who use environmental-centered expressions in their daily life, such as Tenejapan Mayan, made the environmental-centered responses. Li and Gleitman (2002), however, challenged Levinson: in those studies, the Dutch speakers were tested in the labs while the Tenejapan speakers were tested outdoors on the hills. Either the language or the environment could have caused subjects' responses. So they held language constant and manipulated the environments. Using the same 'animal in a row' test on speakers of a single language, English, they found that different problem-solving strategies were used by their subjects with different environmental cues. There were three conditions. In the first condition, subjects were tested in a lab with the blinds pulled down. In the second condition, they pulled up the blinds so the subjects could see outdoor landmarks. In the last condition, subjects were tested outdoors. The subjects in the last two conditions were provided with environmental cues such as tall buildings, and thus were inclined to choose environment-centered reference frame, while subjects who were not cued overwhelmingly chose the viewer-centered framework. The result indicates that language is not the causal factor in the choice of reference frames. Rather, perceptual cues lead people to shift from one perspective to another. Two populations without language, rats and 9-month-old infants, also demonstrate a shift in the choice of reference frames if perceptual cues are provided (reviewed in Li and Gleitman 2002). All in all, these facts suggest human minds, or even animal minds, are basically the same in choosing the reference frame—the choice depends on the cues available in the environment rather than on language.

Besides the relation between spatial language and perception, the relationship between language and cognition is also a captivating topic. The influence of cognition on language is evidenced by the asymmetry between Figure and Ground. Languages unanimously project large, immovable objects as the Ground while realizing small, movable ones as Figure, which could be a universal semantic pattern (Jackendoff 1996a; Talmy 2000). For example, while *the bike is next to the house* is a very natural description of a scene shown in Fig. 5.2, reversing the positions of the two nominal phrases in saying *the house is next to the bike*, namely, using the small, movable bike to locate the large, immovable house renders the sentence odd. The asymmetry has nothing to do with the syntax of English or properties of the physical world. Some deep-level cognitive principles determine the way in which the spatial relationship between two objects is perceived and linguistically encoded. The same situation is found in Mandarin Chinese (Liu 1994). The (b) sentences in (206) and (207) are anomalous compared with the (a) sentences, suggesting the Figure-Ground asymmetry exists in Mandarin.

Fig. 5.2　Figure-Ground asymmetry

(206) a. 自行车在房子旁边。
　　　　Zixingche　zai　　fangzi　pang-bianr.
　　　　bike　　　be at　house　side
　　　　'The bike is next to the house.'
　　b. #房子在自行车旁边。
　　　　#Fangzi　zai　　zixingche　pang-bianr.
　　　　house　　be at　bike　　　side
　　　　'The house is next to the bike.'

(207) a. 城里有公园。
　　　　Cheng　li　　　you　　gongyuan.
　　　　city　　inside　have　park
　　　　'There is a park in the city.'
　　b. #公园外有城市。
　　　　#Gongyuan　wai　　　you　　chengshi.
　　　　park　　　　outside　have　city
　　　　'There is a city outside the park.'

A variety of experimental evidence showed the effect of the Figure-Ground asymmetry in perception, cognitive judgments of distance, and English speakers' linguistic judgments of semantic naturalness (reviewed in Landau and Jackendoff 1993). When a stationary dot was placed within a moving frame, subjects perceived that it was the dot rather than the frame that moved. The perceived movement seems to be induced by a cognitive misjudgment of the small dot as the movable Figure. When adults and children were required to 'make it so the (mobile object) is near the (fixed object)', their reaction time to the semantically natural sentence was shorter than that for the unnatural one. Adults and 2-, 4-, 6-year-olds viewing drawings of pairs of objects were asked 'Which one is near which one?' or 'is the house near the bicycle, or is the bicycle near the house?' Even the youngest children tended to place the smaller and more mobile entity in the subject position and the other entity in the prepositional object position. The cross-linguistic data from English and Mandarin Chinese, and the acquisition data reported in Landau and Jackendoff (1993) suggest that the Figure-Ground asymmetry is a language universal that may be given by human species' shared cognitive ability.

Cognition exerts powerful influence on language as shown above, but there is also evidence pointing to the autonomy of language. In children and adults with Williams Syndrome (WS), a rare genetic deficit, non-linguistic spatial representations are impaired but some aspects of spatial language are relatively spared, which supports the independence of language from the non-linguistic spatial system (reviewed in Landau and Lakusta 2006).[1] Bellugi et al. (1988, cited from Landau and Lakusta 2006) reported that WS adolescents performed at the level of 4-year-olds in

---

[1] There are challenges to this view. Karmiloff-Smith et al. (1997, cited in Laudau and Lakusta 2006), for instance, suggested that aspects of syntax and morphology, e. g. knowledge of relative clauses, are impaired in WS children both quantitatively and qualitatively. Laudau and Lakusta (2006) responded that the task that they used recruits memory and attention, and thus is not a good diagnostic. For example, a child subject in Karmiloff-Smith et al. (1997) was asked to choose one out of four pictures where 'the circle the star is in is red'. The center-embedded structure has great linguistic processing demands, and the task also requires considerable visual-spatial processing and memory.

visual-spatial construction tasks that require the subjects to make a copy of various spatial configurations. Yet in an elicited production task, WS children (N = 12, median age 9;7) and WS adults (N = 13, median age 21;9) were capable of using the correct categories and word orders to express Figure and Ground, and expressing different types of Path with appropriate prepositions (Laudau and Zukowski 2003, cited in Landau and Lakusta 2006, 323). Even though people with WS deviate from normal people in their spatial representation, their spatial language is quite normal. The findings suggest that language is an independent cognitive system.

To summarize, two levels of representation must be differentiated in the present discussion about spatial language: the spatial representation, the end product of perception, and the linguistic representation (Jackendoff 1996b). The two levels interact with each other, as well as with other cognitive processes. The choice of reference frames shows that our interpretation of a spatial expression is constrained by perception, and at a deeper level, by general cognition. Perception cues from the environment affect both cognition and language, as they influence one's ability to solve problems and use language (see Hill 1982; Guo 2008; Li and Gleitman 2002).

At least two language universals have been proposed and received some empirical evidence. The Figure-Ground asymmetry could be a universal semantic pattern. It arises as a consequence of our nonlinguistic representations of space on which language draws. It is an asymmetry in general cognition and influences both perception and language. The second language universal lies in people's similar behavior in choosing the aligned reference strategy in the [+ Motion] perceptual condition, and the facing strategy in the [+ Cover] perceptual condition. These language universals seem to result from human beings' shared perceptual and cognitive systems. One may ask why such language universals are plausible. It is well known that psychological encoding of spatial location and motion evolved long before language. Given the evolutionary primacy of spatial concepts, language universals encoded by genes are not an illusion. Lastly, cognition has primacy over language in some respect, but language may be an independent subsystem of the general cognitive system, interacting with other subsystems, as data from children and adults with Williams Syndrome show.

5.2 Effects of cognitive development on language development

The investigation of how cognitive and perceptual development influence child language development is an integral part of the study of the relationship between cognition, perception and language. The answer to this question in the context of Mandarin Chinese can be found through examining three aspects: Mandarin-speaking children's use of reference frames/strategies and their responses to perceptual cues in interpreting projective localizers (Ls) *qian* 'front' and *hou* 'back'; their acquisition sequence of Ls; and their knowledge of the Figure-Ground asymmetry. We will review research findings in these three directions.

5.2.1 Frames of reference and reference strategies used by children

Linguistic systems and general cognition interact to determine the properties of spatial language. In this section, previous studies into the cognitive determinants of frame-of-reference acquisition will be discussed. Much attention in the field has centered on the age at which children are able to use the spatial terms in a nonegocentric way. Piaget (1923/1959) and Piaget and Inhelder (1948/1956) have shown that young children are egocentric in thinking. In other words, they have difficulty adopting the viewpoints of others. Decentering takes place after the preoperational period, which is roughly between ages 2 and 7. For instance, based on a longitudinal study of two 6-year-old boys in one month, Piaget (1923/1959) found that more than 40% of both children's utterances were egocentric ones, which were not addressed to anyone and did not call for reaction. The egocentric language includes repetition, monologue and collective monologue in which children repeat the words that they hardly understand, accompany their games with word-play or talk aloud to himself in front of others. The reason for this egocentricity is that children younger than 7 or 8 are neither fully individualized nor socialized (ibid., 42). Besides, children are surrounded by adults who not only know everything but also do everything to understand the child. Therefore, children seem to have the impression that people can read their thoughts (ibid., 102). Based on many experiments in the development of spatial cognition, Piaget and Inhelder (1948/1956) found that egocentrism preceded decentered spatial cognition. The initial egocentric attitude encourages a child to accept her own perspective as the only one possible, and decentering is not achieved until the age of 7 or 8 (ibid., 194). For instance, children up to 6;6 tended to draw the shadow of an object as similar to the shape of the object perceived from where they stand, without considering the relative positions of the light, the object, and the plane that the shadow falls on.

However, this Piagetian view has been subject to all kinds of critiques in psychological and psycholinguistic studies. Some studies have shown that children can break away from his own perspective, and take an object-centered perspective in using spatial expressions. Based on placement or act-out tasks given to 45 children aged between 2;6 to 4;2, Kuczaj and Maratsos (1975) found that young children tended to adopt the RE's reference frame before the viewer's reference frame. The competence of placing an object in relation to a non-fronted object is a late development, suggesting that it was easier for the children to capture the meaning of *front*, *back* and *side* based on the intrinsic characteristics of the RE, rather than constructing the front-back-side axes on the basis of themselves. This study demonstrates nonegocentricity in using spatial language before 4;0. Similarly, based on experimental data from 21 Mandarin-speaking children in three age groups (2;8 – 2;11, 3;0 – 3;3, and 3;4 – 3;6), Li (1988) found that children acquired the correct use of reference strategies and perspectives before 4;0. In his experiment, subjects were required to say whether the Figure was in front of or behind the RE for each arrangement of the toys. When the RE was non-featured, i. e. without inherent front and back, the subjects could only use the viewer-centered perspective, but they had two options when using this perspective—imagining the non-featured RE as a person facing them, namely choosing the facing strategy, or projecting their own orientation to the RE in the same direction, i. e. taking the aligned strategy. It was found that the subjects who used the aligned strategy decreased from 80% to 37% from the youngest to the oldest age group, and those who chose the facing strategy increased from 0 to 63% across age groups. When the RE was featured, the subjects could either use the viewer-centered perspective or the object-centered perspective. There were also two situations: in canonical encounter situations where the front of a featured RE faced the subject, the use of the speaker's perspective decreased from 40% to 13% from the youngest to the oldest age group; in non-canonical encounter situations, the use of the RE's perspective increased from 20% to 75% across age groups. With the aligned strategy, the child views the RE as aligned in the same direction as him- or herself, which is an indication of egocentrism. The facing strategy requires the child to imagine that the frontward direction of the RE is counter to his own frontward direction. The shift from the aligned strategy to facing strategy and from the speaker's perspective to RE's perspective reflects a process of decentering in cognitive development. Chinese children in Li (1988) seemed to acquire reference strategies and perspectives in their fourth year.

Decentering is an important sign of progress in cognitive development. We are concerned with children's choice of frames of reference or reference strategies with projective localizers *qian* 'front', *hou* 'back', *zuo-bian* 'left' and *you-bian* 'right'. If children are really egocentric up to 8 as proposed by Piaget and Inhelder (1948), one would expect to see a non-adultlike choice of reference frame that ignores the inherent orientation of the RE. Li (1988) suggested that Chinese children acquired the decentered reference strategy and perspective in interpreting *qian* 'front' and *hou* 'back' in their fourth year as shown by a comprehension experiment. However, this study still leaves room for improvement: it did not include an adult control group and simply assumed that adult Chinese speakers use the same facing strategy as English speakers; and the sample size was not large enough to allow for statistical analysis.

In an attempt to improve on previous studies, Deng and Yip (2016) designed a modified forced-choice experiment, and tested 79 2- to 6-year-olds, together with 20 adults. They found that slightly more Mandarin-speaking adults were found to use the facing strategy in comprehending *qian* 'front' and *hou* 'back', rather than the aligned strategy which is associated with egocentricity, under normal perceptual conditions. However, 3-year-olds (N = 15) used the facing strategy considerably less frequently than 4- to 6-year-olds (N = 23, 25, 9, respectively) and adults (N = 20). Under the [+ Cover] and [+ Motion] perceptual conditions, the same contrast between children younger than 4;0 and older children was found. Under the [+ Motion] condition, the differences in using facing strategy between 3-year-olds and other child groups were significant ($p < .05$, $p < .01$, $p < .01$, respectively). In a word, compared with older children and adults, the 3-year-olds were found to be still under the spell of egocentrism, in line with Li (1988).

Zuo 'left' and *you* 'right' can also be used to test children's choice of frame of reference. Previous studies have shown that these two localizers are difficult to acquire, but few have worked on children's choice of perspectives in using *zuo* 'left' and *you* 'right'. To interpret them, one needs to consider whether the RE has intrinsic orientation. For instance, in example (208a), one only needs to locate the monkey by using one's own field of orientation because the moon *per se* does not have one. In contrast, one could use either his own frame of reference or that of the little sheep to locate the little monkey in interpreting (208b). Can children shift from viewer-centered perspective to the object-centered perspective when the RE has intrinsic orientation as in the case of (208b)? If so, it would be strong evidence for the ability to use other people/entity's field of orientation, or non-egocentricity. Those who can use the RE's frame of reference to understand *zuo* 'left' and *you* 'right' are more decentered than those who always use their own perspective.

(208) a. 猴子在月亮左边。

   House zai yueliang zuo-bian.

   monkey at moon left-side

   'The monkey is to the left of the moon.'

b. 猴子在小羊左边。

   Houzi zai xiao yang zuo-bian.

   monkey at little sheep left-side

   'The monkey is to the left of the little sheep.'

Deng and Yip (2016) found that five- and six-year-olds (N = 18) did not use the object-centered perspective to the same degree as adults in their interpretation of *zuo* 'left' and *you* 'right'. The difference is statistically significant. Children tended to ignore the RE's inherent left and right and rely on their own body as the origin of the reference frame, indicating adherence to egocentrism up to six. Admittedly, there was great individual variation: two out of the three 3-year-olds in this study could shift from the viewer-centered to the object-centered perspective when the RE was featured. They treated featured and featureless entities differently in their choice of frame of reference, suggesting early sensitivity to the object-centered perspective and a fast pace in cognitive development. In other words, some children decenter earlier than others. Furthermore, comparing the age of decentering for *qian* 'front' and *hou* 'back' in Li (1988) and that for *zuo* 'left' and *you* 'right', it is found that cognitive complexity, as in the case of the latter pair in contrast to the former pair, slows down the process of decentering. The child needs to acquire a wide range of semantic structures. They may decenter early with some structures, but take a longer time to decenter with others whose complexity calls for more cognitive resources. Children will finally acquire adult-like interpretations of *zuo* 'left' and *you* 'right' after they overcome egocentrism.

The egocentricity of children could also be tested by studying children's use of spatial deictic pronouns. In using space deixis, the speaker needs to use his own body, or the ego, as point of reference and make distal-proximal distinctions. The deictic system is probably most primitive psychologically in the system of spatial designation (Miller and Johnson-Laird 1976). If Mandarin-speaking children are egocentric, then they may tend to use significantly more deictic pronouns *zher* 'here' and *nar* 'there' than adults. This is confirmed in Deng and Yip's (2015) corpus study, based on the Beijing corpus in the Child Language Data Exchange System (CHILDES) (Tardif 1993, 1996; MacWhinney 2000).

Language bears the imprint of perception and general cognition. Perception cues are argued to influence our choice of reference frames and strategies. There are studies showing children being sensitive to perceptual cues in using spatial expressions. In Richards, Coventry and Clibbens (2004), 80 children from four age groups (means 4;1, 5;5, 6;1, and 7;1) were shown videos in which puppets placing objects with reference to a bowl. When the Figure moved together with the bowl, children tended to use *in the bowl* to describe the spatial relation, but when the Figure moved independently of the bowl and other objects inside the bowl, many of them shifted to use *on/above the bowl*. Similarly, *in the bowl* was used significantly more when the Figure was the same as the other objects in the bowl, compared to the scene where the other objects in the bowl were different from the Figure. In both cases, the spatial relation between the Figure and the RE is the same, but the environmental cues that children perceived affect their conceptualization of the scene and ultimately affect their choice of spatial prepositions *in* and *on/above*. This is evidence that children as young as 4;0 alter their production of spatial prepositions under different perceptual cues.

Cross-linguistically, situations with [+ Cover] or [+ Motion] features are reported to induce people from different linguistic backgrounds to make consistent choice of reference strategies in using *in front of* and *behind* and their translational equivalents. However, few acquisition studies have been done in this domain. To fill the gap, Deng and Yip (2016) attempted to investigate whether Mandarin-speaking children will shift their reference strategies in interpreting *qian* 'front' and *hou* 'back' under the [+ Cover] or [+ Motion] perceptual conditions, and behave the same as adults in Hill (1982) and Guo (2008). Their experiment shows that [+ Cover] perceptual cue induces more uses of the facing strategy in interpreting *qian* 'front' and *hou* 'back' for Mandarin-speaking children and adults, in line with what Hill (1982) and Guo (2008) reported for Hausa, English and Mandarin adult speakers. The results indicate that shared perceptual mechanisms give rise to similar behaviors cross-linguistically in interpreting some spatial terms. However, Deng and Yip (2016) did not confirm Guo's (2008) finding that the [+ Motion] perceptual cue induces more uses of the aligned strategy in adults. The different results of the two studies can be explained by task effect. Instead of pictures, Guo (2008) used verbal description to elicit responses from adult subjects. For instance, adult subjects were asked whether *Zizhuyuan* (a place name in Beijing) was behind or in front of the National Library in Beijing if the subject were to start from Peking University and take a taxi. This method cannot be used on children as it is unlikely that they know the relevant locations of the three places. As there are no perceptual cues from the picture, Guo's method did not effectively test the perceptual condition. Deng and Yip (2016), however, used pictures and videos to provide the perceptual cues, and thus more effectively reveals children and adults' choices of reference strategy under the influence of perceptual cues.

In summary, perceptual cues are found to influence the choice of reference strategies in children and adults. Childhood egocentricity also influences children's choice of frames of reference and reference strategies, especially for young children.

5.2.2 Acquisition sequence of localizers

There is a rich body of literature on the developmental sequence of various spatial expressions cross-linguistically. Bowerman's (1989) cognitive theory is influential in this field. Its main contention is that the semantic organization of language is a reflection of deep-level properties of perception and cognition, and that initial lexical, morphological, and syntactic development is a process of learning to map linguistic forms onto pre-established concepts. This theory predicts universal tendencies in learning spatial expressions because there are such tendencies in the development of spatial cognition. Piaget and Inhelder's (1948) research on the child's conception of space shows that topological relations such as enclosure/containment are conceptualized earlier than projective notions such as axial dimensions of a reference entity. It follows from Bowerman's (1989) theory that the acquisition order of spatial terms should mirror sequence in cognitive development, namely, from topological notions to projective ones.

This prediction is borne out by Windmiller (1976) that showed that the English-acquiring child's understanding of projective prepositions depends on the stage of cognitive development that she is in. Windmiller established the stage of cognitive development by carrying out a non-linguistic cognitive task on 24 children, and then used an act-out task to find out the spatial prepositions that they could understand. Based on their scores in the cognitive task, subjects were assigned to five stages with mean ages 2;11, 3;6, 4;5, 5;9, and 7;1. Only subjects of the last stage fully understood projective prepositions such as *in front of* and *behind*, when the reference entity did not have inherent front and back. The prediction that follows from the cognitive theory is also confirmed by other empirical studies showing the same sequence in the emergence of spatial expressions across languages. Johnston and Slobin (1979) found that locative markers are acquired in an order that is remarkably consistent in English, Italian, Serbo-Croatian and Turkish. They tested for each language 48 children aged between 2;0 and 4;8 with the elicited production task. A general acquisition order, determined by conceptual complexity, was identified: (1) *in*, *on*, *under*, and *beside*, (2) *between*, *back* and *front* with featured objects, (3) *back* and *front* with non-featured objects. Topological notions of containment, support and occlusion predict early acquisition of *in*, *on* and *under*, while projective *front* and *back* are acquired later. Bowerman, de Leon, and Choi (1995) collected spontaneous data from English, Korean and Tzotzil children (age range 1;2 - 3;0) and elicited production data from English, Dutch, Korean and Tzotzil (age range 2;0 - 3;5). They spotted a common tendency—words for the topological spatial relations 'separating' and 'joining' are prominent in early vocabularies. In sum, as reviewed in Bowerman (1996), there is a cross-linguistic tendency for children to first produce words for topological notions of containment ('in'), support ('on'), and occlusion ('under'). Next come words expressing proximity ('beside'), and words conveying projective order ('front') appear later.

Relative cognitive simplicity of topological relationship compared with projective relationship determines the acquisition sequence of topological expressions preceding the projective ones. But how can we measure the cognitive simplicity within topological expressions or within projective ones? Due to its abstract nature, however, cognitive complexity is not easily calculated. H. Clark's (1973) Complexity Hypothesis makes it concrete and turns the cognitive theory into a potentially falsifiable scientific hypothesis. The Complexity Hypothesis is built on the Semantic Feature Hypothesis proposed by Clark (1973) which assumes that children use the unmarked member of a pair of antonyms to cover the meaning of both terms. Bearing on the acquisition of spatial terms, H. Clark's (1973) Complexity Hypothesis states that in antonymous pairs of spatial terms, the positive member should be acquired before the negative member. 'Within the field of vision' is positive and 'not within the field of vision' is negative. For instance, *in front of* is positive, while *behind* or *in back of* is negative; *up* is positive and *down* negative. The hypothesis predicts the semantically simpler term in an antonymic pair being acquired earlier than the other. For instance, in the pair of *on top of* and *underneath*, the positive preposition *on top of* was comprehended by more children than the negative *underneath* as reviewed in H. Clark (1973).

In English, *the side* is different from *beside* in being defined negatively as not being *front* or *back* (see H. Clark 1973). Therefore, *the side* is cognitively more complex than *front* and *back*, and is predicted to be acquired later. By testing 45 children aged between 2;6 and 4;1 with five different tasks, Kuczaj and Maratsos (1975) found that *the side* is indeed acquired later than *front* and *back*. In a typical trial, the subject was asked to place an object in front of, in back of, and at the side of his body or an object with or without an inherent front. For children aged between 3;6 and 4;1, they could put things correctly in front/back of themselves 100% of the time, but they could only place things correctly at their sides 77% of the time. The number of subjects that were found to know the front and back of their own body and fronted objects is 35 whereas the number of those that knew the side of their own body and the sides of fronted objects is 17. The data point to the difficulty in understanding *the side* compared with *front* and *back*, supporting H. Clark's (1973) hypothesis that *the side* is cognitively more involved than *front* or *back*. Congruent with Kuczaj and Maratsos' (1975) findings, Li (1988) found that 80% of his subjects aged between 2;8 and 2;11 could differentiate the front and back of objects when asked to point out a certain side of an object, but none of them could point out which side is *pang-bian* 'side'. *Pang-bian* was acquired late, as only 75% of his subjects aged between 3;4 and 3;6 could identify the sides.

There is another pair of Ls in Chinese through which one may find the effect of cognitive complexity on linguistic development: *zuo-bian/you-bian* 'left/right' vs. *pang-bian* 'side'. *Zuo* and *you* are more cognitively involved than *pang-bian*. They break the semantic field of *pang-bian* into two symmetrical parts. Which part is called *zuo* 'left' and which is *you* 'right' are arbitrary conventions. As reviewed in Miller and Johnson-Laird (1976, 397 - 398), children cannot identify their own right and left hands until the age of five, they cannot use the terms correctly with respect to a person facing them until 7;0 or 8;0, and even many adults have trouble with *right* and *left*. The late acquisition of *right* and *left* was echoed in the study of Zhang, Ding, and Lin (1987) on Chinese children from 2 to 6, with 10 to 12 subjects in each age group.[①] An act-out comprehension task and an elicited production task revealed that no 2- or 3-year-olds comprehended or produced *zuo* 'left' and *you* 'right'. Only 30 to 40% of 4-year-olds were able to do so. At 6 years of age, 75% of children

---

[①] The experiment was carried out in Fuzhou, a southern city in China. The authors did not mention if the subjects spoke Mandarin or other dialects.

comprehended *zuo* 'left' and *you* 'right' and 83% of them could correctly produce them. The finding clearly shows that Chinese children do not develop a steady understanding of *zuo* 'left' and *you* 'right' until 6. The concepts of left and right are more complex than the side, therefore *left* and *right* are acquired even later than *the side*.

Besides cognitive complexity, other factors may also play a role in initial spatial language development. Slobin (1973) reviewed cases where formal complexity in a specific language overrides semantic or cognitive complexity, giving rise to exceptions to the universal course in acquiring spatial terms. For instance, two Serbo-Croatian-Hungarian bilingual girls at 2;0 productively used Hungarian case endings on nouns indicating 'into', 'out of', 'onto' and 'on top of', but they had barely begun to use Serbo-Croatian locative expressions which have greater formal complexity. The relative formal complexity of Serbo-Croatian locative expressions, in comparison to Hungarian ones, is reflected in two aspects: in Hungarian, the locative marker is bound to the noun, and the choice of formal markers is semantically consistent, while in Serbo-Croatian the locative marker is divided between preposition and inflection, and the choice of these markers is less principled and orderly. Slobin (1973) argued that the two bilingual children had acquired the relevant notions as they could express them in Hungarian, but the formal complexity of the corresponding expressions in Serbo-Croatian slowed down their acquisition. The effect of formal complexity is also evident in Sinha et al. (1994). They analyzed the longitudinal data from two Danish children (age range 1;1 - 2;8), and found that in Danish, the first acquired particles were from the main group, and the subgroup particles derived from the main group through prefixation, suffixation, or both, were acquired later. In Johnston and Slobin's (1979) experiment, the factor of lexical diversity, or the existence of competing forms of the same notion, also decelerates acquisition rate.

Another factor in spatial language acquisition is the language-specific properties of the language being acquired. Korean, English, and Tzotzil children encode Path differently, as the ambient languages have different ways to express Path. Choi and Bowerman (1991) examined longitudinal data from two English-speaking girls and eight Korean children aged from 1;2 to around 2;0. They found that English- and Korean-speaking children under 2; 0 produced Path expressions that were most typical in their language. By about 20 months English-speaking children combined Path particles, e.g. *out*, *up*, and *down*, productively with verbs. Korean children made an adult-like distinction between spontaneous and caused motion at the very beginning. They used transitive Path verbs only for caused motion and never overgeneralized them to spontaneous motion. Children learning Korean encounter the notion of Path mostly conflated with spontaneous and caused Motion, and often with specific properties of Figure or Ground, so they were late in acquiring 'pure' Path markers. An obvious effect of exposure to typologically different languages was also found in Bowerman, de Leon, and Choi (1995). English-speaking children prefer Path particles while Tzotzil-speaking children opt for Path verbs because Tzotzil has Path verbs, in addition to Path particles. In a word, the properties of the ambient language, or the input properties, play a significant role in spatial language development.

There seem to be exceptions to the universal acquisition order of spatial terms, which calls Bowerman (1989) and Johnston and Slobin (1979) into question. Based on a study showing different acquisition orders across languages, and great individual difference within a language, Sinha et al. (1994) claimed that the divergence was attributed to the interaction between cognitive and linguistic complexities, mediated by input frequency. In Sinha et al. (1994), the two Danish children, recorded fortnightly from 1;1 to 2;8, were found to acquire *op* 'up' and *ned* 'down' earlier than *i* 'in' and *på* 'on', while previous studies report that *i* 'in' and *på* 'on' are the first acquired in Scandinavian languages.

There are also individual differences between the two Danish children: e. g. the girl acquired *af* 'off', her second locative particle, at 1;2, but the boy acquired it at 1;10 as his fifth locative particle. The explanation of the divergence based on linguistic complexity and input frequency in Sinha et al. 's (1994), however, is not satisfactory, as *i* 'in' and *på* 'on' are not more complex than *op* 'up' and *ned* 'down' in form, and frequencies of the locative particles in child-directed speech have not been analyzed in their study. The factors of formal complexity and input need to be carefully examined to account for the individual differences within a language and the cross-linguistic variation.

Spatial language acquisition is an important domain to provide empirical evidence for the dependence of linguistic on cognitive development. In studying languages such as English and Danish, however, any statement about the relationship between linguistic and cognitive development may be confounded by formal complexity. For instance, the English preposition *in* is acquired before *in front of*, but it is difficult to determine if it is because *front* is cognitively more complex than *in*, or because *in front of* is more complex than *in* in form. Mandarin localizers, on the other hand, are equal in formal complexity. Each localizer that encodes a spatial notion is monosyllabic, and may have a few disyllabic derived variants. However, there is no derivational relationship between each monosyllabic localizer. All the monosyllabic localizers share the same morphological complexity and the same is true for disyllabic ones. In this regard, Mandarin will be an ideal test ground for the investigation of the relations between cognitive development and language acquisition, as the factor of formal complexity is controlled.

Studies on Mandarin-speaking children in 1980s and 1990s confirmed some predictions of the complexity hypothesis proposed by H. Clark (1973): *li* 'inside' is acquired before *qian/hou* 'front/back', and *pangbian* 'side' follows *qian/hou* 'front/back' (reviewed in Lee 1996).

However, there is conflicting evidence for some of these predictions. Based on a case study, Jia (2010) found that the 'negative' term *hou* 'back' was acquired earlier than its 'positive' counterpart *qian* 'front'. Her finding was not supported by Zhou and Wang (2001) who identified the opposite acquisition sequence. In other words, there are conflicting results with respect to the complexity hypothesis.

Despite some minor differences, we found a similar acquisition sequence in four recent studies on Mandarin-speaking children as summarized in (209), the first three being corpus studies and the last one an experimental study. In (209), the monosyllabic localizer stands for itself and its disyllabic derived forms, ' > ' stands for 'be acquired earlier than', and the comma between localizers means that they are acquired around the same time. All the acquisition sequences have something in common: *li* 'inside' is acquired earlier than *shang* 'top' and *xia* 'bottom', which in turn are acquired earlier than *qian* 'front' and *hou* 'back'; moreover, *pang* 'side' is acquired earlier than *zuo* 'left' and *you* 'right'.

(209) a. li > shang > wai > xia > qian > hou

         (Zhou and Wang 2001, 122 – 123, 130)

  b. li, shang > wai, xia > qian, hou > zhong, pang > zuo, you

         (Kong and Wang 2002)

  c. li > shang > xia > hou > zhong > qian > wai > pang > zuo, you

         (Jia 2010)

  d. li > shang, xia > wai > zhongjian > qian, hou > pang > zuo, you

         (J. Zhang, Ding, and Lin 1987)

However, these studies generally do not look systematically into adult input. Without ruling out the possibility of input effects, one cannot safely draw the conclusion that the acquisition order of spatial expressions is determined by cognitive complexity. Deng and Yip (2016) is a serious attempt to examine the distribution of localizers in adult input to determine whether children's use of localizers is modeled after adults or follows an inherent maturation path constrained by their cognitive development. They conducted a corpus study to examine naturalistic speech from Mandarin-speaking children in the Beijing corpus in CHILDES (Tardif 1993, 1996). The corpus contains 50 sessions of longitudinal data from 10 children recorded in their homes. There are generally five sessions for each child with one month interval between each session, starting from around 1;9 and ending around 2;2. Children sampled in the Beijing corpus are representative of Mandarin-speaking children at the same age range in general (J. Chen 2008). Previous studies used age of first occurrence to determine the acquisition order (see Jia 2010; Zhou and Wang 2001; Kong and Wang 2002). Deng and Yip (2016) did not use this method, because the sample size for each child in the Beijing corpus was not large enough to determine the time of first emergence of each localizer. There are only four to six recordings for each child with one month interval between each session. Within one month, the child may have acquired some localizers successively, but the data may suggest that these localizers have emerged simultaneously in one session. It is also possible that a localizer may have emerged in the child's repertoire, but is absent in the limited recordings. Therefore, Deng and Yip (2016) counted the relative frequency of various localizers in children's corpus data. They counted the relative frequency of localizers in two ways. First, the total number of tokens of a particular localizer in the utterances produced by all the children is calculated. Second, the number of children that used a given localizer is counted. Sinha et al. (1994) assumed that an item used with a high frequency is acquired earlier than an item that occurs with low frequency. By extension, the greater the aggregate usage of a given localizer among the children, the earlier the acquisition of that localizer. Based on the total frequencies and the number of children that produced a given localizer, a frequency order is derived as shown in (11) where the number in the brackets is number of children that produced at least one token of the localizer.

(210) li(7), wai(7) > shang(6), xia(6) > hou(3), qian(3) > you (2) > pang(1) > zuo(0), zhong(0)

(Deng and Yip 2016)

The frequency order corresponds well with the acquisition orders reported in previous studies on Chinese-speaking children based on age of first occurrence shown above, whereby *li* 'inside' emerges earlier than *shang* 'top' and *xia* 'bottom', followed by *qian* 'front' and *hou* 'back', and *pang* 'side', *zuo* 'left', and *you* 'right' emerge late. The sequence of acquisition is consistent with that reported for other languages: first acquired are words for topological notions of containment (*in*), support (*on*), and occlusion (*under*), while words conveying projective order (*front*) appear later (see Johnston and Slobin 1979; Bowerman 1996). The acquisition order seems to be constrained by cognitive development: topological notions are less cognitively complex than projective ones, and thus acquired earlier (Windmiller 1976; Johnston and Slobin 1979; Bowerman et al. 1995). Deng and Yip (2016), however, took into account the factor of adult input, and found that the frequencies of localizers in child utterances generally match those in adult input. For instance, the localizer *li* 'inside' was used most frequently by both children and adults; children used fewer tokens of *qian* 'front' and *hou* 'back' than *li* 'inside', *shang* 'top' and *xia* 'bottom', just as adults did. It is hard to determine whether the acquisition sequence is determined by cognitive complexity, input frequency, or both. Nonetheless, children used *wai* 'outside' more frequently than adults (25% vs. 9%), and *shang* 'top' less frequently (12% vs. 28%). The mismatches between child production and adult input suggest that input alone cannot explain the acquisition order of some localizers.

To sum up, Mandarin-speaking children's localizers are shown to follow a similar sequence of emergence to that for English-speaking children's spatial prepositions. Cognitive complexity of the relevant notions may explain the cross-linguistic uniformity in the acquisition sequence. Input seems to interact with cognition in the acquisition of some Mandarin localizers, but cannot account for the acquisition sequence of some others.

5.2.3　Early awareness to Figure-Ground asymmetry

As introduced in Section 5.1, the Figure-Ground asymmetry is found in English and Mandarin (Miller and Johnson-Laird 1976; Talmy 1983; Liu 1994). There is experimental evidence of its effect on perception, and linguistic judgments of semantic naturalness for English adults and children (reviewed in Landau and Jackendoff 1993). It is natural to infer that the Figure-Ground asymmetry is a language universal given by the shared cognitive constraint of the human species. If this is the case, we expect Mandarin-speaking children to demonstrate this knowledge at an early age.

The expectation is borne out by Deng and Yip (2016) which investigated Mandarin-speaking children's sensitivity to this asymmetry. Their experiment on 77 children aged between 2 to 6 shows that knowledge of the Figure-Ground asymmetry enables 3-year-olds to accept Figure in the subject position and Ground in the object position, rather than the other way around. We take this as evidence that the Figure-Ground asymmetry is a language universal given by human beings' shared cognitive mechanism.

5.2.4　Summary

The connection between language universals and child language acquisition has been drawn since Jakobson (1968). Structures that are frequently found across languages turn to appear early in child language development. This section reviews two such language universals. 3-year-olds in Deng and Yip (2016) rejected sentences that violate the Figure-Ground asymmetry, lending support to the asymmetry being a language universal given by human beings' shared cognitive mechanism. In addition, Deng and Yip (2016) found that young children used more facing strategy in interpreting *qian* 'front' and *hou* 'back' under the [+ Cover] perceptual condition, just like adults, in line with Hausa, English and Mandarin adult speakers in Hill (1982) and Guo (2008), suggesting that shared perceptual mechanisms give rise to the same choice of reference strategy cross-linguistically in interpreting spatial terms.

Findings from Mandarin-speaking children show that the development of cognition plays a significant role in their language development. Mandarin-speaking children's localizers are reported to follow a similar sequence of emergence to that of English-speaking children's spatial prepositions. In interaction with input frequency, cognitive complexity predicts Mandarin children's acquisition sequence of localizers. A second case showing cognitive influence is the effect of egocentricity on the ways in which children use localizers. It requires considerable cognitive ability for the child to shift away from the egocentric perspective, as children up to 6; 0 generally ignore the RE's inherent left and right and rely on the viewer-centered reference frame in interpreting *zuo* 'left' and *you* 'right'.

Chapter 6 Beyond the Domain of Spatial Language

This study is a systematic exploration of the semantic domain of space. We have examined the syntax and semantics of Mandarin spatial expressions in comparison with other languages and dialects through the perspective of event semantics. The previous chapters discuss the linguistic encoding of space in Mandarin, especially the ambiguities of Mandarin *zai*-PPs, distribution of *zai*-PPs, the aspectual properties of the Mandarin locative subject construction, and the role of perception and cognition in spatial language. We have shown that the distribution and interpretation of spatial expressions hinge on verbs, and fundamentally, the types and structures of the events that the verbs encode. In addition, we have investigated spatial expressions in the larger context of the general cognitive system, including perception. In this sense, the current study goes beyond the domain of spatial expressions. In sections 6.1 and 6.2, we discuss the major theoretical contribution of the present study. The last section summarizes the other contributions.

6.1 The application of event semantics to the study of spatial encoding in Mandarin

The major theoretical contribution of the current study lies in demonstrating the explanatory power of event semantics in the domain of spatial language. In particular, it explains as well as describes a wide range of data in Mandarin spatial language. The word order and interpretation of the spatial PPs headed by zai '(be) at', and the locative subject construction in Mandarin seem to be two different linguistic phenomena, yet the theory of event semantics enables us to provide a unified account of them.

The first event-semantic principle that we identified is (sub)event modification. 'Event' refers to a particular type of entities that figure in the denotations of verbs. The interpretation of spatial PPs offers a view of the psychological reality of events. Spatial PPs do not modify any particular participant in an event, but the event *per se* (Davidson 1967; Parsons 1990). In Mandarin, all preverbal zai-PPs are potentially ambiguous when they precede transitive verbs: as modifiers of the event, they could be associated with either of the event participants—Agent or Theme. Moreover, the directional reading of spatial PPs can be attributed to the complex event structure of the verb. In the event structure of a complex event, there is a process subevent and a result state subevent. When the result state subevent is modified by zai-PPs, the change-of-state or directional reading arises, but when the process subevent is modified by zai-PPs, the sentence receives a locational reading. Without the notion of event, event structure and (sub)event modification, the semantics of zai-PPs cannot be adequately explained.

Mandarin demonstrates Location-V and V-Goal word order regularity. However, there are exceptions to the otherwise systematic semantics-to-syntax mappings: the posture V-Location and Goal-placement V structures. The irregularity can be explained by subevent modification. Posture verbs and manner-of-motion verbs can occur with postverbal zai-PPs without a result-location meaning, as in their event structure, there is no result state for the zai-PP to modify. Placement verbs can take preverbal zai-PPs to express Goal, as in their event structure there is a result subevent and the *zai*-PP can modify the result state.

The second semantic principle is aspect shift. Verbs belong to a default event type, but can undergo aspect shift and behave as verbs belonging to another event type (Fong 1997; Rothstein 2004). Aspect shift is possible between some event types because they have overlap in their event structures (see Pustejovsky 1995). A crucial piece of evidence for aspect shift is that the 'posture verb-*zai*' construction can express the result location of a direction. The posture verb is normally state verb, and its cooccurring *zai*-PP is unbounded, not able to turn the eventuality into a telic one. The directional/result-location reading arises because the posture verb undergoes aspect shift from State, its default event type, to Achievement, the derived one. The two-argument locative subject construction presents a dynamic state or a result state. However, some activity verbs, for instance, manner-of-motion verbs, occur in this construction, because they can shift into States in the presence of the durative aspect marker *-zhe*. Moreover, the perfective aspect marker *-le* triggers verbs with complex event structure to shift into result state verbs, and the corresponding locative subject sentence with *-le* presents a result state.

Besides the semantics of V-*zai* and locative subject constructions, event semantics also describes or explains syntactic constraints on them. The taxonomy of verbs or verb phrases can be based on their event structures; using these criteria, verbs are categorized into at least four different event types—State, Activity, Accomplishment and Achievement (Dowty 1979; Smith 1997; Rothstein 2004). The event type of a verb determines whether or not it can occur in a V-*zai* construction or a two-argument locative subject construction. Only verbs that have a dynamic State or result state component in their event structures can take postverbal *zai*-PPs or appear in a two-argument locative subject construction. Two-argument locative subject sentences present a dynamic state or a result state that is relevant to the speech time or the reference time. States, Accomplishments and Achievements can enter into this construction, because they have a state component in their event structure. The Agent of a transitive verb is associated with a causing activity, so it does not occur in this construction. Unergative verbs such as *xiao* 'laugh' are not allowed in two-argument locative subject sentences because their only argument is an Agent. Transitive verbs must have their Agent dethematized to occur in this construction.

6.2 A better understanding of linguistic space from the perspective of perception and cognition

In this book, three distinct kinds of space have been distinguished: space as it is, space as humans perceive it (P-space) and space as encoded by human language (L-space). Our knowledge of space is constrained by what we are able to ascertain through our perception, so this book has nothing to say about space outside of the realm of the human mind. Linguistic encoding of space (L-space) is greatly influenced by perception and cognition: people's choice of reference strategies is biased by perceptual cues; they tend to conceive small, movable things as the Figure, and large, immovable things as the reference entity-this is also the tendency in expressing such spatial relationships verbally; real world knowledge in our long-term memory can help to disambiguate preverbal *zai*-PPs, and explain the ungrammaticality of some V-*zai* structures and locative subject sentences.

However, L-space has properties that cannot be explained by perception and cognition. Even though our species share similar, if not identical, perceptual ability, languages differ in the linguistic encoding of space. L-space has its unique properties in contrast to perception and cognition. For instance, Mandarin does not have the English-type ambiguities in the adjunction site of prepositional phrases (PPs) in V-DP-PP sequences. P-space is unambiguous, but L-space has some notable, structured ambiguities. The present study has identified at least four such ambiguities: ambiguity caused by choice of reference frames; ambiguity resulting from adjunction sites of spatial modifiers; ambiguity caused by aspect shift of the verb that a spatial modifier accompanies; and ambiguity caused by free associations between the spatial modifier and the subevents. A number of clarifying factors help to constrain these ambiguities, however, including syntactic, semantic, and cognitive principles, contextual cues, and real world knowledge. The unique properties of L-space, in contrast to P-space, suggest that the linguistic system is an autonomous subsystem of cognition (see Landau and Lakusta 2006).

6.3 Other contributions

While the main part of the book uses notions of event, (sub)event modification and aspect shift to explain the syntax and semantics of spatial PPs and locative subject sentences, we are also concerned with other aspects of L-space in Mandarin.

Spatial relations are encoded by three categories in Mandarin. There are differences between Mandarin and English in each of the three categories: Mandarin locative verbs do not require obligatory presence of Location; most Mandarin spatial Ps demonstrate both prepositional and verbal properties as a result of grammaticalization; and Mandarin localizers (Ls), the counterpart of English Axial Part expressions, occur after DPs that refer to reference entities.

Mandarin Ls provide axial part or topological information about the RE. An L follows a RE-denoting DP and converts it into an LP. The LP can function as the object of a spatial P, yielding an adjunct. It could also be an argument occupying the subject and direct object positions in the sentence. As to locative subjects, in addition to two-argument locative subject sentences (LSSs), we also discussed one-argument ones whose predicates are adjectives or stative verbs encoding static States or result states. The two-argument LSSs are derived from the interaction between thematic hierarchy and information structure. Mandarin and English LPs or AxPartPs can serve as the locative subject whereas PPs serve as the locative topic. English locative topics subsume a broad range of spatial relations, including Locations, Source, and Goal. However, we found that Goal phrases headed by *dao* 'to' cannot be used as locative topics in Mandarin. Different from English, the semantic primitives Location and Goal can be realized as direct objects in Mandarin. Locative objects should be differentiated from space-related non-canonical objects. Nevertheless, both types of objects are assigned undifferentiated Case by preceding verbs and get licensed. We showed that the locative objects are not the result of ellipsis from postverbal spatial PPs.

A thorough understanding of various aspects of L-space in Mandarin enables researchers to gain insight into language specificity, and language universals underlying superficial variation. The potential language universals discussed in this study include aspect shift of the verb (Fong 1997; Smith 1997; Rothstein 2004), spatial PPs as event modifiers (Parsons 1990), and knowledge of the Figure-Ground asymmetry (Miller and Johnson-Laird 1976; Talmy 1983; Jackendoff 1996a). However, we also identified some language-specific properties and complexities of Mandarin: some common nouns have inherent locative meaning, place names cannot be followed by the localizer *li* 'inside', limited classes of verbs can be followed by *zai* '(be) at', and there is a division of labor between *zai* '(be) at' and *dao* 'reach, to' in the postverbal position.

Besides theoretical analysis, this book also associates child language acquisition with the research of spatial language. On the one hand, a theoretical perspective helps to shed light on superficially messy child data and single out an underlying pattern. Firstly, the LP-formation rule and the division of labor between *zai* '(be) at' and *dao* 'reach, to' in postverbal position pose problems for preschool children, as they embody language-specific complexities of Mandarin. There is no universal principle to accommodate each in an across-the-board manner. Instead, learning the syntax and semantics of each noun and verb through experience is an indispensable part of acquiring these rules and structures. Thus children have not fully grasped the LP-formation rule and the division of labor between *zai* and *dao* by 6 years of age. Secondly, it requires considerable cognitive ability for the child to escape from the egocentric space. Therefore, children younger than 4; 0 used the aligned reference strategy more than adults in interpreting *qian* 'front' and *hou* 'back', and children up to 6; 0 generally ignore the RE's inherent left and right and rely on the viewer-centered reference frame in interpreting *zuo* 'left' and *you* 'right', suggesting childhood egocentrism. On the other hand, empirical evidence from child language lends support to a theoretical contention. For instance, children as young as 3; 0 accept Figure in the subject position and Ground in the object position, rather than the other way around, supporting the Figure-Ground asymmetry as a language universal.

To conclude, the core issues addressed in this book include the ways in which spatial notions are expressed in Mandarin in comparison with other languages. We have discussed ambiguities in L-space, word order and interpretation of spatial phrases headed by *zai* '(be) at', and syntax and semantics of locative subjects and locative objects, mainly from the perspective of event semantics. This theoretical perspective enables us to explain the semantics of *zai*-PPs, the constraints on verbs that can take postverbal *zai*-PPs, and the restriction on verbs that occur in the locative subject construction. We expect to see more research on Mandarin spatial language, and the application of event semantic theories to other fields in Chinese linguistics in the future.

References

Afarli, Tor A. and Fufen Jin. 2010. The syntax of presentative sentences in Norwegian and Mandarin Chinese: Toward a comparative analysis? In *Chinese Matters: From Grammar to First and Second Language Acquisition*, eds. Chris Wilder and Tor A. Åfarli, 111 – 130. Trondheim: Tapir Academic Press.

Alferink, Inge and Marianne Gullberg. 2014. French-Dutch bilinguals do not maintain obligatory semantic distinctions: Evidence from placement verbs. *Bilingualism: Language and Cognition* 17: 22 – 37.

Ashcraft, Mark H. 2006. *Cognition* (4th ed.). Upper Saddle River, NJ: Pearson Prentice Hall.

Bach, Emmon. 1986. The algebra of events. *Linguistics and Philosophy* 9: 5 – 16.

Baker, Mark C. 1988. *Incorporation: A Theory of Grammatical Function Changing*. Chicago: University of Chicago Press.

Barrie, Michael and Yen-hui Audrey Li. 2012. Noun incorporation and non-canonical objects. Paper presented at WCCFL 30.

Bierwisch, Manfred. 1996. How much space gets into language? In *Language and Space*, eds. Paul Bloom, Mary A. Peterson, Lynn Nadel and Merrill F. Garrett, 31 – 76. Cambridge, MA: The MIT Press.

Bowerman, Melissa. 1996. Learning how to structure space for language: A crosslinguistic perspective. In *Language and Space*, eds. Paul Bloom, Mary A. Peterson, Lynn Nadel, and Merrill F. Garrett, 385 –

436. Cambridge, MA: The MIT Press.

——. 1989. Learning a semantic system: What role do cognitive predispositions play? In *The Teachability of Language*, eds. Richard L. Schiefelbusch and Mabel L. Rice. Paul H. Brookes Publishing Co. (reprinted in Paul Bloom, ed. 1994. *Language Acquisition: Core Readings*, 329 – 363. The MIT Press).

Bowerman, Melissa, Lourdes de Leon, and Soonja Choi. 1995. Verbs, particles, and spatial semantics: Learning to talk about spatial actions in typologically different languages. In *The Proccedings of the 27th Annual Child Language Research Forum*, ed. Eve Clark, 101 – 110. Stanford CA: Center Study Language & Information.

Bresnan, Joan. 1994. Locative inversion and the architecture of universal grammar. *Language* 70 (1): 72 – 131.

Bresnan, Joan and Jonni M. Kanerva. 1992. The thematic hierarchy and locative inversion in UG: A reply to Paul Schachter's comments. In *Syntax and Semantics* 26: *Syntax and the Lexicon*, eds. Timothy Stowell and Eric Wehrli, 111 – 125. New York: Academic Press.

Brown, Roger William. 1973. *A First Language: The Early Stages*. Cambridge, MA: Harvard University Press.

Carlson, Greg N. 1977. A unified analysis of the English bare plural. *Linguistics and Philosophy* 1: 413 – 57.

Chao, Yuen Ren. 1968/2004. *A Grammar of Spoken Chinese*. Berkeley: University of California Press. Reprinted in *Chao Yuan Ren Quenji (Di San Juan)* [The collected works of Chao Yuen Ren (Vol. 3)]. Beijing: The Commercial Press.

Chappell, Hillary and Alain Peyraube. 2008. Chinese localizers: Diachrony and some typological considerations. In *Space in Languages of China: Cross-linguistic, Synchronic and Diachronic Perspectives*, ed. Dan Xu, 15 – 37. New York: Springer.

Chen, Changlai. 2002. *Jieci yu Jieyin Gongneng* [Prepositions and the introductory function]. Hefei: Anhui Jiaoyu Chubanshe.

Chen, Chung-yu. 1978. Aspectual features of the verb and the relative position of the locatives. *Journal of Chinese linguistics* 6: 76 – 103.

Chen, Fanfan. 2008. The expression of spatial relationship of entities in Chinese as a second language and its development. *Shijie Hanyu Jiaoxue* [Chinese teaching in the world] 3: 114 – 124.

Chen, Jidong. 2008. *The Acquisition of Verb Compounding in Mandarin*. Doctoral dissertation, Max Planck Institute for Psycholinguistics and Free University Amsterdam, the Netherlands.

Cheung, Sik Lee. 1991. *The Acquisition of Locative Constructions by Cantonese Children*. Doctoral dissertation, Stanford University.

Choi, Soonja and Melissa Bowerman. 1991. Learning to express motion events in English and Korean: The influence of language-specific lexicalization patterns. *Cognition* 41: 83 – 121.

Chomsky, Noam. 1981. *Lectures on Government and Binding*. Dordrecht: Foris.

Chu, Zexiang. 2004. Hanyu 'zai + fangwei duanyu' li fangweici de yinxian jizhi [The presence or omission mechanism of the localizer in the 'zai + localizer phrase' structure in Chinese]. *Zhongguo Yuwen* [Studies of the Chinese language] 2: 112 – 122.

——. 1996. 'Zai' de hangaiyi yu jushou chusuo qian 'zai' de yinxian [The semantics of zai and its presence or absence in the sentence-initial position]. *Hanyu Xuexi* [Chinese study] 4: 33 – 6.

Cinque, Guglielmo. 2010. Mapping spatial PPs: An introduction. In *Mapping Spatial PPs: The Cartography of Syntactic Structures (Vol. 6)*, eds. Guglielmo Cinque and Luigi Rizzi, 3 – 25. Oxford, New York: Oxford University Press.

Clark, Eve V. 1973. What's in a word? On the child's acquisition of semantics in his first language. In *Cognitive Development and the Acquisition of Language*, ed. Timothy E. Moore, 65 – 110. New York;

London: Academic Press.

Clark, Eve V. and Kathie L. Carpenter. 1989. The notion of source in language acquisition. *Language* 65 (1) (reprinted in Paul Bloom. ed. 1994. *Language Acquisition: Core Readings*, 251 – 284. The MIT Press).

Clark, Herbert H. 1973. Space, time, semantics, and the child. In *Cognitive Development and the Acquisition of Language*, ed. Timothy E. Moore, 27 – 63. New York; London: Academic Press.

Davidson, Donald. 1967. The logical form of action sentences. In *The Logic of Decision and Action*, ed. Nicholas Rescher, 81 – 95. Pittsburgh: University of Pittsburgh Press.

Demuth, Katherine, Malillo Machobane and Francina Moloi. 2003. Rules and construction effects in learning the argument structure of verbs. *Journal of Child Language* 30: 797 – 821.

Deng, Xiangjun. 2014. *Space, Events and Language Acquisition in Mandarin*. Doctoral dissertation, the Chinese University of Hong Kong.

——. 2011. Chusuo jieci duanyu yuxu de lishi yanhua [Diachronic change of the word order of spatial prepositional phrases]. Ms. The Chinese University of Hong Kong.

——. 2010. *The Acquisition of the Resultative Verb Compound in Mandarin Chinese*. MPhil. thesis, the Chinese University of Hong Kong.

Deng, Xiangjun and Virginia Yip. 2016. Cognition and perception in the linguistic encoding of space in child Mandarin. *Journal of Chinese Linguistics* 44(2): 287 – 325.

——. 2015. The linguistic encoding of space in child Mandarin: A corpus-based study. *Linguistics* 53(5): 1079 – 1112.

Dikken, Marcel den. 2010. On the functional structure of locative and directional PPs. In *Mapping Spatial PPs: The Cartography of Syntactic structures (Vol. 6)*, eds. Guglielmo Cinque and Luigi Rizzi, 74 – 126. Oxford, New York: Oxford University Press.

Ding, Shengshu et al. 1961. *Xiandai Hanyu Yufa Jianghua* [Talks on modern Chinese grammar]. Beijing: The Commercial Press.

Djamouri, Redouane, Paul Waltraud and John Whitman. 2013. Postpositions vs. prepositions in Mandarin Chinese: The articulation of disharmony. In *Theoretical Approaches to Disharmonic Word Orders*, eds. Theresa Biberauer and Michelle Sheehan, 74 – 115. Oxford: Oxford University Press.

Dowty, David. 1979. *Word Meaning and Montague Grammar: The Semantics of Verbs and Times in Generative Semantics and in Montague's PTQ*. Dordrecht: D. Reidel.

Erbaugh, Mary S. 1982. *Coming to Order: Natural Selection and the Origin of Syntax in the Mandarin-speaking Child*. Doctoral dissertation, University of California, Berkeley.

Ernst, Thomas. 1988. Chinese postpositions? -Again. *Journal of Chinese Linguistics* 16 (2): 219 – 245.

Fan, Jiyan. 1982. Lun jieci duanyu 'zai + chusuo' [On preposition phrase 'zai + location']. *Yuyan Yanjiu* [Language research] 2: 71 – 86.

Fan, Xiao, ed. 1998. *Hanyu de Juzi Leixing* [The sentence types in Chinese]. Taiyuan: Shuhai Chubanshe.

Fang, Jingmin. 2004. Xiandai hanyu fangwei chengfen de fenhua he yufahua [Differentiation and grammaticalization of locative terms in modern Chinese]. *Shijie Hanyu Jiaoxue* [Chinese teaching in the world] 2: 5 – 15.

Feng, Shengli. 2008. Yunlü yufa lilun yu hanyu cifa he jufa yanjiu [The theory of prosodic grammar and the research of Chinese morphology and syntax]. In *Dangdai Yuyanxue Lilun he Hanyu Yanjiu* [Contemporary linguistic theory and Chinese research], eds. Yang Shen and Shengli Feng, 83 –95. Beijing: The Commercial Press.

——. 2003. Prosodically constrained postverbal PPs in Mandarin Chinese.

Linguistics 41 (6): 1085–1122.

Fong, Vivienne. 1997. *The Order of Things: What Directional Locatives Denote*. Doctoral dissertation, Stanford University.

Gass, Susan M. 2003. Input and interaction. In *The Handbook of Second Language Acquisition*, eds. Catherine Doughty and Michael H. Long, 224–255. Malden, MA: Blackwell Pub.

Goodluck, Helen. 1991/2000. *Language Acquisition: A Linguistic Introduction*. Oxford; Cambridge, MA: B. Blackwell; Beijing: Foreign Language Teaching and Research Press.

Grimshaw, Jane B. 1990. *Argument Structure*. Cambridge, MA; London: The MIT Press.

Gruber, Jeffrey. 1965. *Studies in Lexical Relations*. Doctoral dissertation, MIT.

Guo, Rui. 2008. Kongjian canzhao lilun yu hanyu fangwei biaoda canzhao celue yanjiu [Spatial reference theory and the research of spatial reference strategies in Chinese]. In *Dangdai Yuyanxue Lilun he Hanyu Yanjiu* [Contemporary linguistic theory and Chinese research], eds. Yang Sheng and Shengli Feng, 120–135. Beijing: The Commercial Press.

——. 2002. Shiti he weizhi: hanyu mingci gongneng de fenhua [Entity and position: the differentiation of the functions of Chinese nouns]. In *Zhongwai Wenhua Jiaoliu yu Aomen Yuyanwenhua Guoji Yantaohui Lunwenji* [The proceedings of the international conference on cultural communication between China and other countries and language and culture in Macaw], eds. Bainian Song and Yongxin Zhao, 280–286. Macaw: Macaw Institute of Science and Technology Press.

Hauser, Marc D., Noam Chomsky and W. Tecumseh Fitch. 2002. The faculty of language: What is it, who has it, and how did it evolve? *Science* 298: 1569–1579.

He, Leshi. 1985. '*Zuo Zhuan*', '*Shi Ji*' jiebing duanyu weizhi de bijiao

[The comparison of the positions of the prepositional phrases in '*Zuo Zhuan*' and '*Shi Ji*']. *Yuyan Yanjiu* [Linguistic research] 1: 57 – 65.

Herskovits, Annette. 1986. *Language and Spatial Cognition: An Interdisciplinary Study of the Prepositions in English*. Cambridge: Cambridge University Press.

Hickmann, Maya. 1995. Discourse organization and the development of reference to person, space and time. In *The Handbook of Child Language*, eds. Paul Fletcher and Brian MacWhinney, 194 – 218. Oxford; Cambridge, MA: Blackwell pub.

Hill, Clifford. 1982. Up/down, front/back, left/right: A contrastive study of Hausa and English. In *Here and There: Cross-linguistic Studies on Deixis and Demonstration*, eds. Jürgen Weissenborn and Wolfgang Klein, 13 – 42. Amsterdam: John Benjamins.

Hoffmann, Thomas. 2011. *Preposition Placement in English: A Usage-Based Approach*. Cambridge; New York: Cambridge University Press.

Hsieh, Miao-Ling. 2010. Post-verbal locative/directional phrases in child Mandarin: A longitudinal study. In *Chinese Matters: From Grammar to First and Second Language Acquisition*, eds. Chris Wilder and Tor A. Åfarli, 111 – 130. Trondheim: Tapir Academic Press.

Huang, Cheng-Teh James. 2009. Lexical decomposition, silent categories, and the localizer phrase. *Yuyanxue Luncong* [Collected papers on linguistics] 39: 86 – 122.

——. 2007. Hanyu dongci de tiyuan jiegou yu qi jufa biaoxian [The thematic structures of verbs in Chinese and their syntactic projection]. *Yuyan Kexue* [Linguistic sciences] 6(4): 3 – 21.

——. 1994. More on Chinese word order and parametric theory. In *Syntactic Theory and First Language Acquisition: Heads, Projections, and Learnability*, eds. Barbara Lust, Margarita Suñer, and John Whitman, 15 – 35. Hillsdale, NJ: L. Erlbaum Associates.

——. 1987. Existential sentences in Chinese and (in) definiteness. In *The Representations of (In)definiteness*, eds. Eric J. Reuland and Alice G. B. ter Meulen, 226-253. Cambridge, MA: The MIT Press.

——. 1984. Phrase structure, lexical integrity, and Chinese compounds. *Journal of the Chinese Language Teachers Association* 19: 53-78.

——. 1982. *Logical Relations in Chinese and the Theory of Grammar*. Doctoral dissertation, MIT.

Huang, Cheng-Teh James, Yen-hui Audrey Li, and Yafei Li. 2009. *The Syntax of Chinese*. Cambridge, UK; New York: Cambridge University Press.

Huang, Guoying. 1985. Xiandai hanyu de qiyi duanyu [Ambiguous phrases in modern Chinese]. *Yuyan Yanjiu* [Language research] 1: 69-89.

Huang, Shuan-Fan. 1978. Historical change of prepositions and emergence of SOV order. *Journal of Chinese Linguistics* 6: 212-242.

Jackendoff, Ray. 1997. *The Architecture of the Language Faculty*. Cambridge, MA: The MIT Press.

——. 1996a. Semantics and cognition. In *The Handbook of Contemporary Semantic Theory*, ed. Shalom Lappin, 539-559. Oxford, UK; Cambridge, MA: Blackwell.

——. 1996b. The architecture of the linguistic-spatial interface. In *Language and Space*, eds. Paul Bloom, Mary A. Peterson, Lynn Nadel, and Merrill. F. Garrert, 1-30. Cambridge, MA: The MIT Press.

——. 1983. *Semantics and Cognition*. Cambridge, MA: The MIT Press.

——. 1972. *Semantic Interpretation in Generative Grammar*. Cambridge, MA: The MIT Press.

Jakobson, Roman (1968). *Child Language, Aphasia and Phonological Universals*. The Hague: Mouton.

Jia, Hongxia. 2010. Putonghua ertong fangweici fazhan de ge'an yanjiu

[Development of locality postpositions of an infant Chinese speaker: a case study]. *Shijie Hanyu Jiaoxue* [Teaching Chinese in the world] 4: 514 – 524.

Jiang, Zixin. 1991. *Some Aspects of the Syntax of Topic and Subject in Chinese*. Doctoral dissertation, the University of Chicago.

Jin, Changji. 1996. Hanyu Jieci he Jieci Duanyu [Chinese prepositions and prepositional phrases]. Tianjin: Nankai Daxue Chubanshe

Johnston, Judith R. and Dan I. Slobin. 1979. The development of locative expressions in English, Italian, Serbo-Croatian and Turkish. *Journal of Child Language* 6: 529 – 545.

Koenig, Jean-Pierre, Gail Mauner, and Breton Bienvenue. 2003. Arguments for adjuncts. *Cognition* 89: 67 – 103.

Kong, Linda and Xiangrong Wang. 2002. Ertong yuyan zhong fangweici de xide he xiangguan wenti[The development of localizers in child language and relevant issues]. *Zhongguo Yuwen* [Studies of the Chinese language] 2: 111 – 117.

Kracht, Marcus. 2002. On the semantics of locatives. *Linguistics and Philosophy* 25 (2): 157 – 232.

Kratzer, Angelika. 1995. Stage-level and individual-level predicates. In *The Generic Book*, eds. Gregory N. Carlson and Francis J. Pelletier, 125 – 175. Chicago: University of Chicago Press.

Kuczaj Stan A. and Michael P. Maratsos. 1975. Child development: On the acquisition of *front*, *back* and *side*. *Child Development* 46: 202 – 210.

Kwan, Wing Man Stella. 2005. *On the Word Order of Locative Prepositional Phrase in Cantonese: Processing, Iconicity and Grammar*. MPhil. thesis, University of Hong Kong.

Lakoff, George, and Mark Johnson. 1980. *Metaphors We Live By*. Chicago: University of Chicago Press.

Lam, Chi Fung. 2013. *The Cartography of Spatial Adpositional Phrases in*

Mandarin and Cantonese. Doctoral dissertation, Università Ca' Foscari Venezia.

Landau, Barbara and Ray Jackendoff. 1993. "What" and "where" in spatial language and spatial cognition. *Behavioral and Brain Sciences* 16: 217 – 265.

Landau, Barbaraand Laura Lakusta. 2006. Spatial language and spatial representation: Autonomy and interaction. In *Space in Languages: Linguistic Systems and Cognitive Categories*, eds. Maya Hickmann and Stéphane Robert, 309 – 333. Amsterdam; Philadelphia: J. Benjamins.

LaPolla, Randy J. 2009. Chinese as a topic-comment (not topic-prominent and not SVO) language. In *Studies of Chinese Linguistics: Functional Approaches*, ed. Janet Xing, 9 – 22. Hong Kong: Hong Kong University Press.

Larson, Richard K. 2004. Sentence-final adverbs and 'scope'. In *Proceedings of NELS* 34, eds. Keir Moulton and Matthew Wolf, 23 – 43. UMass: GLSA.

——. 1988. On the double object construction. *Linguistic Inquiry* 19: 335 – 391.

Lee, Thomas Hun-tak. 1996. Theoretical issues in language development and Chinese child language. In *New Horizons in Chinese Linguistics*, eds. Cheng-Teh James Huang and Yen-hui Audrey Li, 293 – 356. Dordrecht: Kluwer Academic Publishers.

Levin, Beth and Malka Rappaport Hovav. 1996. Lexical semantics and syntactic structure. In *The Handbook of Contemporary Semantic Theory*, ed. Shalom Lappin, 487 – 507. Oxford, UK; Cambridge, MA: Blackwell.

——. 1995. *Unaccusativity: At the Syntax-lexical semantics Interface*. Cambridge, MA: The MIT Press.

Levinson, Stephen C. 2003. Language and mind: Let's get the issues straight! In *Language in Mind: Advances in the Study of Language and*

Thought, eds. Dedre Gentner and Susan Goldin-Meadow, 25 – 46. Cambridge, MA: The MIT Press.

——. 1996a. Language and space. *Annual Review of Anthropology* 25: 353 – 382.

——. 1996b. Frames of reference and Molyneux's question: Crosslinguistic evidence. In *Language and Space*, eds. Paul Bloom, Mary A. Peterson, Lynn Nadel, and Merrill F. Garrett, 109 – 169. Cambridge, MA: The MIT Press.

Levinson, Stephen C. and David P. Wilkins. 2006. The background to the study of the language of space. In *Grammar of Space: Explorations in Cognitive Diversity*, eds. Stephen C. Levinson and David P. Wilkins, 1 – 23. Cambridge: Cambridge University Press.

Li, Charles N. and Sandra A. Thompson. 1981. *Mandarin Chinese: A Functional Reference Grammar*. University of California Press.

Li, Jingxi. 1924. *Xinzhu Guoyu Wenhua* [New Mandarin grammar (5th edition)]. Shanghai: The Commercial Press.

Li, Peggy, and Lila Gleitman. 2002. Turning the tables: Language and spatial reasoning. *Cognition* 83: 265 – 294.

Li, Ping. 1990. *Aspect and Aktionsart in Child Mandarin*. Doctoral dissertation, Leiden University.

——. 1988. Acquisition of spatial reference in Chinese. In *Language Development*, eds. Peter Jordens and Josine Lalleman, 83 – 99. Dordrecht: Foris Pub.

Li, Yen-hui Audrey. 1990. *Order and Constituency in Mandarin Chinese*. Dordrecht: Kluwer Academic Publishers.

Lightfoot, David. 1999. *The Development of Language: Acquisition, Change, and Evolution*. Malden, MA: Blackwell Publishers.

Lin, Tzong-Hong Jonah. 2008. Locative subject in Mandarin Chinese. *Nanzan Linguistics* 4: 69 – 88.

——. 2001. *Light Verb Syntax and the Theory of Phrase Structure*.

Doctoral dissertation, University of California at Irvine.

Liu, Danqing. 2008. Syntax of space across Chinese dialects: Conspiring and competing principles and factors. In *Space in Languages of China: Cross-linguistic, Synchronic and Diachronic Perspectives*, ed. Dan Xu, 39 - 67. New York: Springer.

——. 1999. Yuxu gongxing yu qiyi jiegou: Hanyu zhong ruogan qiyi jiegou de leixingxue jieshi [Language universal and ambiguous structure: the typological explanation for some ambiguous structures in Chinese]. In *Zhongguo Yuyanxue de Xin Tuozhan: Qingzhu Wang Shiyuan Jiaoshou Liushiwu Sui Huadan* [New developments in Chinese linguistics: in celebration of Professor Shiyuan Wang's 65th birthday], eds. Wuyun Pan and Feng Shi, 231 - 243. Hong Kong: The City University of Hong Kong Press.

Liu, Feng-Hsi. 2009. Aspect and the postverbal *zai* phrase in Mandarin Chinese. In *Studies of Chinese Linguistics: Functional Approaches*, ed. Janet Zhiqun Xing, 103 - 129. Hong Kong: Hong Kong University Press.

——. 2007. Auxiliary selection in Chinese. In *Split Auxiliary Systems: A Cross-Linguistic Perspective*, ed. Raul Aranovich, 181 - 205. John Benjamins Publishers.

——. 1998. A clitic analysis of locative particles. *Journal of Chinese Linguistics* 28 (1): 48 - 70.

Liu, Ningsheng. 1994. Hanyu ruhe biaoda wuti-de kongjian guanxi [How do Chinese express spatial relationships between entities]. *Zhongguo Yuwen* [Studies of the Chinese language] 3: 169 - 179.

Liu, Yuehua et al. eds. 1998. *Quxiang Buyu Tongshi* [A general explanation of the directional complements]. Beijing: Beijing Language and Culture University Press.

Löbner, Sebastian. 1989. German schon-erst-noch: An integrated analysis. *Linguistics and Philosophy* 12: 167 - 212.

Lü, Shuxiang, et al. eds. 2010. *Xiandai Hanyu Babai Ci (Zeng Ding Ben)* [800 words in Modern Chinese (revised edition)]. Beijing: The Commercial Press.

MacWhinney, Brian. 2000. *The CHILDES Project: Tools for Analyzing Talk (3rd ed.)*. Mahwah, NJ: Lawrence Erlbaum.

Mai, Ziyin. 2007. *Jieci 'Zai' de Yinxian Yanjiu* [A study of the occurrence of the prepositional *zai*]. MA thesis, Peking University.

Marcus, Gary F., S. Vijayan, S. Bandi Rao, and P. M. Vishton. 1999. Rule learning by seven-month-old infants. *Science* 283: 77 – 80.

Marr, David. 1982. *Vision: A Computational Investigation into the Human Representation and Processing of Visual Information*. San Francisco: W. H. Freeman.

Miller, George A. and Philip N. Johnson-Laird. 1976. *Language and Perception*. Cambridge, MA: Belknap Press of Harvard University Press.

Mulder, Rene and Rint Sybesma. 1992. Chinese is a VO language. *Natural Language and Linguistic Theory* 10 (3): 439 – 76.

Nam, Seungho. 2000. A typology of locatives and event composition in English. *Language Research* 36 (4): 689 – 714.

Pan, Haihua. 1996. Imperfective aspect *zhe*, Agent deletion, and locative inversion in Mandarin Chinese. *Natural Language and Linguistic Theory* 14: 409 – 432.

Parsons, Terence. 1990. *Events in the Semantics of English: A Study in Subatomic Semantics*. Cambridge, MA: The MIT Press.

Peyraube, Alain. 1994. On the history of Chinese locative prepositions. *Chinese Languages and Linguistics* 2: 361 – 387.

Piaget, Jean. 1923/1959. *The Language and Thought of the Child* [Language et la pensée chez l'enfant, translated by Marjorie and Ruth Gabain, reprinted in 2010]. London: Routledge & Kegan Paul.

Piaget, Jean and Bärbel Inhelder. 1948/1956. *The Child's Conception of*

Space (translated by F. J. Langdon and J. L. Lunzer, reprinted in 1997). London: Routledge.

Pinker, Steven. 1989. *Learnability and Cognition: The Acquisition of Argument Structure.* Cambridge, MA: The MIT Press.

Pustejovsky, James. 1995. *The Generative Lexicon.* Cambridge, MA: The MIT Press.

——. 1991. The syntax of event structure. *Cognition* 41: 47 – 81.

Qi, Huyang. 1998. *Xiandai Hanyu Kongjian Wenti Yanjiu* [Research on spatial issues in modern Chinese]. Shanghai: Xuelin Press.

Quine, Willard V. 1985. Events and reification. In *Actions and Events*, eds. E. LePore and B. McLaughlin, 162 – 171. New York: Basil Blackwell.

Radford, Andrew. 2004. *Minimalist Syntax: Exploring the Structure of English.* Cambridge; New York: Cambridge University Press.

Rappaport, T. R. 1999. Structure, aspect, and the predicate. *Language* 75: 653 – 677.

Richards, Lynn V., Kenny R. Coventry, and John Clibbens. 2004. Where's the orange? Geometric and extra-geometric factors in English children's talk of spatial locations. *Journal of Child Language* 31: 153 – 175.

Rosen, Carol G. 1984. The interface between semantic roles and initial grammatical relations. In *Studies in Relational Grammar* 2, eds. David M. Perlmutter and Carol G. Rosen, 38 – 77. Chicago: University of Chicago Press.

Rothstein, Susan D. 2004. *Structuring Events: A Study in the Semantics of Lexical Aspect.* Malden, MA: Blackwell.

Schütze, Carson T. 1995. PP attachment and argumenthood. In *Papers on Language Processing and Acquisition*, eds. Carson T. Schütze, Jennifer B. Ganger, and Keven Broihier, 95 – 151. MITWPL.

Shi, Dingxu. 2000. Topic and topic-comment constructions in Mandarin

Chinese. Language 76 (2): 383 – 408.

Sinha, Chris, Lis A. Thorseng, Mariko Hayashi, and Kim Plunkett. 1994. Comparative spatial semantics and language acquisition: Evidence from Danish, English, and Japanese. *Journal of Semantics* 11 (4): 253 – 287.

Slobin, Dan I. 1997a. The universal, the typological, and the particular in acquisition. In *Crosslinguistic Study of Language Acquisition* (Vol. 5) , ed. Dan Slobin, 1 – 40. Mahwah, NJ: Erlbaum.

——. 1997b. The origins of grammaticizable notions: Beyond the individual mind. In *Crosslinguistic Study of Language Acquisition* (Vol. 5) , ed. Dan Slobin, 265 – 324. Mahwah, NJ: Erlbaum.

——. 1973. Cognitive prerequisites for the development of grammar. In *Studies of Child Language Development*, eds. Charles A. Ferguson and Dan I. Slobin, 175 – 208. New York: Holt, Rinehart & Winston.

Smith, Carlota S. 1997. *The Parameter of Aspect* (2nd *Edition*). Dordrecht; Boston: Kluwer.

——. 1991. *The Parameter of Aspect*. Dordrecht; Boston: Kluwer.

——. 1990. Event types in Mandarin. *Linguistics* 28: 309 – 336.

Soh, Hooi Ling. 2009. Speaker presupposition and Mandarin Chinese sentence-final -*le*: A unified analysis of the "change of state" and the "contrary to expectation" reading. *Natural Language and Linguistic Theory* 27 (3): 623 – 657.

Song, Gang. 2009. *Putonghua Ertong Zaoqi Dongci Xide: Fanchou, Lunyuan Jiegou yu Jufaxiansuo* [Early verb acquisition in child Mandarin: category, argument structure and syntactic cue]. Doctoral dissertation, Beijing Language and Culture University.

Stowell, Tim. 1981. *Origins of Phrase Structure*. Doctoral dissertation, MIT.

Styles, Elizabeth A. 2005. *Attention, Perception and Memory: An Integrated Introduction*. New York: Psychology Press.

Sun, Chaofen. 2008. Two conditions and grammaticalization of the Chinese locative. In *Space in Language of China: Cross-linguistic, Synchronic and Diachronic Perspective*, ed. Dan Xu, 199 – 227. New York: Springer.

Svenonius, Peter. 2010. Spatial P in English. In *Mapping Spatial PPs: The Cartography of Syntactic Structures (Vol. 6)*, eds. Guglielmo Cinque and Luigi Rizzi, 127 – 160. Oxford, New York: Oxford University Press.

Sybesma, Rint. 1999. *The Mandarin VP*. Dordrecht; Boston: Kluwer Academic Publishers.

Tai, James H-Y. 1985. Temporal sequence and Chinese word order. In *Iconicity in Syntax*, ed. John Haiman, 49 – 72. Amsterdam: John Benjamins.

——. 1975. On two functions of place adverbials in Mandarin Chinese. *Journal of Chinese Linguistics* 3: 154 – 179.

——. 1973. A derivational constraint on adverbial placement in Mandarin Chinese. *Journal of Chinese Linguistics* 1(3): 397 – 413.

Talmy, Leonard. 2000. *Toward a Cognitive Semantics (Vol. 1&2)*. Cambridge, MA: The MIT Press.

——. 1985. Lexicalization patterns: Semantic structure in lexical forms. In *Language Typology and Syntactic Description*, ed. Timothy Shopen, 57 – 149. Cambridge: Cambridge University Press.

——. 1975. Semantics and syntax of motion. In *Syntax and Semantics (Vol. 4)*, ed. John P. Kimball, 181 – 238. New York: Academic Press.

Tardif, Twila. 1996. Nouns are not always learned before verbs: Evidence from mandarin speakers' early vocabularies. *Developmental Psychology* 32: 492 – 504.

——. 1993. *Adult-to-child Speech and Language Acquisition in Mandarin Chinese*. Doctoral dissertation, Yale University.

Teng, Shou-hsin. 1975. On location and movement in Chinese. *Gengo Kenkyu* 67: 30 – 57.

Vendler, Zeno. 1957. Verbs and times. *Philosophical Review* 66 (2): 143 – 160.

Verkuyl, Henk and Joost Zwarts. 1992. Time and space in conceptual and logical semantics: The notion of path. *Linguistics* 20: 483 – 511.

Wang, Huan. 1980. Zai shuoshuo 'zai' [A revisit to zai]. *Yuyan Jiaoxue yu Yanjiu* [Language teaching and research] 3: 25 – 29.

——. 1957. Shuo 'zai' [On zai]. *Zhongguo Yuwen* [Studies of the Chinese language] 2: 25 – 26.

Wang, Jianjun. 2003. *Hanyu Cunzaiju de Lishi Yanjiu* [The diachronic research on Chinese existential sentences]. Tianjin: Tianjin Guji Chubanshe.

Wang, Mingquan. 1990. With or without *li*. *Journal of the Chinese Language Teachers Association* XXV (2): 91 – 95.

Wang, Yuan. 2011. Jingxing ti yuyi yanjiu pingshu [A review of the semantics of the progressive aspect]. *Waiguoyu* [Journal of foreign languages] 34 (3): 31 – 39.

Windmiller, Mara. 1976. A child's conception of space as a prerequisite to his understanding of spatial locatives. *Genetic Psychology Monographs* 94: 227 – 248.

Wu, Hsiao-hung Iris. 2012. P-incorporation and locative inversion. Paper presented at IACL 20.

——. 2015. The fine structure of spatial PPs in Mandarin Chinese. In *The Cartography of Chinese Syntax: The Cartography of Syntactic Structures* (*Vol.* 11), ed. Wei-Tien Dylan Tsai, 209 – 234. New York: Oxford University Press.

Wu, Jiun-Shiung. 2007. Semantic difference between the two imperfective markers in Mandarin and its implication on temporal relations. *Journal of Chinese Linguistics* 35 (2): 372 – 398.

Wu, Xieyao. 2006. *Xiandai Hanyu Cunxianju* [Existential sentences in modern Chinese]. Shanghai: Xuelin Chubanshe.

Yang, Suying and Haihua Pan. 2001. A constructional analysis of the existential structure. In *Studies in Chinese Linguistics II*, ed. Haihua Pan, 189 – 207. Hong Kong: Linguistic Society of Hong Kong.

Yip, Virginia and Stephen Matthews. 2007. *The Bilingual Child: Early Development and Language Contact*. Cambridge: Cambridge University Press.

Zhang, Chen. 2002. *Hanyu Jieci Cizu Cixu de Lishi Yanbian* [The historical evolution of the word order of Chinese prepositional phrases]. Beijing: Beijing Language and Culture University Press.

Zhang, Jingguang, Huiyun Ding, and Jing Lin. 1987. 2-6 sui ertong dui kongjian cihui de lijie he chansheng de chubu shiyan yanjiu [A preliminary experimental study of the comprehension and production of spatial terms for 2- to 6-year-olds]. *Fujian Shifan Daxue Xuebao* [Journal of Fujian Normal University] 1: 118 – 124.

Zhang, Niina Ning. 2002. Movement within a spatial phrase. In *Perspectives on Prepositions*, eds. Hubert Cuyckens and Günter Radden, 447 – 463. Tubingen: Niemeyer.

Zhou, Guoguang and Baohua Wang. 2001. Ertong Yuyan Zhong de Fangsuoju [The spatial constructions in child language]. In *Ertong Jushi Fazhan Yanjiu he Yuyan Xide Lilun* [The study on Chinese children's development of constructions and the theory of language acquisition], 117 – 131. Beijing: Beijing Language and Culture University Press.

Zhou, Jing and Chien-ju Chang. eds. 2009. *Hanyu Ertong Yuyan Fazhan Yanjiu: Guoji Ertong Yuliaoku Yanjiu Fangfa de Yingyong yu Fazhan* [Research on the language development of Chinese children: the application and development of the research method of international child language corpora]. Beijing: Educational Science Publishing House.

Zhou, Wenhua. 2011. *Xiandai Hanyu Jieci Xide Yanjiu* [Research on the acquisition of prepositions in modern Chinese]. Beijing: Shijie Tushu Chubanshe.

Zhu, Dexi. 1982. *Yufa Jiangyi* [Notes on grammar]. Beijing: The Commercial Press.

———. 1978. Zai heiban shang xiezi jiqi xiangguan jushi ['Write on the blackboard' and relevant sentence types]. *Yuyan Jiaoxue yu Yanjiu* [Language teaching and research] 3: 58 – 70.

Zwarts, Joost. 2005. Prepositional aspect and the algebra of paths. *Linguistics and Philosophy* 28: 739 – 779.